RISING SON

RISING SON

A US Soldier's Secret and Heroic Role in World War II

SANDRA VEA

SASQUATCH BOOKS
SEATTLE

For Alan

Printed in the United States of America

Published by Sasquatch Books

SASQUATCH BOOKS with colophon are registered trademarks of Penguin Random House LLC

23 22 21 20 19   9 8 7 6 5 4 3 2 1

Editor: Gary Luke
Production editor: Bridget Sweet
Design: Tony Ong
Copyeditor: Jeanne Ponzetti
Front and back cover photographs: the Abe family
Author photograph: Sockheng Nay
All interior photos courtesy of the Abe family, with the exception of pages 180–182 and 210 (Paul J. Mueller Collection, US Army Heritage and Education Center, Carlisle, Pennsylvania), pages 211 and 273 (US National Archives and Records Administration), and page 298 (Kathie Abe).

Library of Congress Cataloging-in-Publication Data
Names: Vea, Sandra, author.
Title: Rising Son : A US Soldier's Secret and Heroic Role in World War II / by Sandra Vea.
Other titles: Masao
Description: Seattle : Sasquatch Books, [2019] | "An earlier version of this book was published in 2016 under the title Masao." | Includes bibliographical references.
Identifiers: LCCN 2018027947 | ISBN 9781632172419 (hardback)
Subjects: LCSH: Abe, Masao, 1916-2013. | World War, 1939-1945--Military intelligence--United States--Biography. | Japanese American soldiers--Biography. | United States. Army. Infantry Division, 81st--Biography. | World War, 1939-1945--Participation, Japanese American. | World War, 1939-1945--United States--Japanese Americans. | Japanese Americans--History--20th century. | BISAC: BIOGRAPHY & AUTOBIOGRAPHY / Cultural Heritage. | HISTORY / Military / World War II. | BIOGRAPHY & AUTOBIOGRAPHY / Historical.
Classification: LCC D769.8.A6 V43 2019 | DDC 940.54/8673092 [B] --dc23
LC record available at https://lccn.loc.gov/2018027947

ISBN: 978-1-63217-241-9

Sasquatch Books
1904 Third Avenue, Suite 710
Seattle, WA 98101
(206) 467-4300
SasquatchBooks.com

CONTENTS

Acknowledgments   vii

Preface   ix

Prologue   xi

PART I

Chapter One   The Beginning   3

Chapter Two   Loss of Home   26

Chapter Three   Home in Japan   37

PART II

Chapter Four   United States Under Attack   63

Chapter Five   The Aftermath   86

Chapter Six   Life of Loneliness   112

Chapter Seven   Finding His Way   136

Chapter Eight   Battle   178

PART III

Chapter Nine   Beginning of the End   277

Chapter Ten   Final Journey   294

Epilogue   297

Bibliography   299

ACKNOWLEDGMENTS

I am forever grateful to Masao Abe for humbly sharing his life story and recollections as a Military Intelligence Service soldier during World War II. Before he died, Masao was one of the last three soldiers of the ten-man Interrogation/Interpretation Team that was attached to the Eighty-First Infantry Division. The others have also provided great insight: Saburo Nakamura generously shared his memories before he died in 2015, and Hiroki Takahashi has shared poignant stories, written by hand. It was an honor to gain knowledge from all three of these brave and venerable men.

Doris Okada Abe, Masao's wife of sixty-three years, was kind enough to describe bits of her life. Alan Abe made this project possible and kept propelling it forward. Michael Abe and Kathie Abe were sources of strength. Pat and Stephanie Abe have provided valuable input and shared family photos. Sherman Abe, Anna Pusina, and Kathleen Greinke, the children of Tatsuo Abe, have been wonderful guides and provided intricate details and documents about their parents' internment and imprisonment. Phyllis Mizuharo Hirata was gracious with encouragement and information. Dawn Marano was invaluable as an editor, as were Leah Campbell and Barbara McPherson. I also want to thank the professionals at Sasquatch Books who worked on this manuscript and patiently guided me through the publishing process. First and foremost is Gary Luke, editor; also Bridget Sweet, production editor; Tony Ong, designer; and Jeanne Ponzetti, copyeditor.

Richard Thompson, librarian for the City of San Bernardino Historical and Pioneer Society, and Sue Payne, from the Arda Haenszel California Room in the San Bernardino Public Library, sent information and pictures. Jevin Orcutt from the Army Heritage Center Foundation assisted with images from World War II and the Eighty-First Infantry Division. Mark Vanderveen, University of Washington professor, was helpful with regard to military affairs in Japan during the 1930s. Mark Wittow, intellectual property attorney, provided wisdom and expertise with regard to some of the photos. Lieutenant Colonel Michael Yaguchi, United States Air Force (retired), has been an integral part of the development of the book. Michael provided feedback and also connected me with others. He has been a constant source of encouragement. The input and suggestions by Bobby C. Blair, coauthor of *Victory at Peleliu*, and Terry Shima, World War II veteran and recipient of the 2012 Presidential Citizens Medal, were so valuable with regard to military and historical accuracy.

My hope is that these fine soldiers of World War II, soldiers who fought in near isolation in the South Pacific, finally have their loyalty, valor, and accomplishments recognized.

PREFACE

Thirty years. He couldn't speak of his specific assignment in World War II for thirty years after the war ended. Masao, like six thousand other Military Intelligence Service (MIS) soldiers, almost all Japanese American, was operating under a shroud of secrecy during the war. But Masao's assignment in the MIS was unique: he was embedded in a combat unit on the ground, facing an enemy that looked like him, and surrounded by the mindset that "the only good Jap is a dead Jap." Only a handful of the MIS soldiers served in this way. They are among our bravest combat soldiers from that time, and their stories remain untold.

Masao's medals speak to his heroics during the war. Among the many medals he wore on his service cap were the Combat Infantryman Badge, Purple Heart, Bronze Star Medal, Asiatic-Pacific Campaign Medal with two Bronze Campaign Stars and Bronze Arrowhead Device, Army Good Conduct Medal, World War II Victory Medal, Army Commendation Medal, American Defense Service Medal, and the Philippine Liberation Medal with one Bronze Campaign Star. He was bestowed the Congressional Gold Medal in 2010, an honor he was proud to receive. After Masao passed, we discovered that he had not earned just one Bronze Star Medal, but three. All three Bronze Star Medals were awarded for meritorious achievement as a result of active and heavy ground combat in the South Pacific. Masao died not knowing what a hero he was, but had he known, he would have humbly shrugged it off.

By the time Masao was in his nineties, I had entered the picture and started to ask questions about the war. Not only was he delighted to have an interested listener, he could remember details from seventy-five years ago with little effort. His war stories were fascinating, but he also had poignant memories of his uncle, with whom he lived in California. His uncle was imprisoned during the evacuation, while his aunt and little cousins were interned. Like thousands of other Japanese and Japanese Americans who lived along the West Coast, their lives were forever changed.

A word regarding the genre of this book: I was honored to meet, and came to love, Masao Abe during the last years of his life. It quickly became clear to me that his was a story that deserved to be told in its own right, but also because one of its central messages concerning the respectful, civil, and humane treatment of Americans, immigrant-Americans, and others in our country of various ethnicities, races, and religions is as critical today as it was in Masao's time. The book is a biography, faithfully representing the hundreds of hours of Masao's vivid storytelling that I recorded. Taking my creative license from the genre of the nonfiction novel, first introduced by Truman Capote with his book *In Cold Blood*, I have reimagined portions of Masao's story, rendering those in fictionalized form, although carefully attending to the "facts" of those stories as he told them.

After his wife, Doris, passed away, I spent two days a week with Masao, mostly to keep him busy, as he was lost without his wife of sixty-three years. What started out as simple interviews to record his thoughts about the war turned into a friendship unlike any I've ever experienced. In the end, I realized what a gift I had in my time with Masao. Those three and a half years, the last of his life, were an absolute treasure. He shared so many untold anecdotes about what had happened on the islands of Angaur, Peleliu, and Leyte in the South Pacific—but I also saw a warrior who had become vulnerable to the inevitability of aging. That he let me walk with him during these moments of loss is what I remember most.

Masao is gone now. I miss him every day. And I miss his stories about World War II.

PROLOGUE

We were taking Masao Abe on his final journey, approaching the TSA officer, attempting to make eye contact. Like so many of those guys, he looked sick of his job and worked pretty hard to avoid meeting our gaze. Clearly, he didn't want to answer yet another stupid question or take one more insult about the ridiculous security measures from an airline passenger.

Alan stopped in front of him, holding up the line. "The ticket agent told us to check in with you. I have an urn."

"What?" He looked beyond annoyed.

"You know. An urn." Alan's voice was anything but confident.

"We have his father's ashes." I meant to sound unintimidated by this guy, but my voice almost quivered, which surprised me. *I hope this guy isn't going to be a jerk. That's the last thing we need.*

I saw Mr. TSA peek over Alan's shoulder to the pack on his back. The American flag, folded into the military triangle and protected in a plastic cover, protruded from his backpack. He softened and gave the slightest nod.

"Follow me."

At the conveyor belt line, he motioned for us to stop.

"Go ahead and get your things in the bins." We did as instructed, a little confused, but he seemed to have a plan. He motioned for his fellow TSA workers to join him as he pulled out his wallet to remove a shiny coin. Two other TSA workers, both young men, gathered near him.

"These folks are taking a loved one to his final resting place." He looked at us. "Here's what we're going to do. We will place this coin underneath the urn while it goes through the scanner. We need to make sure the coin is visible." We nodded, indicating we understood. He gestured to me. "You'll go first. After your things are off the belt at the other end, we'll send your father through alone. Nobody else will have anything on the conveyor belt." His eyes shifted to Alan. "Only your father. Out of respect."

Alan and I looked at each other. My eyes started to sting.

"Okay," I heard Alan squeeze out, trying to avoid a complete breakdown. I fought to choke back my own tears.

"I'm so sorry for your loss." We both nodded. Our faces must have revealed the long trail of grief we had followed for weeks.

At the far end of the conveyor belt, I glanced back at Alan while I collected my bins and waited for the people in front of me to remove their items. It seemed like they were taking forever. I bit my tongue and smiled at them when they looked at me, and they eventually moved on. I turned toward Alan and the TSA officer on the other end. The TSA officer motioned that the conveyor belt was clear.

Masao's urn was carefully placed on the belt that then started to move. In the few moments as the urn came through, a silence fell around us. Fellow passengers seemed to take note and were quietly observing. I watched as the urn lit up the security screen, the coin visible on the bottom. I hadn't realized that the two younger TSA workers were now beside me; both donned fresh gloves. The urn came through, and the TSA officer carefully picked it up to retrieve his coin. He then brought the urn in my direction.

"Excuse me, ma'am, we'll take it from here." One of the younger TSA workers took the urn. "We just need to scan the outside as well."

"Of course." I was relieved that there was more to the process, so Alan could get through security and join me on the other side. Alan picked up his bins, and we hurried to follow the young TSA men to a nearby station.

"This won't hurt anything," one of them said as the other used a cotton-like swab to rub the outside of the urn, "we're just testing for certain materials." They couldn't have been any more careful or sensitive.

Alan and I both nodded, each trying hard to control the emotion that was in our throats. I looked at Alan and saw that his eyes were moist but his tears were contained. He looked at me too. We didn't have to say a word. This was hard.

"Sandie," he whispered. I softly put my hand inside his. "I'm glad you're doing this with me."

I nodded. "Me too."

The TSA workers completed their scan, gently picked up the urn, and walked over to Alan. "We're sorry for your loss."

Alan took the urn. It was all he could do to nod.

"Thank you," I choked out as I watched Alan arrange his backpack. The TSA guys waited while we organized everything; I think they wanted to be on standby in case we needed anything. It was quite impressive how they treated us that day.

"Thanks," Alan said as he heaved the pack on his back. He looked for the first TSA officer, who was watching from a distance, and we waved to him as well. Step one in the final journey was now complete. Try as I might to hold them in, tears fell from my eyes as we walked to the gate. I looked at Alan, only to find him in even worse shape.

PART 1

CHAPTER ONE

THE BEGINNING

I first met Masao and Doris Abe, the parents of my partner, Alan, in 2007. My initial impression of them was that Masao was a warm and gentle man who had a great sense of humor, and Doris was a tough, no-nonsense type. It wasn't until we'd had dinner together several times that the notion of Masao's service during World War II came up.

"They were called landing craft." Masao was trying to explain the reality of battle to someone who had no military knowledge.

"Like those boat things you see in the movies?" My question felt as clumsy as it sounded.

"Heh! I guess so."

"Was this in Europe?"

"Nah. South Pacific." Masao sipped on his tea as though we were talking about nothing more than the weather. "It was an island called, what's the name now, ah, Angaur. Tiny island."

Having little knowledge of World War II other than what I learned in high school several decades earlier, I wasn't sure where to begin. I looked at Masao, at his gentle face, and couldn't begin to see him on the battlefield and, yet, I knew he had a story to share.

"Do you remember being on the landing craft?"

"Heh! Sure I do." He smiled. "You want to hear about it?"

I nodded, eager to learn more. "I'd love to hear about it."

Masao looked away, his expression changed. He was calling up his past and reliving it right there at the restaurant table. "I was scared shitless, boy."

SEPTEMBER 17, 1944—SOUTH PACIFIC

Navy destroyers sat off shore of the small South Pacific island, pummeling it with shell fire, bombarding it mercilessly. Fighter planes screeched overhead attacking from the air. Masao was bunched in with hundreds of other soldiers on the deck of a transport ship, waiting for orders.

"*Move out!*" A higher rank yelled the order from behind Masao.

The soldiers, in rows eight wide, hurled themselves onto Jacob's ladders and climbed down to hovering landing craft. Masao climbed down the rope fixture with ease, glancing at smoke rising from the tiny island.

He jumped into the landing craft and held onto the side while he found his footing and squeezed in among other soldiers. In a flurry, the landing craft deployed along with several others, forming a ring at sea and awaiting orders to go ashore. Relentless explosions continued in the distance as the craft rocked in the swells. Tension mounted with every passing second.

For Masao, the intensity was amplified. He was the only Japanese American on the sea vessel, and, in fact, only one of ten Japanese American soldiers in the division, the Eighty-First, a division with some 25,000 soldiers. Only the highest-ranking officers and essential combat personnel were aware of his purpose with the military, and he'd already felt the confused and suspicious glances coming from the occasional soldier, although many figured he was Chinese or Korean—anything but Japanese.

"Wave Three, commence to Blue Beach," a voice on the commander's radio ordered. The landing craft broke from the ring and headed to a beach in the distance. Fear escalated rapidly. Masao's heart was pounding faster and harder than ever before. He glanced at soldiers near him. They looked just as scared.

The tempo of the naval gunfire intensified. Fires burned all over the island. Black smoke billowed into the clear sky, and debris and chunks of trees fell with a splash in the surf as the beautiful paradise was quickly demolished. The landing craft was a thousand yards from shore now. Landing Craft Infantry, gun boats, and mortar boats took position in front of the craft. As landing crafts neared the beach, naval air fire concentrated on the shore, clearing the way for ground troops.

On the beach army tanks dragged themselves out of the surf and onto land, taking position to protect the dismounting men. The landing craft approached the beach facing relentless rapid fire and mortar rounds by the enemy. With a loud bang, the ramp of the craft released, making way for the men to jump off.

"Let's go, let's go, let's go!" yelled a soldier near Masao.

On the beach, Masao slammed his body down against a sandy ridge. Other soldiers lined up beside him. Machine-gun fire hit all around. Shards of coral scattered in all directions, spraying the men with razor-like fragments.

Masao looked back to the surf as the landing craft's ramp went up and it retreated back to the sea, leaving the men to fend for themselves. Bodies littered the beach. Some soldiers never even made it on shore, their bodies now floating with the tide. *This can't be real*, Masao thought. Navy fighter planes flew overhead, thrashing the enemy with gunfire as they hid in caves. Tanks advanced off the beach from all directions. Masao watched a Tech Sergeant, the leader in charge of the company he was assigned to, scurry down the coral ridge. The Tech Sergeant grabbed the radio and tried to communicate in the midst of the explosions.

Masao waited and watched, his hands glued in a firing position on his rifle.

★ ★ ★

"I had my hands just gripped on that rifle, boy," Masao recalled as he watched the waitress set his food down in front of him. I was enthralled with the details he shared about that day in battle so long ago and disappointed his story had been interrupted by the arrival of our order. It seemed like it was just getting good.

"Can I hear more about this, Mas?"

"Ah," he brushed me off, "later."

I wanted to learn about World War II and the secret operation of which he was a part, and at the same time, I realized I would need to know about Masao's life in full to be able to understand why he, a Japanese American soldier, was chosen to serve in the South Pacific—a battlefield where the enemy looked like he did. Before the night ended, Masao assured me that he would be happy to fill me in on his life's story, and I was delighted he was allowing me to record his history.

Nisei. The literal meaning is "second," as in second generation. Masao was born on November 16, 1916, to his parents, Tomie and Yasoshichi, both *Issei*, or first generation. They were among the growing population of Japanese people who lived in southern California.

"It was called, uh, Fourth Street School," Masao told me as the waitress poured tea while we were out for Japanese food one night. "I was the only Japanese in my class."

"What? I thought the school was near Little Japan, or Japantown—whatever you called it." I was merely trying to understand his life, but I quickly found that I would be astounded by much of his childhood history.

"Heh!" he chuckled. "It was. But most of the Japanese people lived away from that area. We didn't call it anything. Japanese people, they just had their shops there, a-no?"

"So, no other Japanese attended that school?"

"There were a few, a-no? But I was the only one my age."

"So, who were your pals, then?"

"Oh, anyone. A lot of Spanish-speaking people there, you know?"

"I didn't know. Did you speak Spanish?"

"Nah."

"Japanese, though, right?"

"Nah. My parents didn't teach it to me."

"Did they speak English pretty well?"

"My dad did. But my mom, it was kind of hard to understand her." I was amused by this. I wondered if Masao had the upper hand with his mom due to her limited English; he seemed like the mischievous type.

"What was it like back then?"

"Back when?" He had nine decades to choose from. I quickly discovered that I would need to be precise in my questions.

"Well, let's start in San Bernardino when you were little. What do you remember about that part of your life?"

"Heh! I was just a little guy, a-no? Let's see now . . ."

SEPTEMBER 1925—SAN BERNARDINO, CALIFORNIA

The heat was oppressive. It was a sweltering ninety-three degrees outside, but inside Fourth Street School where Masao attended third grade, the temperature must have hit a hundred. Children sat at their wooden desks and halfway listened to their teacher. Roughly a third of the students sitting in Masao's classroom were people of color: mostly Latinx, one or two African Americans, and one Japanese child—Masao. He glanced slyly at Josué, the boy sitting next to him. They smirked at each other; seeing or hearing something that only the eyes or ears of eight-year-old boys can detect, something that amused them.

"Class dismissed," their teacher announced. And with that, the children sprang from their desks eager to get out of the stuffy building.

Masao, already wearing glasses, and Josué erupted through the doors of the school and ran together like little boys do. They giggled all the way in a sprint to the end of the sidewalk, their bulky leather shoes not slowing them down in the least. At the street, they parted ways. Josué would walk to the barrio, Masao to Little Japan.

"See ya," Masao called after Josué.

"*Hasta mañana*," Josué called back as he trotted off.

Masao walked the five blocks to his house, a two-bedroom, one-bathroom bungalow that sat right behind the San Bernardino courthouse on Arrowhead Avenue. The yard was as neat and tidy as the inside of the house, which his mom kept spotless. Masao came in through the back door to the kitchen where his mom was working. Like any boy, he tossed his metal lunch pail on the floor and immediately took off his shoes to get some relief.

"Masao. Put pail here." His mother, Tomie, spoke softly in her broken English as she placed her hand on the kitchen counter. Masao complied and hurriedly set his lunch pail on the counter as his mother wanted, part of their afternoon routine. In his bare feet, he scurried to his room to put his shoes away before his mom could get after him about that. Then he came back to the kitchen to eat his afternoon snack that she had carefully prepared and had waiting for him. He sat at the table along with his two little sisters, Yoshiko, then five, and Yuriko, three. He largely ignored them as he ate his sliced apple.

"After snack, you go store," his mother gently demanded.

"I don't want to help daddy today. It's too hot," Masao stammered.

Tomie looked at her only son and smiled. "He need your helping."

"He needs your help," Masao corrected with a sigh. "Okay. I'll go."

Tomie was trying her hardest to learn the language of the country she had come to a decade earlier, but it was a struggle given that she had limited interaction with English-speaking people. She would sometimes listen to the radio to try to pick up words, but the announcers spoke so fast that she would become frustrated and give up. Besides, she was raising three children, keeping the house clean, cooking meals, and helping in the family grocery store from time to time. Who had the time to learn English?

"My son," she cooed as she gently stroked Masao's thick black hair. Still working on his snack, Masao didn't notice the sadness in her eyes.

A few minutes later, Masao had his shoes back on and was towing his Liberty Coaster wagon the half-block down to Third Street. He passed by the dry cleaners on Arrowhead where the owner, Mr. Kamimura, waved to him. Once he turned the corner onto Third Street he was in a different world. This was Little Japan. Japanese merchants littered Third Street for blocks, but the concentration of Japanese businesses was located within the few blocks between Arrowhead and D Streets. He made his way inside Star Cash Grocery that was owned and operated by his father, Yasoshichi, and uncle, Tatsuo. The grocery store was as neat and tidy as the Abe home.

"Little man here!" Tatsuo's English was broken, his having arrived just four years earlier. A strikingly handsome Yasoshichi looked on, admiring the fondness Tatsuo shared with him for Masao.

"Masao. Take these potatoes to Mr. Hirata." He was already loading up Masao's wagon. "Then you come back and sweep." Masao, used to taking orders from his father, helped him load the potato sacks onto the wagon.

Out on the sidewalk, Masao, in an attempt to avoid the chore of sweeping, decided to take the long way to the Hirata Deli that was just across the street. He meandered along, waving to the merchants along the way. They all knew him and greeted him as he passed by: Mr. Sawada owned the café next door to the grocery store, Mr. Ohashi owned the barber shop next to the café, Mr. Nakabayashi ran the pool hall, and Mr. Uyeda owned the café at the end of the block. Everyone knew Masao and Masao knew them all, by name. It was a tight-knit community.

★ ★ ★

Back at Masao and Doris's apartment, Alan hung up his parents' coats and put their leftovers away. I was in my own world, thinking about San Bernardino in the 1920s. I lingered along the wall that displayed family photos. Then I noticed it: the picture of his days at Fourth Street School. I took the old photo out of its spot, stuck in the frame with another picture, and had a closer look. There he was, his little face looking back at me from days long gone. Masao's memory served him remarkably well. The way he described Little Japan all those years ago proved to be amazingly accurate, according to historical

Masao (first row, fifth from right) in the Fourth Street School class photo, 1921

records. I was content knowing that I had embarked on Masao's story and looked forward to our next dinner with anticipation.

Alan and I were sound asleep when his phone rang. He jolted awake and grabbed the phone, glancing at the number.

"It's Dad," he was alarmed. "Dad?"

"Mommy fell." I could hear Masao's voice in the stillness of the night. He sounded shaky and the fear in his voice was evident. "She's bleeding from her head," he continued.

"I'm on my way. Call 911." Alan was quickly getting dressed while holding the phone with his neck.

"What?" Masao sounded confused.

"I'm on my way, Dad. Call 911!"

Doris was in the hospital for days; then she was moved to a long-term care facility. Unfortunately, she had entered "health impairment limbo": lacking an ailment that can be treated, she was sent to a place, it seems, where folks go when they are waiting to die, depressing places despite the efforts of those in charge to create a positive and upbeat atmosphere. Doris hated it there.

I visited her with Alan, and sometimes with Alan and Masao, and even by myself. But the interviews with Masao had all but stopped—the attention was on Doris and her health. That was all that mattered to Masao, and it was all that mattered to Alan.

"How did your dad get here from Japan?" I asked Masao over lunch one day before going to visit Doris. It was an attempt to regenerate our conversation about his life.

"Well, let's see now. He came here when he was just a youngster. Fifteen or sixteen, I guess."

Ignorant of history, I had no idea what circumstances would bring someone to the United States during that period, but Masao, too, was probably uncertain of the context. As it turned out, the year Masao's father stepped ashore in Seattle was the same year the United States started to turn up the heat to stop Japanese immigration.

"He came to work on the railroad, I think," Masao said, attempting to piece together his father's history.

1907—FUKUSHIMA-KEN, JAPAN

Sixteen-year-old Yasoshichi balanced on the top rung of a wooden ladder and reached for ripe cherries in the thick of a tree. He came down the ladder, loading his burlap bag to the top with his last handful of cherries. As he carefully poured the cherries from his bag into a wooden bin, he noticed his father approaching. Something about his father's face concerned Yasoshichi, so he put his bag down.

"*Ohayou gozaimasu.*" Yasoshichi met his father with the formal "good morning" greeting. His father, Mataemon, nodded. He admired his son's handsome young face.

"Let's walk," Mataemon motioned. Yasoshichi brushed off his hands and joined his father. They strolled through Mataemon's apple and cherry orchard as Mataemon contemplated how to phrase what was on his mind. Yasoshichi, the oldest of ten children, had been on walks with his father before. Usually, these thoughtful walks meant the introduction of some rite of passage he would soon experience, such as how to properly pick cherries, then apples, then how to sell or barter their goods with others in the small village of Senoue in the prefecture of Fukushima-ken. One such walk introduced Yasoshichi to the art of bartering with folks from other villages, an exciting event for Yasoshichi because he had never traveled outside Senoue. But this walk seemed different. It was clear his father's heart was heavy.

"My son. The time has come for you to work away from the family orchard." This caught Yasoshichi's attention. He had heard of other young men traveling to glorious faraway places. Maybe his father would send him to Tokyo or other parts of Japan to work on the railway. He listened with much anticipation.

"There is a group going to America. You will go with them." Mataemon gazed at the ground as he strolled and spoke, as though carefully choosing his words while thinking through the necessary steps of his plan. Yasoshichi could hardly believe his ears. America! He had heard stories about this land. A land where gold lined the streets and every man had the chance to earn money beyond his wildest dreams. He could surely make enough to make his father proud; he would return to Japan a wealthy man and be the envy of everyone in Senoue—no—Fukushima!

"When will I go?" Yasoshichi tried to control his excitement, but it bled through in his voice, and his father detected it.

"There is a long process. Be patient."

"Yes, father."

The long process included an extensive board examination of character. The Japanese government wanted their subjects treated better, once in the United States, than Chinese countrymen had been treated previously. This examination was intended to ensure ethical, virtuous, and conservative behavior while abroad. It was a laborious course of action that exhausted the mental capacity of many young men. Yasoshichi endured, but not without question.

"Why must they put me through all of this?" Yasoshichi asked while he and his father waited in the hall of the local municipality for yet another board review.

"America is growing rapidly," Mataemon explained. "It has been necessary for them to gather workers from around the world to fill the jobs."

Yasoshichi nodded, waiting for his father to continue.

"For many years, Chinese countrymen filled much of this demand, especially on the shores of the west, where you will go. But problems occurred with the Chinese."

"What problems?" Yasoshichi asked after giving this some thought. He wanted to be aware so that he wouldn't make the same mistakes.

"I am not certain. I have heard that the United States people became angry that the Chinamen were taking all the jobs. And the Chinamen were working harder and working longer hours. So it made the United States people uncomfortable with Chinamen. They made laws to prevent any more travel from China to America. So for many years, no more Chinese people have gone to America. Only Japanese can go. But that is ending soon."

Yasoshichi didn't know what to make of this. "Why?"

"Same reasons. Taking jobs, working hard. Only Chinese countrymen got in a little bit of trouble with drinking and gambling. The Japanese government wants to make sure Japanese countrymen don't do those sorts of things. That's why you go through all of this."

Yasoshichi nodded. The last thing he wanted to do was to bring shame to his family or to Japan.

"Will I be treated well in America?"

"If you act well, you will be treated well."

"Then I will act well," Yasoshichi assured him. And this made Mataemon smile.

Yasoshichi, having been a good student, son, and citizen, passed the exam and was cleared for travel to the United States. And so, in November of 1907, Yasoshichi's journey began from his small village. Some friends had a horse-drawn carriage and took Mataemon and Yasoshichi to the train station in Fukushima, eight kilometers away from Senoue. Yasoshichi was happy to get the ride so he wouldn't have to walk with his luggage along the dirt roads. Besides, this way, his father could come along to bid him farewell.

At the Fukushima train station, Mataemon handed him a roll of money.

"Spend wisely. Act honorably."

"Of course, father." Yasoshichi bowed out of honor. In his western suit that they had bartered for, he looked out of place at the train station where everyone else was in traditional kimono wear.

"Go now," Mataemon said with a wave of his hand. Yasoshichi locked eyes with his father while he picked up his luggage. His eyes spoke for him; he was both eager and anxious about the journey that awaited him, not to mention the new world. He bowed again and headed to the train.

When Yasoshichi stepped off the locomotive at the Shimbashi Station in Tokyo, his eyes were wide with wonder at the huge buildings, the vastness of the city, and the streets littered with people who bustled along in the growing and industrialized metropolis. On his long walk to Yokohama Harbor to meet the Methodist missionary group he would be traveling with and catch the steamship *Kaga Maru*, his feet craved a ride on a *jinrikisha*. But he remembered his father's words, "spend wisely," so he kept his money in his pocket and lugged his suitcase along.

NOVEMBER 1907—PORT OF SEATTLE

Yasoshichi could not begin to imagine how grueling his voyage across the sea would be. He endured days of travel in steerage, bearing living quarters no larger than a coffin and experiencing seasickness throughout the journey. On November 14, the ship finally pulled into the Port of Seattle.

Seattle, in 1907, was sprawling. While half the population of Tokyo, it was a busier city. Construction was going on in just about every block. Cable cars whizzed by, people filled the streets, and there were more motor-powered vehicles than Yasoshichi had ever seen. Just a few blocks from the pier where he disembarked stood the Pike Place Market, having opened for the first time earlier that year. It bustled with merchants, including Japanese farmers. As the missionary group made their way to the flourishing Nikkei community known as Japantown, where Japanese immigrants had formed a tight-knit town within the city, he noticed where cable track had been laid in a massive expansion. *My fortune is coming*, he thought.

The main passenger terminal for the interstate railway system was located a short distance from Japantown. As a result, numerous hotels were built in the area surrounding the terminal; some of those hotels would be standing as long as a century later. Yasoshichi stayed at one of them, but not for long. It was less than a week before he found employment on a railway. He worked on various railroads from that point forward and for the next several years, moving his way south.

He soon found out that there was nothing glorious about working on a railroad. There were no streets lined with gold, and he was toiling long hours for practically nothing. Although he saved every penny and rarely spent money on anything other than absolute necessities, it dawned on him that it would take years for him to become the wealthy man of his dreams. He also began to notice that he, and other railroad workers who were of color, were treated quite differently than their white counterparts. He was doing his best to act honorably; he didn't gamble, he didn't drink, and he worked hard. And yet, he was treated as though he were some sort of a scoundrel. He was eager to find a different vocation that would allow him to follow his dream and be treated well because, after all, he was acting well.

The railroad work led him to the San Diego area, where he found his way to Imperial Valley and the town of Brawley, the site of the Takahashi Company, a farm and packing enterprise. Yasoshichi, happy to find a Japanese employer, worked for Takahashi and was eventually promoted to management. As a manager he was able to save more money, and when the Takahashi Company changed hands, Yasoshichi moved on. Through networking, he discovered a small store in San Bernardino that he became interested in purchasing. San Bernardino was considered a small town at that time, yet already boasted a Chinatown, and a strong Nikkei community was forming. It was the perfect setting for him to make his mark. So, in 1920, at the age of twenty-nine and with his hard-earned savings, Yasoshichi became the proud owner of Star Cash Grocery. The block on which his store was located would eventually become the central area for Japanese businesses. It must have been comforting for a young Yasoshichi to settle in a town that had welcomed other Japanese businessmen in its ranks and had such a strong Japanese presence. He had established his home in America.

★ ★ ★

Back in the restaurant, Masao ate the last bit of rice in his bowl. I was always amazed at the artful way the elder Japanese people used their chopsticks. He gently set them down. He was still deep in thought, back in San Bernardino all those years before.

"Maybe it was because his own life was so tough that my old man did what he did to me," he said thoughtfully, looking off in the distance at nothing in particular. But what he said caught my attention, and I waited for him to continue. He sipped his tea. It was the kind of sip he would take before telling another story. But instead of telling me the story about his dad, Masao snapped out of the past and looked at me as though I had just entered the room and sat down. Try as I might, I couldn't get Masao to share the details of the seemingly awful deed his dad had committed. He was in a hurry to go see Doris, the love of his life, who had spent weeks in long-term care.

Eventually, Alan found a retirement home that provided assisted living so his parents could be reunited, something that delighted Masao. It was moving day and Alan, along with his two brothers, were at their apartment, packing.

"How can I help?" I called out to Alan as I entered Masao's apartment.

"You can take him to lunch if you want." Masao's eyes lit up and he hustled to get his jacket. After we settled in the car, I asked him where he wanted to go.

"We go casino."

"Casino? I was kind of hoping you would tell me more about your parents."

"Ah. We talk on the way." He motioned as a way to hurry me.

I took out my tape recorder and turned it on, hoping to hear more details about his childhood. There wasn't much conversation in the beginning of our twenty-minute drive up the mountain to the closest casino. I was caught off guard and didn't have any questions prepared. After about five miles, I remembered our last conversation. About that same time, Masao decided on a topic.

"Did I tell you about my mom?" he asked. I could tell that he wanted to provide me with something about his life to make my time worthwhile, interview-wise. I think he felt he was manipulating me in some way by having me drive him to the casino. I was just happy to hear more of his story.

"No, not yet. We were last talking about your dad." I was trying to steer him back to the terrible deed, but no such luck.

"Heh!" He was somewhat embarrassed by what he was about to reveal. "My mom, she was a picture bride." He looked at me for my reaction. There wasn't any reaction other than confusion. I had no idea what he was talking about. I shook my head and shrugged, like a five-year-old would shrug, to indicate my ignorance.

"My dad. He wanted a wife. So he sent for her."

"What? Like some sort of mail-order bride?" Masao laughed at this while nodding, still uncomfortable with this piece of his family's history.

"How did that work back then? I can't even imagine."

Masao was really amused. "Well, he wrote letters back home and there was a woman, a-no, who arranged marriages. Heh!" He chuckled more. "My mom. She was a *picture* bride!"

1914—TSUKIDATE, FUKUSHIMA-KEN, JAPAN

Seventeen-year-old Tomie Haga had closed herself off in the far end of the home so she could concentrate on her sewing. Considered quite the seamstress, once she was working on a project, she didn't like to be interrupted. Weeks before, her mother had surprised her with a trip to the city of Fukushima to buy fabric for a new kimono. Her mother let her pick out a beautiful purple and light-blue fabric that boasted stripes. Used to wearing drab gray kimonos, Tomie was thrilled to finally make something that would get her noticed.

Her mother approached her so quietly, Tomie didn't even notice until she spoke.

"Tomie. You are making good progress, yes?"

Tomie stopped and turned toward her mother. "Yes, Mommy. I will be done well before New Year's Day," she reported proudly.

"Come, please. I have someone I want you to meet." Tomie's mother motioned with her hand.

In the sitting area, tea had been served. A woman in a stunning kimono sat on her knees. Tomie had never witnessed anything like her. She had her hair worn *shimada* style, up off her face in elaborate buns and adorned with *kanzashi*, various styles of hairpins. Her makeup was flawless and her skin—perfect. Tomie immediately felt "country" and unsophisticated. The woman looked up. Tomie instinctively lowered her eyes and bowed out of respect.

"Tomie, this is Hayashi-san. Hayashi-san, my first daughter, Tomie." Tomie's mother was talking but Tomie couldn't hear anything; she couldn't take her eyes off this woman.

Hayashi-san's eyes slowly assessed Tomie's appearance from head to toe. Tomie tried not to notice.

"She is pretty, Haga-san." Her voice was like silk. Tomie blushed, felt herself blush, and then looked down.

"You are kind, Hayashi-san," Tomie's mother said as she poured more tea. Tomie felt trapped in her body, not sure if she should sit or simply run out of the room under the pressure of being in the presence of someone so magnificent and who was attributing any beauty at all to her. Tomie was naturally beautiful, although completely unaware of it. There was softness in her perfectly almond-shaped, mocha-brown eyes. Her face was put together in an almost symmetrically perfect way, and her nose was small— not too pointy, not too short. She felt herself bow to signal appreciation for the compliment.

"Tomie, your mother tells me that you sew." Hayashi-san's silky voice filled the room.

"Yes, Hayashi-san, I make my own kimonos, of course, and those of my siblings," she reported.

"Very good." Hayashi-san smiled, and that elicited another bow from Tomie. Then Hayashi-san gave the slightest of nods to Tomie's mother.

"Tomie, you can continue on your project," Tomie's mother suggested, an order put in a polite manner. Tomie understood. She bowed again as she made her way out of the room.

Tomie stared at Hayashi-san from behind the *fusuma*. The sliding wall was made of rice paper, yet Tomie couldn't hear their conversation. Still, she couldn't take her eyes off this handsome woman in her spectacular kimono and perfect hair. *Why did my mother have to shoo me off?*

A few days later Tomie modeled her newly made kimono for her mother and father. She had finished it a week ahead of the big day.

"I will be the envy of all the girls on New Year's Day," Tomie announced. Her parents smiled; their oldest daughter was their pride and joy.

"Tomie. Come, sit." Her father patted his hand on the pillow next to him after she had finished her debut. Tomie did as she was told. It was a perfect chance for her to see how this new kimono would wear. She decided, as she sat, that it was perfect.

"Tomie." Her father's voice was suddenly compromised.

"What is it, father? Are you ill?"

"No, my child. My health is fine." He paused before he continued. "Tomie, the time has come for you to marry."

Tomie was confused by this. "But I have not been courted, father," she reminded him.

He nodded that he understood. "We have arranged for you to marry."

At first, she thought she was hearing things. She had barely talked to boys, much less anticipated being courted. But *married*! "I don't want to marry, father, I want to stay with you."

Her father scratched his head. This was going to be more difficult than he thought. "My dear, Hayashi-san has arranged for you to marry the son of a councilman."

The son of a councilman! Her mind started to spin. Maybe this would mean that she would take on the attributes of someone as grand as Hayashi-san.

"In Tsukidate?"

"No, Senoue." Her mind settled a little bit with this. Senoue was just a carriage-ride away; she could even walk home if she was desperate.

"I don't want to leave my family," she succumbed, "but if I must, I'm happy I will be close by."

Her father looked helplessly at his wife. "Tomie, this son of a councilman lives . . . in America."

"America!" The breath was sucked out of her body. She couldn't even imagine how far away this was. "I—I don't want to go. I won't go! Haven't you heard the stories about the brides they send to America? Some are left to rot, never claimed by their husband. Some are stuck with an old man who purports to be young in his photos. Is this what you want for your daughter? Helpless and alone in a country that is foreign to her?"

Her parents had no answer for Tomie, for they had also heard the stories of disappointed brides who had been sent to America. But arranged marriages had become common practice since so many Issei men had taken work overseas. The Japanese government thought it prudent to formulate a strategy to unite Japanese men with Japanese women. The only problem was the Pacific Ocean that separated the men living abroad from the women still in Japan. To complicate matters, Japanese men living in the United States had limited means to return to Japan to be married. While earnings were better in the United States than in Japan, any savings required hard work and long hours. There was no time for the luxury of traveling to Japan, losing weeks of work for the purpose of marriage. A much simpler solution was born: the "picture bride."

They let her sob in between them and when she looked up with longing eyes, she didn't get the assurance she was hoping for. They, themselves, were torn about this decision and knew it was a gamble. At the time in Japan, there wasn't much of a future for girls in general, but girls coming from small towns had very little chance of meeting the right man for marriage. They had taken all the precautions they could and had gone as far as traveling to Senoue to meet Mataemon. They felt assured that Tomie would embark on a better life with Yasoshichi in America than she would if she remained in Japan.

"It is decided, my daughter." Tomie's father's voice was gentle but firm.

Later that night, alone in her room, Tomie sobbed quietly. She looked at her new kimono, the one she had been so proud to wear. It was all a farce. This kimono that she had put her heart and soul into making, this kimono was intended only for her first meeting with her new husband, a total stranger. This kimono of beautiful colors would not be enjoyed on New Year's Day; its purpose had been entirely different and unbeknownst to Tomie. She now hated this kimono and everything it stood for.

Tomie, with a dozen or so other brides, endured the same grueling voyage across the Pacific as Yasoshichi had years earlier. She arrived in San Pedro, California, on February 18, 1915, as Tomie Abe, having been married by proxy in Japan. In the kimono she hated, she was taken to the immigration office on Terminal Island to wait for her new husband. Other husbands came to claim their brides and with each union, Tomie became more anxious. One husband was a good twenty years older than he had portrayed himself in the photo held by his helpless bride. Tomie saw the sheer distress in the young bride's eyes, utterly powerless to do anything but go with the old man. She waited nervously for this son of a councilman.

When Yasoshichi entered the room, she hoped that he was the one, her husband. He checked in with the immigration officer speaking fluent English. The immigration officer shuffled papers around and then pointed at Tomie. Her heart fluttered. Could she have such good fortune? This was a handsome man, seven years her senior, and he had secured a good vocation. He looked over at Tomie, and their eyes met for the first time. With papers in hand, he walked over to her and extended his hand to help her up.

"Tomie. I am Yasoshichi," he said in perfect Japanese. She bowed. He continued, "You must be tired after such a long voyage."

"Thank you, yes."

"We have three hours travel ahead of us," he said as he picked up her suitcase, "much easier travel than the steamship, however." And with this, he smiled at her, and her heart knew in this moment she was with a good man.

Yasoshichi took great care of Tomie as they arrived at the train station. Tomie's eyes were wide with wonder at the modern Los Angeles of 1915. While railroads in Japan were plentiful, Los Angeles boasted a whopping fifty-two rail routes and hundreds of departures a day, making this city one of the busiest hubs in the country. Los Angeles county possessed the highest number of automobiles in the state—something that was astounding for Tomie to see.

"Much to learn, no?" Yasoshichi noticed how intrigued Tomie was with the modern state of America. Tomie nodded. Indeed, she had much acclimation ahead of her—a new world, a new language, and a new husband.

★ ★ ★

LEFT: Tomie, Masao, and Yasoshichi in San Bernardino
RIGHT: Tomie with son Masao

At the new retirement home, Alan greeted us in the lobby and we all headed up to see their new place. Masao hobbled along at lightning speed on his cane—I had never seen him move so fast. I figured he had to go to the bathroom, but I was wrong. He was in a hurry to get to Doris. That was all he wanted.

Doris was in a hospital bed in her room. Masao was excited to see her and immediately went to her without even so much as looking around at the new place his sons had arranged so nicely. When Alan and I peeked in on them, Masao was sitting by the head of her bed. They were holding hands and comforting each other. The way they were looking at each other seemed to transcend time; it was as if they were young and seeing each other for the first time.

CHAPTER TWO

LOSS OF HOME

"Mas, do you remember when we were talking about your dad?" I asked when we were all out to dinner one night.

"My dad. Jeez." He started down the trail of thought from his childhood. I was happy to see the look on his face that told me he was ready to revisit the past.

"My dad. He was a different kind of father than I am."

"What did he do?" I asked, almost afraid to hear the answer. Masao settled into a thinking posture, his eyes drifted off into the distance, and I knew he was reliving something. He shook his head.

"When I was eight," he started, looking at me to make sure I was listening. "When I was just a little boy, my whole family took a trip to Japan." I nodded; I was with him so far. I was eagerly waiting for the punch line and was about to get it.

"The whole family, we went. We were there a few weeks, maybe months, I don't remember. I didn't know any Japanese but for some reason, my dad started me in school over there. The kids—they were mean, boy, *really* mean."

1925—SAN BERNARDINO

Masao and Josué sprinted to the end of the school sidewalk as usual. Josué won by a hair.

"See you tomorrow," Josué puffed as he caught his breath.

"Uh-uh. Remember? I'm taking a trip with my family."

"Oh, yeah. Where are you going again?"

"Japan." Masao could tell by Josué's confused face that he needed to fill in the details a little bit more. "It's where my parents are from."

"Is it by Mexico?"

"Nah. I don't think so. We have to take a boat to get there."

"When are you coming back?"

"I don't know. By Christmas, I hope."

"That's too long."

Masao shrugged, "See ya, Josué."

"See ya, Mas."

Masao kicked a can all the way home, then picked it up and put it in the trash behind his house. He came in through the back door and set his lunch pail on the counter. His mother, who was always in the kitchen to greet him, was not to be seen.

"Mommy?"

Tomie came out of the bedroom, wiping her eyes and nose with an embroidered handkerchief. Masao wondered if he was in trouble.

"What's wrong?"

"No. I okay," she lied. "I fix snack." And she immediately busied herself at the kitchen counter.

Masao went to put his shoes away and noticed that his mom had been packing his suitcase. He slowly swung open his closet door and saw that there was nothing left inside. On his bed, two suitcases were waiting to be closed up.

Back in the kitchen, his snack of apple slices was waiting. He sat at the table and ate, not thinking too much about anything.

"After snack, you go store," his mother was saying.

"Okay. Hey, Ma, why are you packing all my stuff? Are we going to be there that long?"

But his mom didn't answer him. She was at the sink with her head down. Masao figured she didn't understand him, because her

English was a little on the sparse side and sometimes this was how she coped—by ignoring.

A few minutes later, he was on his way to Star Cash Grocery, wagon in tow. As usual, all the merchants along the way waved to him. He rounded the corner to Third Street and pulled his wagon inside his father's store. Tatsuo was the first to greet him.

"Ah. Masao!"

"Hi, uncle." Masao eyed the fresh apple bananas that had arrived. Sweeter and smaller than a regular banana, it was Masao's favorite fruit.

"Take one, they good," Tatsuo encouraged him. Masao pulled an apple banana off its stalk and peeled it. He sat down in his wagon to enjoy the treat.

"You excited for trip?" Tatsuo took a piece of the fruit for himself and peeled it.

"Nah, what's so special about Japan anyway?"

His dad came out from the back of the store and was ready to bark out orders but decided to give Tatsuo and Masao their moment. When he saw that they were done eating, he gathered some produce.

"Masao. Take this to Mr. Uyeda," he directed as he loaded up Masao's wagon, "then come back to sweep."

Masao pulled his wagon into the café at the end of the block where Mr. Uyeda was waiting for him.

"Ah, thank you, Masao-chan," Mr. Uyeda warmly greeted Masao, helping unload the goods.

"Okay, see ya, Mr. Uyeda." Masao started to leave when he felt a tap on his shoulder.

"I have something for you. For your journey," Mr. Uyeda said as he reached behind the counter and pulled out a small, neatly bundled package. "It's candy."

Masao's eyes lit up. His parents rarely let him eat candy. "Thanks, Mr. Uyeda!"

Yasoshichi (second from left) and Tatsuo (third from left) at Star Cash Grocery

"You take care, now," Mr. Uyeda said to an oblivious Masao, who was clutching his little candy package as though it were a bag of gold.

And as Masao walked back to Star Cash Grocery, the sun was setting.

1925—SENOUE, FUKUSHIMA-KEN, JAPAN

After weeks at sea, there was a buzz of excitement as passengers stood at the rail and watched the ship dock inside Yokohama Harbor. Little Masao, who had grown up with Japanese people who spoke English, realized he was surrounded by the sound of the Japanese language. Only Japanese. Even his parents seemed to be limiting their English. On the long train ride to the little town of Senoue in the north of Japan, Masao noticed the same.

"Doesn't anyone here speak English?" he asked.

His mom smiled at him, "You must be speaking Japanese too one day."

The next morning, at Masao's grandparents' home, Yasoshichi was up early. He and his father had tea together and then walked in the orchard, as they had done many times when Yasoshichi was young. Yasoshichi was impressed with the expansion of roads in the little village since he had departed some seventeen years earlier.

"Was the harvest good this year?" Yasoshichi asked, noticing that the trees had not been pruned. This would be at the top of his list to accomplish while visiting.

"Yes."

They walked along in silence.

"This town in California, it's a good place to live?" Mataemon pondered.

"Yes. Many Japanese live there, father. Tatsuo is quite content," Yasoshichi said. It was important to ease his father's mind.

Mataemon nodded. He hadn't intended for his sons to live in America permanently. But out of economic necessity, that was exactly what happened. And now, two of his sons had chosen America as their home, and a third son was entertaining the idea as well.

Back in the house, Masao woke up. He examined the odd house, one huge room with flimsy doors that slid to cordon off sections. It was bitterly cold inside. He wandered around until he found his mother in the kitchen, along with an older woman who was decrepit and had a sour face. The woman whirled around to look at him with such hostility it made him jump.

"Mommy?" He instinctively went near his mother wondering who this horrible old lady was and more—wanting to get far away from her.

"Ah, Masao. Good morning." She kissed him on the head. The old woman spattered out something in Japanese; her voice was as harsh as her looks. Tomie listened respectfully to this old woman, then nodded.

"Masao, this is grandmother to you," she said. Masao cringed, then tried to hide it. He glanced at his little sisters who sat quietly nearby. Evidently, they had already met this sour woman.

"Nice to meet you," he said and extended his hand to shake hers. But the old woman, his grandmother, pulled back and spat some other Japanese words out at him. Tomie gently guided his hand back at his side.

"In Japan, must have great caring for grandmother. No—this," she motioned with her hand. Masao got it: don't shake hands with old people here.

"Mommy, where is the bathroom?"

"Ah," she guided Masao to the window that overlooked the orchard. She pointed to a little shack in the back area. Masao couldn't believe his eyes. His little sister, Yuriko, muffled her giggles.

"Out there?" He was mortified. This elicited more Japanese that seemed to vomit from his grandmother's mouth. She was the most unpleasant woman Masao had ever encountered. His grandmother was grabbing newspaper from a pile and abruptly handed it to Masao. Then she sharply motioned for him to go.

"I can't read Japanese." Masao was confused but did as his grandmother ordered and headed for the door.

In the outhouse there wasn't a toilet, just a hole in the ground. There was no toilet paper either. That was when it dawned on him: the newspaper *was* the toilet paper. From that first morning, Masao couldn't wait to get back home. He longed for San Bernardino, for their house that had a regular bathroom and no grandmother to torment him.

That night at dinner, Masao quietly observed his grandparents and stuck close to his mother. He had been raised using chopsticks, so that was natural to him and seemed to please his grandmother. But that was the only thing that pleased her.

The meat they served was unlike any Masao had ever tasted. He didn't like it and instead ate the rice. His grandmother noticed this, of course, and that ignited more of her wrath. She spat some Japanese out at his dad, who then took note.

"Eat your meat, Masao," his dad said firmly.

"I don't like it," Masao responded respectfully. "What kind is it?"

"Horse. It's good for you." This made Masao set his chopsticks down. Then there was an eruption of Japanese from his grandmother. His parents went into some sort of explanation, evidently on Masao's behalf, but his grandmother was visibly angry.

"What's the matter, Mommy?" Masao asked timidly.

"She thinks you're a spoiled American," Yasoshichi answered for Tomie. Masao leaned into his mother. He felt ashamed but didn't know exactly why. "Tomorrow, we start you in school," Yasoshichi continued. Clearly, this was not the time to argue. He tried to sink away into his mother's side.

The next morning, his father woke him up early. He had some clothes laid out for Masao: a drab, gray outfit.

"It's your school uniform," Yasoshichi explained.

"Daddy, I don't know Japanese. What am I going to do in school all day?"

"You go to school to *learn* Japanese."

"Are we going to be here that long?"

"Get dressed. Don't argue."

Masao and his father walked the half mile on a trail through a wooded area. Children also walking to school stared at the newcomer. His dad delivered him to the schoolmaster and the two spoke in Japanese. Masao looked around, noticing the stark difference from his school in San Bernardino, where there were a variety of faces and the teachers were nice. Here, everyone looked the same, and there was a harsh feeling to the place.

"Do you remember your way home?"

Masao nodded. His father nodded back, took a moment to assess his son's strength, then left.

The first day was the worst. Masao didn't understand anything that was going on in the classroom, and to make matters worse, children made fun of him. They couldn't understand how someone could be Japanese and not speak the language. At lunchtime, they surrounded him. Although he couldn't understand a word, he knew he was being taunted.

He ran all the way home, holding in his tears. When he came to his grandparents' orchard, he slowed down. He sat down by a tree and it was there, in the safety of the orchard, where he cried. Things didn't get any better as the days wore on. Even on his ninth birthday in mid-November, when one is supposed to celebrate one's own life, one's own existence, Masao endured the relentless teasing.

Over the next several weeks, Masao suffered the same punishing treatment, day after long day. Kids teased him endlessly; every day after school, he sat alone in the orchard. But he began to pick up words, one of which was *chitai*. It was something that the kids yelled at him persistently in the schoolyard.

"What does '*chitai*' mean?" he asked his father at dinner. His grandmother gasped at this and mumbled something under her breath. Tomie's eyes filled with tears. She quietly got up and left the table. Yasoshichi watched her go and then looked at his father, who nodded slightly.

"Where did you hear this word?"

"The kids at school call me that all the time. What's it mean?"

"Masao, you are not *chitai*. It means—slow."

"Slow?"

"Retarded. It means retarded."

Masao swelled with anger. His grandfather noticed and said something in Japanese, with which his father seemed to agree.

"Masao, it won't be long before you are able to speak two languages. The children here, they only have one. You, Masao, you know what it is like in two worlds—they only know one. You are not *chitai*." His father's words calmed Masao for the moment. Yasoshichi gazed at his son. His eyes spoke only love as he softly followed with, "You are brave. Brave and smart."

At bedtime, when his mother came to kiss him goodnight, Masao noticed that she had been crying again.

"Mommy, it's okay. I'll be okay," Masao said. But this just made it worse for her. She sat down next to him and stroked his hair, choking back tears. Masao didn't know what to say to her to make her feel better.

"I'll be okay. I promise," he assured her. He already had a plan for how to deal with the mean kids, and besides, they couldn't stay in Japan forever.

"My son," she said as her tears persisted, "you good boy." She kissed him on the head and quietly got up. Masao watched his mother's silhouette behind the *fusuma*. She collapsed into his father's chest as he shut the *fusuma* that closed off his room. Masao was confused about why the situation with the mean kids bothered his mother so much, but he would show her that he was strong. He would show her that she had nothing to worry about.

The next day at lunch, in the courtyard, he was again surrounded by children. But he was ready.

"*Chitai!*" They shouted from every direction.

"*Watashi wanaidesu chitai!* I am not retarded!" Masao yelled back. "*Watashi wa* American. I am American! I'm from America! I will know things you will never know." And this stifled their voices. They backed down, every last one of them. He had found a way to get some relief from this horrid vacation that seemed to last forever.

In his mind, he must have thought the nightmare would end some day soon, when he and his family would return to the United

States, to San Bernardino where everything made sense. But that would not happen. His nightmare would only get worse. That afternoon when Masao returned home, things had changed. It was the first day he didn't need to stop in the orchard on his way home. He felt vindicated somehow. Maybe now they could go home, content in knowing that he could survive in Japan if need be. Maybe now, his grandmother would let him be.

He walked in the back door and spotted his stern grandmother at the sink.

"Mommy?" he called out. Something felt different. His annoying little sisters weren't there to bother him, he hadn't noticed his father or grandfather outside where they usually were, and his mother wasn't answering him.

"Mommy?" he called out again. He ran through the house looking for anyone; his sisters, his father, his mother, anyone at all.

"Mommy?!" His voice became frantic.

His grandmother gave him a sly look from the sink and sputtered something in Japanese. The only thing he understood was *inaku natta*—gone. His little heart pounded. *This can't be happening,* he thought as he ran to every last corner in the house. Not one piece of luggage remained; even his own suitcases had been taken.

★ ★ ★

Recalling those events seemed to make Masao melancholy. "I was scared. I was just a little boy, just turned nine years old, a-no?" His voice wasn't angry or bitter; he spoke as if speaking of someone else, of some little boy he knew long ago and for whom he felt incredible empathy.

"Why did they do that?" *What possible reason,* I wondered to myself.

"Gee, I don't know. I would never do that to my boys." He was genuinely bewildered by his parents' decision. A mood fell upon the table; a sadness, even grief, about a child who had been left behind. Masao felt it, Alan felt it, and I felt it. Doris nibbled away on her rice.

"It took a long time before I could even communicate with my grandparents," he said as he ate a piece of sashimi. "But my grandmother was mean, boy, *really* mean."

"What about your grandpa?" I asked, hoping for some sort of silver lining to this depressing story.

"He didn't talk much. But I remember that he always ran for village councilman. He was always nervous about winning. Heh!" It's funny that Masao remembered a detail like this. His grandfather's position in the village also factored into Masao's future in a way that nothing else would.

At home, I pulled up the ship's manifest that showed it all: December 14, 1925. Masao's name is vividly absent from the list that contains every other Abe family member on the ship returning to the port of San Pedro, California: Yasoshichi, Tomie, Yoshiko, Yuriko.

No Masao.

CHAPTER THREE

HOME IN JAPAN

"Hey, Mas," I said to get his attention. The four of us were driving back from a casino not far from Seattle, which had become one of Masao's favorite places. "Can you tell me more about your time in Japan?"

"What do you want to know?" he asked, needing a little more help with a direction but definitely in the mood to talk.

"Hmmm. Well, what was school like over there?"

"Heh! It was a lot different then. That was a long time ago. Now . . . let me think. Well, middle school, that's like high school here, a-no? I was in, ah, something like ROTC, military training." He glanced at me sitting in the back seat with Doris.

"Was everyone in military training?"

"Nooo." He said his "no" almost like it was an explanation rather than a finite answer. It was soft and thoughtful and the inflection went up at the end.

"A lot of us boys were in military training. I was in *officer* training. A big shot, a-no?" Masao chuckled at himself. "The military in Japan was taking over everything. There were a lot of assassinations during that time. Jeeezz. Tough times in Japan."

1932—FUKUSHIMA-KEN, JAPAN

As Masao grew up he learned the Japanese language, as well as the culture. The school system in Japan, at that time, was a tracking system.

Students attended primary school and subsequently took a test to enter a specific middle school for five years. Students were tracked depending on how they tested and whether or not they showed promise of academic success in college. For Masao, it was the military track.

In 1931, Japanese troops overran the Chinese province of Manchuria. Around this time, the military grooming of Japan's children intensified in an attempt to prepare Japan for ultimate expansion. Masao, going on fifteen, was in the final stages of being primed for the military. He had entered the officer's training program and, upon graduation, could enter the Imperial Japanese Army as a second lieutenant once he reached the age of the draft, which was twenty.

During this period, the Japanese Ministry of Education compiled and produced all textbooks studied by children in schools. Essentially, the government chose what to feed the minds of its young. The military had a strong influence throughout Japan and permeated education. A heavy emphasis was placed on loyalty to the emperor and the Empire of Japan. Spartan discipline and national spirit also ranked high on the agenda. Most extracurricular activities and social customs revolved around the notion of loyalty to the empire.

Masao's training included military tactics and weapon instruction. He was even involved in sword fighting as part of his school day ritual. In the all-boy program, Masao was indoctrinated into a brotherhood that was often divided, as was Japan as a nation. One day Masao walked with his buddies, Akira and Kunio, through the wooded area near their school. They all wore military uniforms but were kids at heart, joking and laughing. Although they were just fifteen, they had been in training to be warriors and when serious topics emerged, the men in them would come out.

"What do you think about the coup attempt in Tokyo? Our prime minister—gone. Just like that," Akira inserted into their banter. The laughing all but stopped as the three young men debated this.

Masao took a stance. "Those militants are shortsighted."

"Masao, those guys are the future of Japan," Kunio shot back.

"It's going to be hard for them to be the future of Japan from jail," Masao laughed, retorting. But Kunio wouldn't have it.

"Maybe their 'short-sighted' ideas are the right ideas. Maybe their goals for Japan are the correct goals for Japan. Those brave men are going to be the leaders of Japan one day, you'll see. Then we'll go in as officers, and it will be up to *us* to protect our country and the purity of our people."

"No country is pure, Kunio. Look how many countrymen we have living here from around the world. Look at me."

An infuriated Kunio cut Masao short. "You. You are *not* Japanese. You never have been. It's only nationalists, like myself, who are pure in our blood, and who will fight to the death for Japan."

All three boys stopped in their tracks. Kunio often went into tirades, but this personal attack on Masao was unprecedented.

Kunio positioned himself physically and became more of a threat. "You and your American blood will one day have to choose. Do you have the spirit of Japan in your heart? *Do you?*"

Masao was mortified. Never once had Kunio referred to Masao as an American.

"Kunio, he is one of us. He can't help where he was born." Akira came to Masao's defense.

Masao stood speechless, unable to believe that his friend of so many years had turned on him in an instant.

Kunio deliberated for a moment, then stomped off.

"He just gets caught up in the movement," Akira assured Masao, then he ran to catch up with Kunio.

Masao, now alone, looked around. He decided to change his course and instead of following the trail home, he took a different way, to the all-girl school. Outside, he waited patiently for the girl he had met in the village. Finally, school let out and girls poured from the building. A pod of girls, all wearing drab school uniforms, appeared. Masao perked up when he saw her. Miyoko. She approached Masao, and he stood up. It was Masao and Miyoko, in public, yet alone.

"Hello, Miyoko," Masao greeted her with a smile. Miyoko smiled back.

Masao carried her books as they walked the dirt road toward Miyoko's house.

"You look handsome in your uniform." Miyoko admired the boy who had come from America.

"And you . . . look pretty," Masao stumbled on his words.

"Please, tell me more about America."

"I don't remember much about it."

"I love to hear about America."

Masao saw the genuine curiosity in her eyes. It was understandable. Living in Japan at this time was bleak, particularly for women. Ambitious young men had the military waiting for them, but young women had little to motivate them other than young men. Masao wanted to please her, so he pulled up a recollection in his mind.

"I was only eight when I left. But I remember it was always sunny, sunny and warm. It was like a little Japan in the middle of a city. It was nice the way all the Japanese people knew each other. I remember everyone was happy."

"Carreefornia," Miyoko said, trying to impress Masao by reiterating the name of this place where he had lived long ago. Masao smiled at this.

"I think that's how you say it. I've forgotten my English."

"Herreewood," Miyoko continued, showing off her knowledge of American places and names of cities. Masao was confused by this one, though.

"What?"

"Herreewood. You know, where the movie stars live."

Masao chuckled, both at Miyoko's pronunciation and at the fact that he couldn't remember the correct pronunciation.

"I can't remember how to say that either," he admitted. "Hollywood. That's it. Hollywood. California."

"Horr-ee-wood."

"Holl-y-wood. You have to go like this, with your tongue." He tried to show her how his mouth and tongue were positioned.

"Har-he-wood." Miyoko made another attempt, but try as she might, she couldn't pronounce the letter *l*.

"Herreewood is fine," Masao assured her.

"Your family, so far from you. Do you miss them?" Her question elicited a gaze on Masao's face that said it all. He was in love.

"Not anymore."

"And the warm, sunny days of Carreefornia?"

"Japan is my home now."

After spending time with Miyoko, and even though it was just the few minutes to walk her home, Masao felt elated, his confrontation with Kunio a distant memory. When he got to his grandparents' orchard and had the house in sight, he sensed something. He ran up the stairs and into the house, planning his strategy to avoid talking to his grandmother. He still did not care for the old woman, even after living with her for years.

Masao entered the house to find his entire family from America. They had just arrived; their luggage littered the house. Tomie immediately choked up when Masao walked in—she barely recognized her oldest son, whom she hadn't seen in eight years. She embraced him and spoke in Japanese to him for the first time in her life.

"Masao, my son. You're all grown up." She smiled at him.

"Mommy." Masao held her tightly. He had missed her. By the looks of the luggage, they had brought everything with them. His two sisters, now thirteen and eleven, stared at the big brother they barely remembered. His new little brother, Jiro, raced by in a flurry.

Yasoshichi stepped toward Masao; he examined his son in the military uniform. Masao felt the judgment but didn't care. He was just happy to see his mother again.

"We stay here now," his father stated.

Masao nodded. He understood why. Masao's grandfather, Mataemon, was becoming frail and could no longer care for the orchard or garden. As the oldest son, it was Yasoshichi's responsibility to take care of his ailing parents and oversee the family orchard business. Tatsuo would assume responsibility for the store in San Bernardino.

That night the entire family gathered to eat. His younger sisters seemed terrified of their grandmother. Masao, now used to the old lady, largely ignored her, but he knew it would take his sisters a while to get to that point.

"You will take your sisters to school tomorrow," Masao's father stated matter-of-factly.

"Yes," Masao obeyed.

"You have entered military training?"

"Yes. I can join the military as an officer once I am at the age of conscription." Masao stated this confidently, thinking it would make his father proud. Instead, his father looked doubtful.

"Hmm." His father appeared to deeply reflect on Masao's plan.

The next morning, Masao and his father took Yoshiko and Yuriko to school. Masao left them at the primary school and walked to his school, wondering what Kunio's mood would be. His prediction was that whatever had been bothering him would be long forgotten.

Still, it would be hard for Masao to get the image of Kunio's wrath out of his mind.

Kunio was waiting outside the school for Masao. Masao strained to see his friend's face from the distance and felt relieved when he saw him smile. He relaxed even more when he saw Kunio walk his way.

"Good morning, Masao," Kunio bowed. "Please forgive me for yesterday. I get emotional when I think about the current state of our country."

"Of course." Masao responded as the gentleman he was. They both understood, though, that they were leaning toward vastly different political ideologies. Masao had the gift of living in two enormously different cultures and had fond memories of America.

Senoue, Fukushima-ken, Japan, circa 1931
FRONT ROW: Yasoshichi, Jiro, Mataemon, Tayo Anzai (grandmother),
Yoichi, and Tomie
BACK ROW: Masao, Yoshiko, and Yuriko

Kunio had never been outside of Senoue. Their friendship would be forever compromised, and they both knew it.

★ ★ ★

It was a few weeks before I could continue my history lesson with Masao. We were at dinner with Masao and Doris at a cozy little Italian place.

"Last time we talked, your family had all joined you in Japan."

"That's right, they moved over there. All of them. My grandfather was getting too old for the orchard," he recalled.

"So then what happened?"

"Well," Masao started off, "I graduated from officer training school, a-no? I could go into the army as a second lieutenant."

I nodded that I was still with him. Alan arranged his mom's salad that had arrived.

"But my dad, he sent me back," he stated as he unfolded the red cloth napkin that protected the warm rolls in the breadbasket.

"Sent you back here?" I clarified.

"Yep. To the States. He sent me back here," he said while nodding and smearing a huge glob of butter on his roll—my kind of guy.

I was dumbfounded. "Did you want to come back here?"

"Heck no! I wanted to stay in Japan. It was my home by then. I knew the language, my friends were all there. My family was there. I didn't know English any longer, so—no use being here. I was ready to go *fight*. In China." He took a bite of his roll. It seemed more important than my questions.

"I'm so confused," I said. They were really my private thoughts that accidentally spilled out of my mouth. Alan looked at me and smiled at my bewilderment.

"Help me understand the bridge between you wanting to serve in the Japanese military and you actually serving in the US military," I said.

"Heh! I don't know. It just happened that way," he responded. He was sincere about his statement. It was the way life had happened *to him*.

SPRING 1934—SENOUE, FUKUSHIMA-KEN, JAPAN

Outside the school, Masao waited for Miyoko. She emerged, happy to see him.

"Your sisters, their Japanese is getting very good," Miyoko reported. Masao nodded in agreement. "Do they like it in Japan?"

"I don't know, I haven't asked them. It doesn't really matter if they like it or not, they can't go back. Besides, it's safer for them here. America's military is weak." Masao didn't really believe this, but like any young man out to impress a girl, he had to boast a little bit. He was being primed by the Japanese military, after all, to lead soldiers in battle.

"Are you coming to the graduation?" he asked her, hoping that she would attend, hoping that she would see him in the spotlight, accepting his diploma, accepting his future as a leader in the military.

"Yes, of course." She glanced at Masao, shy to speak the words her heart was singing. "I am proud of you, Masao."

Masao liked this. It was quiet as they strolled.

"When I am called to duty I will go proudly. And I will come back for you, Miyoko."

The drab courtyard at Masao's school had been transformed into a spectacular graduation arena. The rising sun flag took center stage, along with another flag laden with *kanji* that espoused loyalty to the emperor. Paper lanterns in vivid colors hung from string above. The front of the courtyard was reserved for the most prestigious men of the village, the schoolmaster, the village councilmen, including Masao's grandfather, and other statesmen. These men were adorned with sashes that crossed the front of their chest and indicated the level of importance they held. On both sides of the courtyard, *taiko* drummers waited for the celebration to begin. In the center of the yard, rows of chairs accommodated the young men: future militants, dressed in their officer wear. Behind them the families gathered to watch the glory unfold.

Masao sat, his hands folded in his lap. He adjusted his glasses when the schoolmaster began his speech about the honor and loyalty that had been instilled into the minds of these young men and about how proud the emperor would be. Masao, only halfway listening, glanced at Kunio, who was all ears. Without straining his head too much, Masao looked back to find Miyoko. There she was, looking at him. He smiled, and she smiled back. After the schoolmaster finished his exhaustive speech, he stepped to the table that held all the diplomas. There was no applause or cheering as he called each young man to the front. This was a serious affair.

Masao's name was called. He accepted his diploma and bowed to the schoolmaster, and then smiled his wonderful big smile. This made his mom happy, and it made Miyoko smile too. A seventeen-year-old Masao had accomplished a great feat—he had learned a second language, a second culture, and was trained as a warrior for the Japanese military. He felt like a man. Now all he had to do was turn twenty so he could put into action all he had learned.

The summer after graduation Masao worked in his grandfather's orchard alongside his father. One afternoon when the sun and heat wouldn't let up, Masao and his father sat under a tree to cool off. They heard someone approach and thought it might be little Jiro, but it was instead a man that Masao didn't recognize. His father knew this man, though, and his face contorted as if this was some sort of uninvited salesman. Osamu Fujita, a stocky man in his thirties, approached Yasoshichi. Masao noticed the scowl deepen on his father's face. This didn't slow Fujita down in the least. He was no stranger to unwelcoming looks on parents' faces. He was there to serve the emperor and took great pride in that effort.

"Abe-san." Osamu greeted Yasoshichi with a bow. Yasoshichi stood up and nodded—he motioned for Masao to stand up as well. Osamu dabbed his sweaty forehead with his handkerchief. "You must be proud of your son," Osamu continued, taking out a small notepad and pencil.

"Yes, very proud," Yasoshichi nodded. Masao had no idea what was happening.

"Tell me, what are your plans this summer, Masao-chan?"

"His plans are to work in the orchard," Yasoshichi answered for Masao. "He is but seventeen, Fujita-san."

"Yes, I am aware," Osamu snapped back. "And this fall, what are your plans this fall?"

Masao shrugged, "I will help my father in the orchard, as he said."

Osamu recorded this in his notebook. Masao looked at his father, who was staring daggers at this man.

"Are you planning travel of any kind?"

"No, no travel," Yasoshichi assured him.

Osamu was skeptical. "And his passport. Where is it located? I would like to take a look at it." Osamu wasn't going to back down from his interrogation.

"It is packed away, Fujita-san. It will take some time to locate. We can have it for you on your next visit," Yasoshichi stated

Masao was surprised to hear his father bend the truth like this. His passports, both his Japanese passport and his American passport, were tucked away in one of his mother's hatboxes, along with all the other family passports.

"Hmm," Osamu said with suspicion. "I will need you to report any travel directly to me," he ordered as he looked directly at Masao.

"Yes," Masao replied as he bowed, sensing his father's irritation.

"I will be back at the end of harvest. Have that passport ready for me to examine. Goodbye for now." Osamu tucked his little notebook away and dabbed his forehead again.

When Osamu was safely out of hearing range Masao looked at his father. "Who was that?"

"Osamu is the military affairs clerk for Senoue," his father said in a dejected tone. "He is here to keep tabs on you for the next two years."

The Japanese military had placed over ten thousand military affairs clerks in villages throughout Japan. These men, like Osamu Fujita, were wholly in charge of keeping track of young men, their whereabouts if they moved, and their ages. Osamu Fujita certainly had Masao on his list of future soldiers who were primed for service in the military. Masao's grandfather, Mataemon, had been the village councilman for a number of years, and this brought even more attention to Masao's name. And because Masao had just graduated from officer training, Osamu was not about to let him out of his sight. He would continue to check on Masao, his conduct, his appearance, his mental state of mind, his whereabouts, and most importantly, his intentions to maintain loyalty to the emperor. With every visit, Masao would become more enthusiastic and Yasoshichi would become more agitated. But the visits continued, season after season.

In November of 1935, after Masao had turned nineteen, his younger sister Yuriko developed acute appendicitis. It came on suddenly. The village doctor provided only minimal relief; the prognosis was grim, and Yuriko died within weeks. The grief of losing little Yuriko permeated the home, and it was during this time that Osamu made another one of his routine visits. The family had just gathered to eat when they heard the knock at the door. Yasoshichi, who had aged years in the span of a few months, opened the door.

"Fujita-san, please, we are mourning the loss of our second daughter. Leave us in peace," Yasoshichi said somberly.

"Of course, Abe-san. I only come to express my condolences," Osamu said as he bowed. The door was opened enough for Osamu to see inside and take note that Masao was still in Senoue. This didn't get by Yasoshichi, who knew that he had to keep this military affairs clerk happy and confident in his findings.

"Thank you." He called to Masao, "Masao, please come." Masao went to the door and greeted Fujita-san with a bow.

"You are nineteen, now, yes?"

"Yes," Masao said proudly.

"No travel plans?"

"No, of course not," Masao answered confidently. Yasoshichi looked on.

"Very well. Again, my condolences, Abe-san," Osamu bowed. Yasoshichi nodded and closed the door. He glanced at Tomie, who looked at her husband helplessly. She couldn't bear to lose another child. They had only one more year before the military would claim her oldest child and from what she knew, he would have little chance of coming out of the military alive.

In early 1936, unrest in Japan was growing, and in February of that year, some nationalistic military officers attempted another coup in Tokyo, assassinating several ministers and hoping to start a new regime. While the coup did not succeed entirely, it managed to mar ginalize the political system, polarize parties, and make it possible for the military to gain control over the political direction of Japan.

This coup attempt, combined with the recent loss of Yuriko, drove Yasoshichi and Tomie to make the decision to send Masao back to San Bernardino. To make matters even more urgent, in Yasoshichi's mind, that persistent Osamu Fujita visited more and more often. He knew exactly when Masao would turn twenty:

November 16, 1936. There would be no turning back once the military had a hold of him. Yasoshichi, acting in his son's best interest and at great risk to himself, arranged for Masao's return to San Bernardino seven months before his twentieth birthday.

It was a cold winter evening in the Abe home. Masao was putting more wood in the stove in an attempt to heat up the house. Grief still lingered from the sudden passing of Yuriko, and Masao was attentive to his mother during this time of deep sorrow. The family gathered at the table to eat; Masao closed up the wood stove and joined them. His father cleared his throat and looked at Tomie, who then looked down.

"Masao. The time has come for you to leave Senoue," Yasoshichi stated as he focused on his bowl of udon.

"Not now, father, I cannot join the military until I am twenty." Masao thought his father was confused.

"No military. You go back to States." The table fell quiet. This was shocking to everyone except for Yasoshichi and Tomie.

"No. Father. I have trained as an officer. The military is expecting me to join, as second lieutenant. I must join. Fujita-san is expecting me as well."

"You go. Tomorrow. Arrangements have been made," Yasoshichi responded without skipping a beat. There was no emotion at all. This was an edict.

Anger descended upon Masao, but Japanese culture defined his actions: respect your parents. He defiantly stood up and stormed out. Tomie started to get up to follow him, but Yasoshichi gently held onto her arm and shook his head.

"He will be fine, let him be," he gently persuaded her. She succumbed and sat down next to her husband. Tears filled her eyes and with that, her children felt her sadness. "It is best." And in her heart, she knew he was right.

That night, in the pitch black, Masao ran through the dark trails and along dirt roads to Miyoko's house. He carefully placed a letter near her door. The following afternoon, just as the *Chichibu Maru* departed Yokohama Harbor, Miyoko found the letter. At first she smiled, excited to hear from her love, Masao. But tears soon followed as she read his words.

> *Miyoko. Our walks together have filled my heart with joy. But in one moment, my father has changed my life forever; he has torn me from the country I love and the girl I adore. By the time you read this I will be on my way to America. Your military officer, his destiny unclear. I will return to Japan someday— I feel it. I can't ask you to wait for me. But I hope you will. Fondly, Your Masao*

And while she read the letter, Masao was at the rail of the ship, anguishing as he watched Japan, and his Miyoko, disappear. His intuition about returning to Japan one day would come to fruition; it just wouldn't occur the way he envisioned.

1939—SAN BERNARDINO

Now back in the United States, Masao tried to acclimate to life in California. He had to relearn English and become reacquainted with the more relaxed Western ways. His Uncle Tatsuo, with whom he lived, had since married Yukie, who was also Issei. But Masao wasn't settled. He longed to return to Japan and made it known to his Uncle Tatsuo, who became like a second father.

While Masao had been in Japan, Tatsuo had established himself as a pillar in the Japanese community. He had become the president of the local Japanese Association and had developed a strong customer base for the little grocery store. Many of his customers were

Latinx, and Tatsuo had even learned some Spanish so he could better relate to them. The nickname his Latinx customers gave Tatsuo and Masao was "Chappo"; Masao soon developed a fondness for Latinx customers, just as Tatsuo had.

Tatsuo had a soft heart for those who struggled. He was the very rare merchant willing to extend credit to local customers. His customers appreciated this about him and always paid him back. On the day they came in to settle their bill, Tatsuo even made sure they had a bag of produce and staples, free of charge.

Locals who were down on their luck came to know Tatsuo as someone who would never turn them away. He would help out locals—including those who were Native American—who would occasionally come around for a serving of wine, even though it was forbidden at the time to sell cigarettes, wine, or alcohol to persons of Native American descent. One day a Native American woman came into the store in need of groceries. Without any money, she had with her a hand-woven basket and asked if she could possibly trade the basket for supplies. It wasn't long before Tatsuo had quite the collection of intricately woven and beautifully designed Indian baskets. At one point, he realized that one of the baskets he had been given was, in fact, a family heirloom. Being a good man, he promptly returned it to the family.

Masao kept himself busy working at Star Cash Grocery and learning the kind and generous ways of his Uncle Tatsuo. In addition to relearning English, Masao picked up some words in Spanish as well. When he was not working at Star Cash Grocery, there were things in San Bernardino that Masao enjoyed. Community gatherings were light-hearted and fun, a stark difference from the militant Japan he had been torn away from. Annual picnics occurred every summer along the Santa Ana River. Folks would come together to enjoy Japanese food, play games, have races, and socialize.

The summer months in San Bernardino were plagued with oppressive heat. To cope with it, Masao would take a break from the grocery store around midafternoon. He took ten cents and went to the theater that was air-conditioned. Occasionally Masao would go to the movies with Jimmy Shimizu, a friend whose father owned the barber shop down the street. Masao thought of Jimmy as a really sharp guy because he attended the San Bernardino Valley College and was majoring in chemistry. While Masao idolized others because of their ability to master college-level courses and pursue post-secondary studies, he was viewed as a *Kibei*.

Kibei was a term used to describe people like Masao, born in the United States and therefore Nisei, but educated in Japan and then returned to the United States. It would seem that Kibei would imply great skill and wisdom, as this small group of Japanese Americans were not only bilingual, but also understood and empathized with two vastly different cultures. But the term Kibei was more often used in a derogatory sense. While Masao should have been honored for his survival and accomplishments in Japan, he was actually looked down upon. He was literally caught between two worlds.

A race at the Santa Ana River annual picnic

Masao with buddy Susumu in front of Star Cash Grocery

The more he encountered dismissive attitudes from both Caucasian and Japanese people in America, the more he wanted to return to Japan.

In San Bernardino, life was complicated for the Japanese population. The Nisei children who had been born of Issei parents were now well into their twenties or thirties and had Western ways baked into their personalities. While they appreciated Japanese traditions, they lived in the West. Their parents would often look on, helplessly, watching their Japanese heritage slip away. But once in a great while, Japanese traditions would take hold and be enforced by the elders. This was the case when Masao asked a girl named Hana out on a date.

Hana's father owned a restaurant down the street from Star Cash Grocery. Masao would routinely see Hana in town. One day when Masao and Tatsuo were stocking a delivery of fresh vegetables, Hana walked by the store with some other girls. Masao stopped what he was doing and watched them pass by, instinctively waving, which then prompted Hana to smile and wave back. Tatsuo took note.

"You like her, no?" Tatsuo asked when the girls were safely out of sight.

"Heh! Well, she's cute," Masao was slightly embarrassed. His English was back, only a slight accent remained.

"You should take her out."

"Nah." Masao quickly shut the idea down.

"No, really. Take her to that new movie that's out. *Gone with the Wind.* "

Masao hadn't really thought about a girl in a serious sense since Miyoko back in Japan. The letters with Miyoko had stopped within a year of his return home. He had heard that Kunio had turned radical, and both Kunio and Akira had been conscripted and were serving in China. Miyoko was working in a factory somewhere making military uniforms, and life in Japan was generally hard.

Masao looked at his uncle, who had never steered him wrong, and pondered the notion of taking this cute girl out on a date.

"Heh, maybe I will."

A few days later, a hesitant Masao approached Mr. Kobayashi to ask his permission. "I'd like to take your daughter, Hana, to see the movie."

Mr. Kobayashi studied Masao and apparently approved. "Okay, you can take."

Masao picked out a night for the movie and primped himself for the date. His Uncle Tatsuo looked on, excited that Masao was finally acclimating to Western life again.

At Hana's house, he knocked on the front door and made sure he was presentable. Hana's Japanese mother opened the door, and when she did, Masao could tell she was traditional.

After the introductions, Hana's mother had news for Masao. "You can't take Hana to the movie. I have three daughters. You will take first daughter, Kay."

Eh? What's this? Masao found it hard to hide the shock on his face, even though he tried. Kay wasn't nearly as attractive as Hana, nor did Masao want to court her. But tradition took over: a Japanese mother took liberties to decide which daughter would be partnered with Masao.

To make matters even more uncomfortable, when they arrived at the theater they had to navigate the rope—the one that separated white people from nonwhites. He stood with Kay, a girl he had no desire to date, in the line established for people referred to as "Oriental" or "Colored," and all he wanted was for the night to end.

★ ★ ★

I listened to the end of Masao's story as we finished our dinner at the Italian restaurant. Looking at his gentle face across the table, I felt incredibly uncomfortable with the notion of him facing segregation of any kind. It must have shown on my face because Masao glanced at me and seemed to understand what I was thinking.

"Well, it was the times. Nothing you can do about it," he said in a tender voice.

This generation of his—they are the salt of the earth, I thought. They know that the liberties of the current generations were built on their backs. And they seem to be okay with that, happy to have been the pawns in the evolution of humans so that their children and their children's children won't have to be treated in such a humiliating manner.

After weeks of watching Doris's health deteriorate, it seemed inevitable that she would not recover. It was a shock, but not a surprise, to receive Alan's text message. "Mom died this morning."

She had died in her sleep, and Masao had been the one to discover her. My immediate concern was for Masao. I thought about Alan too, but knew that he would be consumed by supporting his father and his grief would have to take a back seat. Masao, though. I wasn't confident at all that Masao would make it through this.

"How's he holding up?" I asked when Alan finally called me in the afternoon.

"Not too good." His voice sounded drained. He had gone home for a bit of relief. "I'm going to pick up some Japanese food and take it back a little bit later."

"Are you staying with him tonight?"

"I haven't thought about it. Do you think I should?"

Someone needed to be with Masao that night—the grief would have been too heavy for him to handle alone. "He can't be alone tonight, Alan. He just can't."

He knew I was right. I was beginning to understand Masao at a level that his own sons did not. I wasn't sure when or how it happened, but it had.

"Dad said something about moving back to the facility on Mercer Island. I want him here, though. It's closer to me."

"Move him back, Alan. He wants to be in a space where memories were good. It's where he and your mom were living when things were better. That's why he wants to move there."

Alan spent that night with his dad, and the next night as well. He described the feeling of their apartment as being weighted down with immense sadness, explaining that he and his dad were taking turns sobbing.

Three days later, we all gathered to say goodbye to Doris at the funeral home.

The family, Masao at the helm, was escorted to a room where Doris was waiting, dressed in the pink dress that she had worn at her granddaughter's wedding. I stood at the back of the room while family members mourned. I could hear the sobs of Doris's children and grandchildren, but I could not hear the sobs of her husband. I watched him as he made his way to her casket, where he brought his handkerchief to his eyes every few seconds. I knew he was feeling grief from the deepest part of his soul and that was what finally brought me to tears. I watched him, this man I was learning history from, this man who had endured great losses from the time he was eight and who had braved it all, and I worried that this deep grief might be too much for him. It might be too much.

After several moments, Masao, with his head lowered, turned and made his way out of the room. Alan was right next to him and I followed soon after. I found them outside, in the February cold, sitting on a stone bench. I don't think either of them could feel the bitter weather. They couldn't feel anything but sadness.

From the day that Doris's ashes were ready, Masao wore three things on a gold chain: his Bronze Star Medal, her wedding ring, and a fragment of bone selected from her ashes.

He wore these items, and these items only, around his neck for the rest of his life.

PART II

CHAPTER FOUR

UNITED STATES UNDER ATTACK

We were all worried sick about Masao. Through a team effort, we managed to get him out of his apartment six nights a week. During the summer weeks, I could help a little bit more, and I was happy to do that, given how my enthusiasm for gambling had grown. But, I still waited patiently for more of Masao's stories.

"Masao?" I called out as I went in. No answer. The TV was on, but he was not in his recliner, and I immediately got nervous.

"Masao?" I called, a little louder this time.

"Hey! I'm in bathroom." I noticed the door to the bathroom was wide open. I maneuvered my way to the couch and sat so I couldn't see.

"Okay, uh, take your time."

After a few minutes I heard the flush and out he came. "How's it going today?" I asked as he joined me in the living room.

"Oh, same old, same old." He plopped down in his recliner with a sigh and clicked the TV off.

I often got the feeling he was just waiting to join Doris—that was the feeling today. "Are you okay?" We both knew what this meant. I was asking how his heart was.

"I had a dream about my wife last night." He looked at me, and I nodded with anticipation, letting him know I wanted to hear more.

He was happy to have someone who wanted to listen. "I think she's waiting for me, a-no?"

I nodded. "Of course she's waiting for you. She misses you."

He was still looking at me, hoping I shared his belief that he was somehow communicating with Doris. And, of course, I did believe him. "She misses me, I think," he pondered.

I smiled and nodded. He was off in another world, thinking about happier times with his Doris. It was quiet except for the ticking clock on the wall. We both sat for a few minutes in the silence; I wasn't about to ruin his connection to his wife.

Finally he looked at me. "Well. Shall we go?"

"Where to today?"

"We go casino," he replied, already walking somewhat unsteadily to the closet to get his jacket. I should have known that would be his answer. The casino continued to be the best way for him to get relief. I no longer tried to talk him out of it.

We were on our way up the mountain when I thought, *there's no harm in asking him about the army.*

"Hey, Mas, remember when we were talking about San Bernardino before the war?" He nodded; it looked like a go. "How did you find out you were drafted?"

He looked out the window, calling his history forth, "Let's see now . . ."

SUMMER 1941–SAN BERNARDINO

Masao, now twenty-four, stocked shelves in the grocery store. He had all but succumbed to a life as a would-be grocery store owner. He had watched other Nisei peers go on to college and earn degrees that would lead them to important professions. But with the two languages mixed up in Masao's head, college was too hard. His slight accent had only earned him condescension from his peers.

While other Issei had sent their children, mostly their boys, back to Japan for their education, it wasn't that common, and Masao knew of no one else in the area who had lived in Japan as a youngster. Here he was, a Kibei, unique in a culture that left him out.

He wondered often if he would ever belong.

Masao continued to work at Star Cash Grocery until one day when his uncle came into the store with the mail in hand. "Masao. A letter for you." There was some excitement mixed with stress in Tatsuo's voice. Masao thought it might be word from Japan. Maybe his father had finally decided to let him return, although he was now used to San Bernardino and wasn't sure he wanted to start all over again back in Japan. What hateful word would they have back there to describe him now, being bounced back and forth across the Pacific? Masao took the brown envelope that Tatsuo carefully handed to him and looked at the outside.

"From the US Army." Masao was surprised. He looked at Tatsuo. "Open it!"

Masao slowly opened it and glanced inside. He smiled. "I've been drafted." He looked at Tatsuo, who was also smiling.

"You finally get be a soldier," Tatsuo assured Masao as he patted him on the back. Masao smiled while he mulled this over. He had wanted forever to be a soldier, but all of his visions had been with the Japanese military, wielding swords and bayonets. He had never once given thought to serving in the US military with a bunch of Caucasian guys.

"Well, at least we're not at war," Masao said.

"Not yet, but soon. With Germany or Italy." Tatsuo patted Masao again, and this time Masao nodded.

It was September 10, 1941, when Masao caught the train that would take him to the induction center. On the train platform, Masao said his goodbyes to the many residents and shop owners from Little Japan who showed up to send him off. He shook hands with each one, thanking them for their good wishes. They were all very proud of their Masao Abe. He saved his last goodbye for his precious Uncle Tatsuo. Tatsuo shook his hand and looked directly in his eyes.

"You are American. You must fight like an American and honor this great country."

"Of course, uncle." He didn't want to say goodbye to this wonderful man who had been such a great father figure, so he did what he often did: he ended on a high note. "At least I'll get to see Europe, no?" Tatsuo smiled and nodded. Masao picked up his bag and boarded the train. He sat next to the window so he could see all his friends and family. The train slowly started to move.

"*Banzai! Banzai!*" the townsfolk yelled as the train pulled out. Banzai—ten thousand years—is a traditional Japanese battle call used to wish warriors luck, as in "May you live ten thousand years." Masao waved to his family and friends, who were dressed in their best attire.

Masao leaves for boot camp, September 10, 1941

Dressed in a suit and tie, he sat on the bench and watched the San Bernardino train station until it was no longer in sight. He felt a sadness that he attributed to leaving this world behind. He tried to shake it off with thoughts about the adventures that awaited him, but the sadness wouldn't leave. Somehow he knew things would be different when he returned.

The train took him from the sweltering heat of San Bernardino to the cooler climate of the California coast. He sat with the window open and enjoyed the three-hour journey, which included several stops to pick up other draftees from small towns along the way. As the train approached the seaside, Masao recognized landmarks from the times he had been there before. He reminisced about arriving in San Pedro from Japan, and how he had hated being back in the States. All of that was behind him now. He needed to let go of Japan. He was moving further away from that life from this point forward, and he knew it.

The train slowed and rolled along the piers in San Pedro. For a moment, Masao thought he spotted the *Chichibu Maru*, the last ship that had transported him from Japan across the Pacific. His thoughts drifted as he watched the busy port go by.

He wondered what life in Japan was like and thought about how different his life would have been had he remained in Japan. He assumed he would still be courting Miyoko, maybe even married to her by now. He would be a proud officer, probably stationed in China, writing to his beloved Miyoko from a great distance, promising her his safe return.

The recruit next to him nudged him and pointed out the window, bringing Masao back to America. He looked ahead and spotted what his fellow passenger had noticed, a sign for Fort MacArthur.

"There's no turning back now," the other recruit was saying.

"I guess not," Masao said. The draftees on the train had kept to themselves, each of them nervous for what was to come.

Fort MacArthur was like a well-oiled machine. Recruits were unloaded from the train and funneled into different buildings for the series of tasks: uniform issue, scheduling of the aptitude tests, receiving the appointed time for the medical and physical examination. Masao got sucked along in the crowd, doing his best to follow orders.

On September 11, 1941, Masao took his oath of enlistment and was sworn in. His aptitude test and interview with a career counselor resulted in a path of army medic. He had not considered this before, being a medic, but wasn't opposed to the idea. This meant that he would be sent to a different facility for training.

It wasn't but a few days before Masao was on his way to Camp Grant, located on the outskirts of Rockford, Illinois, about seventy miles west of Chicago. In its day Camp Grant sprawled over eighteen thousand acres and was a boot camp for soldiers during both World Wars I and II.

It took days to get there. A young and spry Masao, dressed in his military uniform, looked out the window of the train as it passed through farmland. One of only a few Asians on the train, he sat with a guy named Bob Fukui. In an attempt to be funny, Bob nicknamed Masao "Kibei Abe." Masao hated this and made a goal to avoid Bob at all cost.

Masao enjoyed the breeze through the open window. The air was cooler than in San Bernardino and not quite as dry. He speculated what this new world of the US military would be like. He hoped he would get the chance to experience real combat if the United States did engage with Germany, as his uncle had predicted.

The train slowed as they passed an air strip, then he saw a white sign ahead: Recruit Reception Center. Masao would learn that the town of Rockford was about four miles north of the camp. He hoped there might be a Little Japan or a Chinatown. He was already craving rice, having gone five days without it now.

Boot camp lasted for weeks. During field endurance training, he was the only Asian in a sea of white privates. As much as he couldn't stand Bob, he would sometimes look to him for a tiny bit of camaraderie.

He eventually met a few Japanese, among other Asians, and so he was able to build a group to call his own. One of their favorite things to do on one-day passes was to head to Rockford to search out anything resembling rice. They had to strike out many times before they found a small Chinese restaurant. Masao wasn't terribly fond of Chinese food, but in the absence of Japanese food for weeks, Chinese seemed like heaven.

His newfound buddies, Rokuro and Shinji, were happy-go-lucky, just like Masao. They would sometimes include Bob, who became more mindful about negative Kibei talk, since both Masao and Shinji were Kibei. Rokuro, one of the few Nisei who lived inland, didn't relate to the concept of Kibei and was happy to ignore the whole thing. They eventually ventured all the way to Chicago when they earned weekend passes. Travel to Chicago became their motivation to do well during the week. Together, the four endured boot camp and medic training. Although they were aware that war could erupt at any moment and they could be shipped out to Europe, for now things were peaceful.

NOVEMBER 21, 1941—WAI MOMI, HAWAI'I

Doris Kimie Okada, eighteen, was born and raised in Honolulu. She was third-generation Japanese, or *Sansei*. Japanese people had originally immigrated to Hawai'i for work. The growing sugar cane industry on the islands required more workers than were available, so many Japanese and Chinese people immigrated to the islands in the mid- to late-1800s.

Fishing and farming on Hawai'i wasn't dissimilar to Japan, and it made the transition easier for those Japanese that chose to settle there. The weather was far more pleasant than the extreme seasons in Japan, which was another lure to making Hawai'i a permanent home. By the 1930s, the Japanese were by far the largest ethnic group inhabiting Hawai'i, including native Hawaiians. Numerous Japanese schools were prevalent, along with clubs, movie theaters, and community centers dedicated to Japanese traditions.

In 1941 Hawai'i was considered a US territory; it would not become a state until 1959. A former kingdom, Hawai'i had been overthrown by the United States in 1893. Although there were significant efforts on the part of Native Hawaiians and their queen to save the kingdom, it became a territory in 1898.

Waikiki, in 1941, was still somewhat undiscovered and considered exotic. The famously pink Royal Hawaiian Hotel was one of two notable hotels on Waikiki beach. They sat alone, surrounded by pristine beaches and lush greenery. The absence of merchants and stores is what drew tourists from the mainland. The closest city was downtown Honolulu, several miles away. Tourists came to surf and sun on the beautiful and untapped wonder of Waikiki, but it was home to Doris.

The oldest of three children, she lived with her parents, both Nisei, in Mo'ili'ili. Doris attended McKinley High, located on King Street in Honolulu, less than a mile from the beautiful Ala Moana Beach and a mere eight or so miles from Pearl Harbor. The magnificent 'Iolani Palace was just down the road.

One of the things Doris loved to do was to pick oysters. In Hawai'i, there was one place and one place only to do that—Wai Momi, Water of the Pearl, or Pearl Harbor. Hawaiian legend had it that the water in this area was the home to the Shark Goddess,

Ka'ahupahau, who was believed to live in a sea cave at the entrance to the harbor, protecting the waters against sharks that preyed on man. Whatever the folklore, these waters were known for generating a wealth of pearl-producing oysters and had been popular among locals for generations.

It was the Friday after Thanksgiving and Doris, along with her friend Helen, arrived on the beach, buckets in hand. Doris loved oysters and she loved to cook, so the combination of collecting and preparing oysters was the making of a great day. They waded along in bare feet and rolled-up dungarees searching for the delectable oysters that they would make for lunch with other friends. It was the perfect November morning. Even with US battleships in the background, it was a peaceful, Hawaiian day.

DECEMBER 1, 1941—SAN BERNARDINO

Tatsuo swept the floor of the Star Cash store. Now that Masao was gone, and Yukie was taking care of their newborn daughter, he was manning the store almost entirely by himself. It was chillier than normal that afternoon, so he went to the storage-area office and found the sweater he kept in the back. He glanced at the only picture in the store, a picture of himself, his older brother, Yasoshichi, and their father. It had been taken when Tatsuo first arrived in the United States in 1920. He could hardly believe he had been in the States for twenty-one years already. He admired a younger Tatsuo who looked so innocent.

Only the railroad-style wall clock made any sound with its continuous and serene ticking, the polished brass pendulum swaying back and forth behind the glass door of the old wooden case. The hand of the clock struck twelve and the prompt but calming chimes sounded the top of the hour. He was wondering where the clock

came from when his thoughts were interrupted as he heard someone enter the store, so he put his sweater on and hurried out.

Ben Miller, a disheveled looking Native American, was trying to
remain invisible just on the inside of the establishment. He wasn't
supposed to be there, he knew that. Nobody of Native American
blood was to be in a store that sold alcohol or cigarettes. In other
establishments, signs were posted to that effect. But in Tatsuo's
store, things were different. Tatsuo smiled.

"Ben, my old friend, how are you?" Tatsuo held out his hand.

"Okay. And you?" Ben's hand reached out to meet Tatsuo's. He
tried to control the shaking as much as he could, but Tatsuo noticed
it anyway. He gently took Ben's hand in both of his and then
motioned to the back of the store.

"Come on. Let's get you fixed up." Tatsuo encouraged Ben to follow. In the storage area, Tatsuo reached for a bottle of whiskey and a
tin cup stored there. He poured a shot for Ben, who chugged it down
in one swallow, closed his eyes and waited for it to kick in. Tatsuo
poured another shot and looked at Ben to see if it was helping. It
seemed to be. Tatsuo pondered Ben's age; he figured that he was in
his early forties, although he looked much older. Tatsuo attributed
his weathered appearance to the rough life Ben led. He was a man
down on his luck and no matter what he did to elevate himself, society wouldn't have it.

"Thank you kindly." Ben's voice was timid, almost ashamed.

"Don't mention it," Tatsuo assured him. And the two sat quietly.
When it was time, Tatsuo made sure Ben had groceries before he left.

"See you again," Tatsuo bid him as he made his way out the back
door into the alley. He watched Ben limp away and wondered what
came first, the alcohol or the shame thrust on Native Americans by
the newly dominant society. In that moment, Tatsuo felt fortunate
to have made his way in a country that wasn't his birth country, but
one that had accepted him on its shores some twenty years earlier.

DECEMBER 7, 1941—HONOLULU

» 7:15 a.m. Hawai'i Standard Time

It was a beautiful Hawaiian morning. The air was a tad crisp, but Doris didn't mind. Her parents had finally been letting her use their car occasionally, something she had been badgering them about for months. Dressed in a cute tennis outfit, she flung her tennis racket into the back seat and jumped in the front. She drove the few blocks to Helen's house, where her friend was waiting.

"Let's go!" Helen smiled as she tossed her tennis racket in the back seat and hopped in the front.

Doris grappled with the four-door Ford as she navigated through the narrow neighborhood streets. It was a short drive to get to the tennis courts at their old high school. The trick was to get there early because everyone in Honolulu had the same idea on the weekends. They were the third car in the parking lot, and there were only four courts, so they hustled to claim one.

On the court they chose sides, knowing one side would inevitably face the rising sun. They positioned themselves on the court, and Doris served the first ball.

DECEMBER 7, 1941—SAN BERNARDINO

» 9:45 a.m. Pacific Standard Time
» 7:45 a.m. Hawai'i Standard Time

Tatsuo kissed his wife, Yukie, and baby Kathleen. Just as he did every day, he walked the short distance from his home on Fourth Street to his store on Third Street, greeting other merchants along the way. He opened the store, turned on the lights, and straightened out some of the produce as he made his way back to the office, where he would brew coffee for himself.

Once his mug was filled, he decided to sit down and read the newspaper, as he did almost every morning before the first customer arrived. Sometimes he would meander down the street and chat with one of the other Japanese merchants, but this morning he just wanted to read the newspaper in peace. He brought his coffee cup and his newspaper out to the front of the store and sat on a stool. It was the perfect location for him to keep an eye out for customers and enjoy the morning at the same time.

DECEMBER 7, 1941—THE PRESIDIO, SAN FRANCISCO

» 9:50 a.m. Pacific Standard Time

» 7:50 a.m. Hawai'i Standard Time

As Japanese fighter planes were almost above Pearl Harbor, operations were status quo on the military base. But as war heated up around the world, the military had implemented precautions. The Fourth Air Force was conducting air defense exercises that began on the sixth of December and were planned to continue until the eleventh. The Navy took over Treasure Island in San Francisco Bay as a military base. Routine test firing of coastal defense guns occurred at Fort Barry, just across the Golden Gate Bridge from the Presidio. And on the Presidio, the US Army practiced war exercises. There was a heightened sense of alert, and while military personnel felt it, they were not privy as to why. For most of the citizens of San Francisco and most soldiers who called that area home, it was business as usual at 9:50 a.m. on December 7.

DECEMBER 7, 1941—CHICAGO

» 11:50 a.m. Central Standard Time

» 7:50 a.m. Hawai'i Standard Time

The four soldiers left base early that morning on a one-day pass. They were eager to get to the city and away from the strict regimental training they had endured for weeks. The bus was full of privates looking to do the same thing that Masao, Rokuro, Shinji, and Bob wanted to do—eat good food. They found a diner that served breakfast all day. The place was packed, though, so they would have to wait their turn.

DECEMBER 7, 1941—HONOLULU

» 7:53 a.m. Hawai'i Standard Time

Doris was ahead forty-love in the first game of their second set when, all of a sudden, they heard loud, cacophonous blasts.

"What's going on?!" Helen ran toward Doris, who looked up when she heard the sound of airplanes flying toward them. She shielded her eyes from the sun to take a closer look. She spotted the distinct red disk on the underside of each airplane wing.

"Are those Japanese airplanes?" Doris uttered with bewilderment. The airplanes flew overhead while explosions continued in the distance. She instinctively looked to where the blasts were coming from and saw billowing black smoke rising. The ground seemed to shake beneath her as she watched the scattered Japanese planes circle and head back toward the smoke. Horrified, she looked at Helen, who was frozen, her mouth hanging open.

"Come on!" Doris shouted as she grabbed their belongings. Helen stood, paralyzed by fear, staring at the sky. Doris took charge, physically taking Helen's arm. "Now, Helen. *Let's go.*"

As Doris pulled Helen to the car, she looked back in horror. The Japanese planes looked like a swarm of bees over Pearl Harbor. More of the thick black smoke rose as the ruthless attack continued. She pushed Helen in the car from the driver's side and jumped in after her. She shoved the car in reverse and it lurched back; the tires spit up gravel as she floored it forward. She glanced over at the others who had been playing tennis, and they just stood there, staring at the sky.

"What are they waiting for?" Doris's voice was shrill.

Helen looked over and saw what Doris was talking about, so she rolled down her window and stuck her head out. "*Get out of here!*" she shrieked. But it did little good; the others didn't seem to feel any urgency. Residents of Honolulu were used to air maneuvers by the American military and even though this was different, they seemed blissfully confident that it was routine. But Doris knew. This was real.

"Don't take Kapiʻolani! King Street. Take King!" Helen was shouting.

Doris used all her might to crank the wheel. They flew by more onlookers who appeared confused and were gazing at the sky in a daze.

The heavy Ford dashed down King Street. Doris swerved to go around cars that had stopped so drivers could get out and gawk at the sky.

"I'm taking McCully," Doris stated. Helen looked confused by this. "It's going to be faster." Helen nodded. She looked out the back of the car and watched the black smoke rise up from Pearl Harbor.

"Do you think the Japanese really just attacked us?" Helen uttered.

"What else could it be?" Doris answered. But Helen was shaking her head in doubt, unable to digest the thought. "I saw it. You saw it too. Those were Japanese airplanes. This is no drill, Helen."

They finally came to McCully and the tires squealed as Doris hurled the car, making the hard right toward Moʻiliʻili. Little did they know that just a short while later, King and McCully, the very intersection they had just passed, would be under assault, a casualty of misfired anti-artillery shells. Businesses and homes went up in flames and the owners were helpless to do anything. Fire personnel were all dispatched to Pearl Harbor—it would be too late by the time they made their way to King and McCully. In all, thirteen buildings were completely destroyed, an entire block decimated. Thirty-one people lost their homes or businesses and four people died. Several other neighborhoods in greater Honolulu, including Waikiki, felt the direct impact of defense missile misfires.

Doris sped all the way home and pulled into her driveway with a screech. Her dad came out of the house with a scowl on his face—this wasn't the way he wanted his car treated. But before he could open his mouth to lecture her, Doris cut him off.

"Dad, something's happened! Look!" She took him by the arm and pulled him out in the street, where there was a view of the sky over Pearl Harbor and the billowing smoke.

The blood ran out of her father's face, and his eyes widened with fear.

"Dad. Those airplanes, they are Japanese. I saw them with my own eyes. They are Japanese." Doris was shaken. Her father took the girls inside the house and immediately tuned the radio to a news channel. The announcer was calling for calm, although he sounded highly anxious and disoriented himself. At about half past eight, the radio announcer proclaimed that the bombing had stopped. There was a collective relief throughout Honolulu, but it was short-lived. It would turn out to be a brief lull in an otherwise furious attack that would continue for another hour or more. The second wave of 170 Japanese airplanes appeared over Pearl Harbor and continued the relentless assault.

All the citizens of Hawai'i could do was watch and wait helplessly.

DECEMBER 7, 1941—CHICAGO

» 1:25 p.m. Central Standard Time

» 9:25 a.m. Hawai'i Standard Time

Their mouths watered as they watched thick Belgian waffles topped with strawberries and fresh whipped cream being served at the table next to them. They figured that their order must be next up. The hungry soldiers had all ordered the Farmer's Breakfast: a stack of hotcakes, two country eggs, ham steak, potatoes, a hot biscuit, juice, and coffee, all for $1.10.

"I'm not too keen on this place. What's taking so long?" Bob sputtered. He had developed the reputation of being a whiner, or a fathead, as others would call him. Masao had gotten used to Bob's inability to cope in the world, but Bob's social ineptitude drove Shinji crazy.

"Ease up, Bob. We're next," Masao assured him. Bob sat back in the booth with a sigh. He was used to being handled by Masao, and as much as he wanted to look down on him for being Kibei, he had actually come to admire Masao's ability to keep things calm, as well as his natural inclination to lead.

"There she is." Shinji noticed the waitress. They all watched as she retrieved their plates from the heating station, grabbed a bottle of ketchup, and headed their way. She set the hot, steaming plates down in front of the young men. Masao got one big bite of ham in his mouth before an army private ran by the front of the diner, instantly stopping when he spotted the military uniforms. He darted in.

"You guys got to get back to base—*pronto*. Something's happened!" He was motioning with his whole arm, and everyone could tell—this was serious.

DECEMBER 7, 1941—SAN BERNARDINO

» 11:25 a.m. Pacific Standard Time

» 9:25 a.m. Hawai'i Standard Time

Tatsuo was bagging up produce for a customer when he noticed commotion across the street in the Hirata Deli. He walked out to see if it was something he needed to attend to. Mr. Hirata was yelling at anyone who would listen, something about a radio. Tatsuo wondered what had driven him to such a state. Then he heard it clearly.

"Turn on your radio!" Hirata was shouting as he looked directly at Tatsuo. Hirata's face was filled with anxiety. Tatsuo immediately went to the back of the store and switched his radio on, tuning it in. Finally, he found a clear signal and the announcer's voice blared.

"The Japanese have attacked the American Naval Base at Pearl Harbor, Hawai'i . . ." In shock, Tatsuo couldn't hear beyond this one sentence. He looked at the radio while he processed the magnitude of the announcer's message.

DECEMBER 7, 1941—CHICAGO

» 1:45 p.m. Central Standard Time
» 9:45 a.m. Hawai'i Standard Time

Masao boarded the bus with all the other army personnel who were on leave. They still had no idea what had happened. The bus driver glared at the four as they went by and maintained his glare while they found seats. Rokuro sat next to Masao.

"What's under his skin?" Rokuro's voice was low; he didn't want any problems. Masao shrugged. The driver started up the bus, then fiddled with his portable radio. He found a station, tuned it in and turned it up, then put the bus in gear.

"The Japanese have attacked Pearl Harbor from the air, and all naval and military activities on the island of O'ahu, Hawai'i . . ." The announcer's voice filled the bus with the horrible news. Masao's face turned white. He looked at Rokuro, who looked like he had seen a ghost.

"My God," was all Masao could utter. He tried to listen to the details of the attack, but all he could think about was the bus driver's glare. He couldn't bear to look around at his Caucasian army counterparts for fear that they would have the same look of hate on their faces. He worried what this would mean for his future in the US military.

The bus ride back to base was the longest of his life. The news reporter kept filling in the details of the morning's attack with gruesome specificity. With each added piece of information, Masao could feel himself sinking further in his seat. The eyes of other soldiers penetrated his existence. Shame grew inside him. While Rokuro sounded American and had no hint of an accent, that wasn't the case for Masao or Shinji. In that moment, Masao envied Bob for having an American name. That made Bob two steps removed from his Japanese ancestry: he didn't have a Japanese name *and* he didn't talk with an accent. Meanwhile, Masao was Japanese. His name was Japanese, his accent was Japanese, and he looked Japanese.

Masao glanced at Shinji and Bob, who were sitting across the aisle. Shinji looked like Masao felt, his head hanging down, his eyes averting any contact with others. Bob, meanwhile, was alert and scanning the bus, seemingly unaware that his roots were Japanese.

"That guy, doesn't he get the connection?" Masao whispered as he nudged Rokuro and motioned toward Bob, who was now poking the soldier sitting in front of him and saying something about the attack that, in Masao's mind, made him look stupid. Rokuro watched Bob make a fool out of himself. Shinji, meanwhile, was trying to become invisible.

"He's an idiot," Rokuro whispered back.

DECEMBER 7, 1941—HONOLULU

» 12:00 p.m. Hawai'i Standard Time

The attack had stopped just before ten, as the last of the Japanese airplanes headed back to the aircraft carrier from whence they came. The massive attack on Pearl Harbor was an incredible success for the Japanese military: twenty-one American ships had been destroyed or heavily damaged, there were over twenty-four hundred military and civilian deaths, and nearly twelve hundred had been wounded in the attack.

After the Japanese airplanes had left the area and some time had passed, people slowly emerged from their homes to assess the damage. Everyone would eventually get to a vantage point where they could see the heavy, thick black smoke rising from Pearl Harbor. Disbelief permeated the area, but a grave reality slowly settled in.

On McCully and King, ashes still smoldered. Buildings had burned to the ground, leaving behind homelessness and grief. The trade winds carried burning debris from McCully and King the few blocks to the Lunalilo School, where fire caught hold.

It seemed that one disaster led to another.

DECEMBER 7, 1941—CAMP GRANT, ILLINOIS

» 4:00 p.m. Central Standard Time

» 12:00 p.m. Hawai'i Standard Time

All soldiers of Japanese descent were ordered to attend a special meeting at the service club on the base at 1600 hours sharp. Masao had been to the service club a few times, once when there was a social mixer for soldiers, and a couple of times when he had wanted to write to his Uncle Tatsuo. Today, the service club had been set up for a formal meeting. Chairs were arranged in rows, and the space easily housed the few dozen Nisei soldiers who were ordered to report. Masao found a seat next to Shinji and glanced at the perimeter of the room, noticing that Caucasian soldiers were stationed strategically.

He glanced at Shinji. "This doesn't look too good," he said in a muffled voice. Shinji nodded in agreement.

A door opened at the far end of the room and a one-star general entered, prompting the entire room full of soldiers to stand at attention and salute. The general walked with purpose to the podium that had been set up for his personal use and took a moment to peruse the soldiers who still stood at attention.

"At ease," he commanded with the slightest nod. His face looked stern. Anxiety grew among the Nisei soldiers, who collectively wondered if they would be immediately dismissed from service. A dishonorable discharge: you are not wanted. They understood this as a distinct possibility and, in their hearts, understood why the American military might take such action. Apprehension filled the room as the general gathered his notes. It seemed to take him forever. There wasn't a sound except for the shuffling of papers at the podium. Finally, the general looked up.

"As you know by now, one of our naval bases has been deliberately and suddenly attacked by the Empire of Japan. They attacked by air with over 190 air squadrons in the first wave and 170 air squadrons in the second and final wave. The military casualties were extensive and the assault was long and brutal, lasting almost two hours from beginning to end." The general paused to let his words resonate throughout the room.

"The targets appear to be military, although there were some civilian casualties. The data is not yet conclusive on that. What is clear is that the attack caused severe damage to American military and naval services on that island. While the base in Hawai'i regains strength and prepares for further attack, bases along the West Coast are also preparing, strategically, for certain and impending Japanese attacks."

Oh my God, thought Masao. This was worse than he imagined. *What about my uncle? I need to talk to him, make sure he's okay*, Masao worried to himself. He had to force his attention back from San Bernardino in order to continue listening to the general.

"Although I'm not certain what course of action the US military will take, I am certain of one thing."

Here it comes, thought Masao, *this is where we find out our destiny. Are we going to be soldiers, or are we going to be the enemy?*

"As long as you men are wearing the US Army uniform, you will be treated like any other American. You are Americans. And your country needs you now."

Pride swelled in the room. The Nisei soldiers didn't even try to hide their smiles and their relief to hear that they were still seen as part of the team, part of the society that they were there to serve. Humble but proud, there was a collective relaxation of shoulders. Their hearts pounded, waiting for the next words from the general they now revered.

"When you get your orders, remember that," the general concluded. He folded up his papers and gave the room a salute that immediately prompted the soldiers to stand erect, tall and confident, in their salute back. They watched until the general left the room. While they congratulated each other and chatted, Masao glanced at the Caucasian soldiers who lined the walls. They didn't look as happy as the Nisei soldiers felt. While part of him was elated, another part of him had an ominous feeling that things were going to get really tough.

DECEMBER 7, 1941—HONOLULU

» 4:00 p.m. Hawai'i Standard Time

The Okada family had remained inside for most of the day. Doris was getting antsy; owing to her naturally curious nature, she wanted to know what was going on. They had been listening to the radio for information, but Governor Poindexter had ordered all commercial radio stations off the air. He feared that the Japanese could pick up the radio frequency and capitalize on public reports that were being broadcast on open air waves. Residents kept their radios on in hopes of getting periodic updates, but only static came through. Yet, Doris continued to mess with the radio. She didn't want to miss anything.

Finally, the radio announcer was back on the air.

"The governor has turned power over to the military." The faint voice of the announcer came through as she fiddled with the dial. Her family all gathered close. Lieutenant General Short was introduced and took over the broadcast. He described how the island would now be under martial law. There would be an island-wide blackout starting at six p.m. Nobody would be allowed out of their homes, no lights of any kind should be used. Not even candles. They weren't going to make it easy for Japan to attack again.

By six p.m., the Okada family, like all the other families on Oʻahu, had turned off every last light in their home, locked their doors, and waited for daybreak. Throughout the night, military police patrolled neighborhoods looking for anyone breaking the rules. Even for very minor infractions, people would be taken to military court and fined hundreds of dollars. But the Okada family obeyed the law, as did most of the residents on the island, and remained in the dark throughout the night. It would turn out to be the first night of many dark nights to come.

At day's end in Honolulu, Hawaiʻi, the deep mourning for those who were lost would be replaced by a determination to become a part of the solution, the cleanup, and military response. Doris wasn't sure just how she would do it, but she was resolute that she would be included in the civilian effort, whether or not her dad approved.

★ ★ ★

Masao returned to the present, looking bewildered. I had pulled off the highway at a truck stop to listen to his riveting account of December 7.

"Where are we?" he asked innocently.

"I just pulled over, we're almost there, though," I assured him.

"We're going casino, a-no?"

I smiled and nodded. "Yeah, I just needed to stop so I could hear everything you were saying," I explained.

"Heh! You've heard it before, it's nothing new."

"It's new to me. I have never heard this before. Never," I attested, but Masao just shrugged. "I didn't know Doris was just a few miles away from Pearl Harbor, for one thing," I continued. "Picking oysters off the beach just a couple weeks before the attack."

"Yep, two weeks before, that's right," he nodded, happy to remember Doris. I had a warm feeling that our conversation, and my interest in it, gave him relief by bringing him closer to the past, his military experience, and thus, Doris. I was happy to be in this role, an unlikely historian keeping his story alive. I admired his face as he lingered in 1941, no doubt picturing his beloved Doris on the beach, picking the oysters she so loved.

CHAPTER FIVE

THE AFTERMATH

"Dad wants to go to Vegas," Alan announced over the phone. At the time I had absolutely no idea that Las Vegas had been a frequent travel destination for Mas and Doris. It had also been a meeting spot for Masao's war buddies. Traveling with Masao required a lot of equipment. He needed his cane, his walker, and a wheelchair. Alan and I became experts in airport navigation and skilled at shielding Masao from ever feeling like a burden. It was worth every last bit of effort to travel with him, and he was always incredibly gracious and thankful.

This would be the first trip of many to Vegas, and we soon developed a predictable routine that included a lot of gambling and eating. Masao preferred to stay downtown, and I was pleasantly surprised at the beautiful accommodations.

"Hey, Mas," I said at dinner during our first trip to Vegas. He sipped from his coffee cup while he fixed his eyes in my direction. I pushed the sugar toward him, instinctively knowing he would want more. He added another spoonful.

"How did your uncle do after December 7?"

"My uncle, jeez. . . . He lived in San Bernardino, a-no?"

I nodded. There was the familiar expression on his face that occurred when he called up memories.

"There was a Japanese Association in San Bernardino. And my uncle, he was the president of it. A leader in that community."

He paused to formulate his thoughts. "I think that hurt him after the attack on Pearl Harbor, a-no?"

I leaned forward and turned all my attention to San Bernardino.

DECEMBER 8, 1941–SAN BERNARDINO

It was a Monday afternoon. Tatsuo locked up Star Cash Grocery a little early that day and headed for the local hall where the Japanese Association meetings were always held. The events of the last two days were to be discussed, and some much-needed support would be shared within the community. His face said it all as he walked down the street: here was a man feeling ashamed of his race, fearful for his future.

People in Little Japan were still reeling from the horrible news about the attack on Pearl Harbor. They were leaning on each other, trying to understand what had happened and how it might affect their future in the States. The Issei were the most worried because they were not citizens. But the many Nisei had grave concerns as well.

The Japanese who lived along the West Coast of the United States and in Hawai'i had immediately become suspect. By the end of the day on December 7, President Roosevelt had ordered the gathering of any Japanese person who was considered a subversive alien. These people would be taken away and detained for two weeks until they were sent to one of the imprisonment camps operated by the Immigration and Naturalization Service, or INS.

Three classifications of Japanese people were considered suspect. Group A consisted of those thought to be highly dangerous saboteurs: local fishermen, produce distributors, farmers, successful and influential businessmen, Shinto priests, Buddhist priests, and members of the Japanese Consulate. Group B had not been under direct surveillance but were thought of as possibly dangerous. Group C were thought of as likely to be involved in sabotage of American military efforts and were closely watched due to their Japanese ties. Groups B and C included Japanese language teachers, teachers of the martial arts, travel agents, editors of Japanese newspapers, community leaders, and of course, Kibeis.

Many of the Japanese that fell into the three classifications were rounded up and turned over to the nearest INS office to be processed. By the early morning of December 8, 1941, less than twenty-four hours after the attack, 736 Japanese, German, or Italian "enemies" had been taken into custody.

Tatsuo had heard about the roundups along the coast, as had many of his friends and business associates. His footsteps were heavy, as was his heart. He wasn't sure what he would say to people, but as the leader of the local Japanese Association, it was certain that the community would be looking to him for answers.

The hall was packed with families. The look on each face was one of anxiety, apprehension, and fear. Tatsuo took center stage at the front of the room. He spoke only English, as a way to include everyone as well as nurture his loyalty to the United States.

"Good people of San Bernardino, and my friends. We're going to need to rely on each other now more than ever, until this gets straightened out," Tatsuo began. People nodded. "Let's begin by just checking in with each other. Let me ask, what immediate needs do you have?" A man named Tom Mitsuhashi raised his hand. Tatsuo nodded.

"My suppliers have cut me off." Mitsuhashi's voice was compromised and weak.

"Me too," café owner Jimmy Sawada added.

"We just have to do our best. If you need supplies for your café, Jimmy, I have produce, staples, and coffee. What I have is yours." Tatsuo tried to sound reassuring.

"Some of our best customers aren't coming around," George Kamimura added.

All Tatsuo could do was nod. There were no answers. It was quiet. "Let's hope this is the worst of it." Tatsuo knew this was not the case, but he felt the need to remain positive, no matter how dire the situation.

"We had a good crop last year. We can share all the canned pears and peaches anyone needs," farmer David Yurimoto stated loudly. This one bright thought seemed to change the mood.

"We have plenty of vegetables," another farmer, Ben Omori, contributed.

"I've got five hogs I can butcher," added Bessie Tamura.

"Let's stick together through this. Cooperate fully with any authorities that might question you. You have nothing to hide, nor do I. We have been good residents of California and of the United States. Some of our children, indeed, my nephew Masao, have been called to military duty. We have done nothing wrong, and we need to stand by that." Tatsuo looked around. Faith in his words seemed to build—maybe, too, a sense of hope.

DECEMBER 8, 1941—HONOLULU

"Dad?" Doris hollered as she came through the door. Her dad came out from the kitchen. "A bunch of people are heading to town, I want to go with them." She strode past him and began rummaging through the cupboards and refrigerator.

"What for?"

"What for? Because all the supply lines to Hawai'i have been cut off, that's what for. There will be a shortage of food, don't you see? I'll go with them and get all the groceries I can."

Her dad thought this through, then grabbed his keys. "We'll both go." This was a pleasant surprise for Doris. Her dad usually dismissed any ideas she had, even when they were brilliant. Her mom, who had been sitting at the table listening, was already writing a list.

As they drove to Honolulu, they witnessed the enormity of the situation. Lines three blocks long formed at gas stations, blocking intersections and creating traffic jams. Everything seemed confusing and chaotic, a drastic difference from the usual relaxed and peaceful Hawaiian ways.

"Try Piggly Wiggly," Doris suggested when they encountered the long lines at May's Market. But at Piggly Wiggly the line wrapped around the block.

"My Lord," Doris said. "Dad, let's try Kaimuki."

"Good idea."

"We might even find a service station to get fuel," Doris thought out loud. They made it to Kaimuki only to face the same disappointment of long lines.

"This is no use. I'll wait in line here. You go try to fuel up." Doris was quick with the plan of action. "Pull over here." Her dad obeyed his bossy daughter; she jumped out of the Ford and headed for the back of the line.

Four hours later they returned home. The car was filled with fuel, and they had the "appropriate" amount of groceries for a family of four. Hoarding was strictly prohibited.

"We're set for now," her dad assessed.

"Yeah, but what about next week?" Doris was already concerned about how her family would survive what was sure to come: severe shortages of everything.

DECEMBER 8, 1941—CAMP GRANT, ILLINOIS

Camp Grant was alive with purposeful activity. Earlier that morning, soldiers had listened with great anticipation and satisfaction as President Roosevelt declared war on Japan. Action was swift, and troops were already receiving orders to be transported to other facilities for combat training. Masao and his friends waited patiently for their orders, watching their Caucasian counterparts pack up and ship out.

No orders came for any of them.

DECEMBER 11, 1941—THE PRESIDIO, SAN FRANCISCO

There was a heightened sense of alert on the base that had become the central hub of military activity along the West Coast. Reports of Japanese submarines off the coast of California were kept from the public, but officers on base were acutely aware of the potential dangers. The entire West Coast was declared a Theatre of Wartime Operations by the Western Defense Command, now under the sole authority of Lieutenant General John DeWitt. One of his first orders as commander in charge was that no vessels of any kind were allowed to sail at night in San Francisco Bay. Military vessels, of course, were permitted.

The branches of the military wasted no time in organizing efforts. A huge submarine net had already been laid across the San Francisco Bay just inside the Golden Gate Bridge. On the other side of the bridge, layers of an extensive mine field had been laid at the mouth in overlapping arches out into the Pacific. Several army regimental combat teams had already been shipped out—their destination, Honolulu. The navy would also send ships loaded with sailors to the same location. Decisions were swift and decisive.

The roundup of enemy aliens that had started on December 8 continued. The Department of Justice, now in charge of this operation, routinely took Japanese, German, and Italian residents into custody. In the coming weeks, the roundup would expand to include all non-citizen resident aliens who were fourteen years old or older who were from enemy nations. All of these aliens were to be moved to the interior of the country and off the West Coast. DeWitt believed that there were about forty thousand people along the West Coast who fit this description. He held the belief that these forty thousand, every one of them, posed an immediate and potential threat to defense measures. He was determined to eliminate that threat.

By the end of the month, there would be an absolute frenzy by military, local police, the Department of Justice, and the FBI to ferret out enemies. Because of the military alert status, these agencies would err on the side of caution and detain even those who clearly posed no security threat at all. FBI agents, who now had the right to search homes at will, frequently imposed their authority on those suspected, with little or no evidence, as enemy aliens. And as the resolve of the US military grew, hope among Japanese Americans waned.

DECEMBER 31, 1941—SAN BERNARDINO

Inventory was disappearing from store shelves all along Third Street, as though the shelves themselves detected what was coming—the vanishing soul of Little Japan. Tatsuo's suppliers had cut him off weeks before. He swept the floor of the store and arranged merchandise to give the appearance of a full inventory. It was December 31, and his mind was on the next day. He was looking forward to the annual gathering of the community to celebrate New Year's Day. Yukie was already busy preparing Japanese food for the big event.

He noticed a shadow of a man out of the corner of his eye. It startled him, until he recognized Ben Miller.

"Ben. How are you, my friend?"

"I think I might be faring better than you these days, sadly," Ben said sincerely.

Tatsuo glanced at Ben's shaky hands. "Come." They walked together to the back of the store, where Tatsuo poured some whiskey for Ben. He then did what he never did: he poured a shot for himself. "I think I'll join you today."

It was quiet. The two men had been rejected by American society under entirely different circumstances, but with a common thread. They sat in silence.

Ben pointed to the picture on the wall. "Who is that, Tatsuo?"

"That's my father and my brother. We look pretty good, don't we? All dressed up." Tatsuo smiled. Ben nodded.

Tatsuo, Mataemon, and Yasoshichi, circa 1920

Ben's appreciation of the picture gave Tatsuo immense comfort.

"I came from Japan in 1920. That picture was taken in San Francisco just after I arrived. My dad, he went back on the same ship that brought me here. It's a long time ago."

"It's a nice photo." Ben was genuine in his compliment. The wall clock ticked. "I feel bad about what's happening here in Little Japan," Ben said. "You're good people. You don't deserve this."

Tatsuo smiled, happy to have compassionate company "Here's hoping it gets better," he said as he raised his cup to toast.

The next morning, New Year's Day 1942, Tatsuo was up early to start the wood stove so Yukie could be comfortably warm when she got up. They were well on their way to making sushi rolls when they saw a car park in front of the house. Two men in suits and one policeman emerged from the car. Tatsuo immediately felt this was the worst event possible. He had heard of Issei being picked up and detained for no reason and hoped this wasn't going to be the case.

He opened the door and greeted the men as though they were guests. They were all business, though, and would have nothing to do with Tatsuo's hospitality.

"Tatsuo Abe?" One of the men asked.

"Yes, I am Tatsuo Abe."

The man held up his badge and some other papers that Tatsuo couldn't even begin to read before all three had entered his home.

"We are FBI and have the authority to search the premises," the agent loudly stated. He motioned for the policeman to stay in the kitchen with Tatsuo and Yukie, who was holding their daughter. "You two stay here. Don't talk to one another," he ordered. Tatsuo looked at Yukie and motioned for her to sit down. The policeman watched their every move. The other two men, one from the FBI, the other from immigration, scoured the home, leaving a trail of clutter in their wake.

"The stove needs more wood. We have in garage. Can my husband or I go get more to keep the house warm for our daughter?" Yukie asked politely, pointing to the dying fire in the wood stove.

The young policeman looked straight ahead, refusing to let humanity enter the room.

"You stay here," he said without any hint of emotion. Yukie held her daughter more tightly. Tatsuo took off his sweater and handed it to Yukie to wrap around Kathleen. It was an hour or more before the other two men came back to the kitchen.

"Stand up," the FBI agent ordered. Tatsuo did as told.

"We're taking you in."

"Why, what have I done?"

There was no room in this investigation for justice or due process. The three men hastily escorted Tatsuo by his arms out to the car. A horrified Yukie looked on.

"Where are you taking him?" she called out in a frantic voice, but they ignored her. She watched as they put him in the car, in between the two men in the back seat, and drove off.

After she warmed the house up again and put Kathleen down for a nap, she spent an hour or more working to make the house tidy. She had been looking out the window at the courthouse, just behind their home, to see if they had taken Tatsuo to the county jail. So far, she hadn't spotted anything. Her plan was to enlist the help of other Japanese in the area. Just when Kathleen was waking up, Yukie looked out the window and spotted the car, the one that had taken Tatsuo away. It pulled up in front of the courthouse. She saw Tatsuo get out of the car in handcuffs. He looked okay; no harm had come to him yet. She sighed with relief and watched as they ushered him into the building.

They would keep Tatsuo in the county jail for twenty-eight days. Yukie would be allowed to visit but was warned that if one word of Japanese was spoken between them, the visits would abruptly end. Since they had never spoken English with each other, it was awkward. Sometimes it took several attempts just to convey simple things, such as the news that she was sure she was pregnant again. This piece of information took five minutes to get straight but delighted them both.

"I'm here with heavy criminal people," Tatsuo reported to Yukie during one of their visits. As it turned out, Tatsuo was in jail cells with rapists and robbers, along with the local drunks during weekends. Yukie gasped at the thought, unable to express her emotions in English. Tatsuo was never formally arrested; they kept him for investigative purposes only. Still, he felt enormous shame in having been put in jail at all.

"Tell everyone, I have done nothing wrong. Nothing." Tatsuo pleaded with Yukie.

She had already taken care of that. She had also taken care of the operations of the grocery store, visiting it daily to make sure everything was in order.

The two kept their hopes up that the investigation would be short. Yukie found out that other Japanese men had been incarcerated too, but the men were separated. Tatsuo had been taken to the San Bernardino jail; Mr. Kitagawa, to the Indio jail; and Mr. Okubo, to the Riverside jail. In the coming months, there would be many more men who would be taken into custody; their fate would sometimes be published in the local newspapers, making the humiliation that much more potent.

In mid-January, Yukie received a postcard in the mail. It was from immigration. It contained specific instructions for her: take Tatsuo's belongings to the county jail on January 28 promptly at noon. She found out that she could also bring him a meal, and she knew he would be hungry for Japanese food.

She prepared a basket of fried chicken; *gohan*, or cooked rice; *takenoko*, or bamboo shoots; and even a few pieces of sashimi. She knew he would be craving rice most of all, so she made sure he had plenty. She made the short walk to the courthouse, carrying the basket, a small suitcase, and pushing Kathleen in a carriage. She arrived at eleven forty-five and waited patiently for Tatsuo, still unsure what was happening. Nobody had told her anything, nor would they.

Meanwhile, Tatsuo was eager to get out of jail. He proudly stepped onto the elevator, a man about to be free. He had proven himself worthy of living in society; he hadn't done anything wrong, and he could never imagine being involved in anything that would bring harm to the United States, the country where he had made his living and enjoyed a good life. The elevator, carrying Tatsuo, an immigration officer, and an FBI agent, arrived at the ground floor, and he stepped off, delighted to see Yukie. He smiled as he approached her and wondered why the law enforcement officers were hovering.

"Here is some food. I make many things you like," Yukie proudly offered as she opened the basket, revealing all the wonderful foods that were Tatsuo's favorites.

His mouth watered at the sight. He was hungry and could have easily devoured everything she brought. Not knowing that Yukie had been instructed to bring a meal and still in the mindset that he must prove his loyalty to the United States, he thought hard about whether or not to accept the food. He badly wanted to go home, to "make free," so he didn't want to be connected with anything Japanese at the moment, not even the food. And the way these officers were hanging around, it was clear they thought something important was in the basket besides food, some sort of device that could aid in the sabotage he had been accused of. He wanted to prove them wrong.

"I sure appreciate you bring *gohan*, chicken, and the rest. But I not hungry in this moment," he lied, hoping to prove that he was in no way connected with Japan. Yukie, dismayed, nodded that she understood, even though she didn't. Tatsuo instinctively went to the carriage to admire a sleeping Kathleen. He leaned down and kissed her on the forehead.

"She's so beautiful," he whispered to himself.

"You sure you don't want any of that Jap food?" the FBI agent barked. And with this question, Tatsuo thought he was surely making the right move by saying no. Maybe this was the final test. Maybe now they would let him resume his life.

"I'm still full from breakfast." His voice reflected the dejection he felt. Yukie detected it, and her heart sank for him.

"Okay, then. Let's go." And before Tatsuo could utter a word, the two men whisked him out the door, where a car was waiting.

In the car, Tatsuo recognized Mr. Kitagawa and Mr. Okubo. He noticed law enforcement officers on each corner of the block, armed with guns, ready to shoot anything or anyone who looked or acted suspicious.

Yukie looked on as the car carrying her husband sped off, watching until she could no longer see it, then turned to ask someone, anyone, where they were taking him. But business as usual had resumed in the courthouse. The excitement was over. No one acknowledged her—she had become an invisible presence. She stood there, helpless, holding the basket of delicious food she had so carefully prepared.

FEBRUARY 1942—CAMP GRANT, ILLINOIS

Masao was still waiting for his orders. Bob had been shipped out to somewhere, to the relief of Shinji and to the dismay of Masao. He wondered what the military saw in an idiot like Bob.

Rokuro had just been handed his orders and was packing. It was just Shinji and Masao left behind. They couldn't help but think they had been passed over because they didn't sound right, as if they were covering up their Japanese accents. And they were. There was an unspoken understanding between them to never talk about how deeply it hurt to be excluded from orders, time and time again.

Mail call sounded, and to his surprise, Masao had a letter from San Bernardino. It was from his Aunt Yukie, although the envelope had been addressed in someone else's handwriting. He found a private spot, made sure no one else was nearby, and opened it. He was almost afraid to get the update; she had last written to him just after Uncle Tatsuo had been arrested in early January. Grateful that they had kept him in San Bernardino, he wondered if perhaps the connection between Tatsuo and an American military nephew would make a difference to law enforcement. Maybe they would let him be.

He pulled out the letter that was written in Yukie's beautiful Japanese *kanji*. She explained the entire ordeal at the courthouse and that she still didn't know Tatsuo's whereabouts. It had been ten days since she had seen him last. She was worried sick but kept things going at the store and managed to keep afloat at home with her little girl. She described how Little Japan had changed, as if it was dying a slow and painful death. Piece by piece, it was withering away, its residents losing faith and hope with each passing day. Many of the Issei men in the San Bernardino valley had been picked up and taken to unknown destinations, leaving the women behind to fill in the gaps of labor and assume the head of the household.

A Caucasian soldier walked near where Masao was sitting, so he lowered the letter inconspicuously, waiting until it was safe again. He continued reading, feeling his aunt's angst, her helplessness, and her attempts to muster strength in the dimmest of conditions. He finished reading and sat there for a moment, unable to function, unable to clearly see the direction he should go. Should he leave the military and go back to California, where he was certainly needed? Or should he stay and prove his loyalty as his other Nisei comrades were determined to do?

He looked at the letter in his hands and admired the beautiful, flowing, and elegant Japanese writing. Japanese. He glanced around and realized the enormity of that moment. Any Caucasian person would assume the worst. They would never believe that this was the letter of a hurting heart, from a wounded woman whose family had been ripped apart by the very government he served, by the country to which he had pledged his loyalty.

He knew what he had to do; he slowly and gently ripped the letter into the smallest of pieces, so no *kanji* were detectable. He would keep it concealed until he could find a barrel fire, either one on base or on a street in Chicago, to dispose of it for good.

★ ★ ★

I was once again mesmerized by Masao's family's legacy.

"He was taken away, just like that." I was astonished.

"Just like that," Mas assured me with a nod. "You know, at Camp Grant, I was there for four months." He looked at me and I nodded. "And, ah, I was never promoted. Other guys, they came in as privates, then promoted to private first class. But me—no."

"What about your friends? Your Nisei buddies. How about them?" I asked. He just shook his head no, and it was a sad no.

"Nope, not a one of us. You know, they said we were American soldiers. But . . ." His voice trailed off. He didn't need to complete the sentence. It was easy to see what was going on. Pearl Harbor had just been attacked; he and his buddies were collateral damage. They knew it, and there was nothing they could do about it.

"Can we pick up where we left off later?"

"Oh, sure." He shifted in his restaurant chair, producing a wince. I had never seen him do this and it scared me.

"What's wrong?"

"My leg. It's been bothering me today."

"Arthritis?"

"No, gunshot."

My eyes must have popped out of my head. "What?"

"Ah. It's not important, let's go gamble." He waved me off as he often did when he had had enough and was already grappling with his walker.

"Mas. You—you can't just—spit things out like that and expect me to just *wait*," I stammered as I followed him, looking to Alan for support. I was beginning to recognize when Masao was done with his storytelling. And he was done. There was nothing I could do to get another sentence of history out of the man at that moment.

November 16, 2010, was Mas's ninety-fourth birthday. The whole family gathered at Alan's brother's house. Everyone wanted to make this birthday special, his first without Doris. Amid the chaos of kids running around and adults catching up over food, I found Mas sitting alone on the sofa.

"I guess we don't get to gamble today," I said.

"Heh! Maybe we go tomorrow." He looked at me to see if that was possible.

"Let's do it," I assured him. He nodded, excited to have something to look forward to.

"When are we going to Vegas again? Soon, a-no?"

"In one more month," I reminded him, "December."

We seemed to be in our own little world, sitting there on the couch. Masao glanced at his family gathered in the kitchen and then looked at me. "You know, my wife, she was from Hawai'i. No seasons, really, in Hawai'i. She had a hard time when we moved here."

"I believe that. It would be hard to move to Seattle from Hawai'i."

He didn't seem to hear me. He was quietly gathering his thoughts.

"After Pearl Harbor, the military was in charge." He paused, as he usually did during his stories. "And, ah, they didn't know what to do with all the Japanese in Honolulu. Heh! There were too many Japanese there." He chuckled at the military's quandary. And then he relaxed and shifted to face me.

FEBRUARY 1942–HONOLULU

Military law had been imposed. Civilians were moved off military bases, a strict curfew had been instituted, and the blackout remained in force. Temporary military headquarters and other buildings were built on nonmilitary sites. Not even the beautiful grounds of the 'Iolani Palace were spared. Schools were routinely seized by the military, forcing students to hold class in unlikely places, such as churches or in parks. Long lines were still the norm at any grocery store, and fuel was rationed.

Buzz about disloyal residents had been flying throughout Hawai'i. There was gossip that Japanese Hawaiians had been in cahoots with the enemy. One rumor was that huge arrows had been carved in sugar cane fields and had pointed Japanese war planes toward military bases during the December 7 attack. Another rumor was that fishing boats floated out to where Japanese submarines waited in order to supply them with food. After a careful investigation by military officials, none of these rumors were ever substantiated.

Doris felt immune to any of the hatred that enveloped the island, directed at those of Japanese descent. "I was born on this island, a territory of the United States. I'm a citizen, Dad. Nobody is going to arrest me for anything," she said, attempting to ease her father's mind.

"There's still talk about sending us away, Doris. Let's not bring any attention to ourselves. It's better to play it safe and stay out of the way." But his reasoning was not going to faze Doris in the least. She was determined to be a part of civilian efforts.

"Dad. We're what—30 percent of the total population of Hawai'i?"

"Forty."

"You think the pineapple and sugar plantations can operate without 40 percent of its workforce?"

"We don't all work at plantations."

"You know what I mean, Dad. There's too many of us to take away. It's just not going to happen."

Doris's mom, who was mending a hole in a sock, looked up from the kitchen table. Her daughter made sense, even though she was a bit of a hothead.

"Doris, there are rumors that there were citizens among those that General Short took away," Doris's mom injected. She rarely spoke in such a manner, so Doris took note.

"What do you mean 'took away'?" Doris was unaware of such a move on the part of the military.

"He ordered hundreds of people into custody. Mostly Japanese people, but a few Germans and Italians," her mom clarified. "It was just after the attack. December 10. They live to this day behind barbed wire."

"How do you know this?" Doris wasn't convinced. She had no idea her mother was keeping up with the news at all, much less in such a detailed way.

"It was in the newspaper. You need to slow down and read. Listen. So you make sound decisions," her mother cautioned her.

"You think we're going to be sent away?" Doris asked. It was the first time she let worry enter her mind.

"No. Too many of us, like you said," her mom assured her. "One hundred forty thousand people, it's too many to move. Too many workers to lose."

Doris slumped down in a chair at the kitchen table next to her mother. "This war is wrecking my life. I just want to be with my friends. They're all getting involved, and I'm stuck here at home."

Her mother looked at her father. "You are a good citizen to want to help. Just slow down, look for a proper way to help. Don't use service as a means to be with your friends. Be sincere about it," her mother advised Doris, to the annoyance of her husband. And that was that. Doris had the green light to go ahead in a proper way, whatever that meant.

Doris had heard of hundreds of civilians, many of them Japanese Hawaiian, helping soldiers clear the land and lay barbed wire. Barbed wire was laid in the beaches just offshore around O'ahu as well. She thought through this notion and decided laying barbed wire wasn't for her. Another civilian job she would put on her reject list was digging trenches. In case of another attack, trenches would provide some cover for residents, as would the many shelters that were being built in the ground. People were also called on to assist in making camouflage, huge chunks of which were made to protect certain areas or buildings from being recognized from the air. While she knew how to sew, she thought that the making of camouflage net might be beyond her skill. She decided that anything physical probably wasn't for her. She kept looking.

Censorship of both incoming and outgoing mail had been implemented. While the military mail was handled by military officials, mail of a nonmilitary nature was handled by a civilian office. Office work was right up her alley, so this went on her growing list of possibilities. As it turned out, Doris would be a welcomed volunteer anywhere.

FEBRUARY 1942—CAMP JOSEPH T. ROBINSON, LITTLE ROCK, ARKANSAS

Being one of the last Nisei to receive orders at Camp Grant had been depressing. But once he got off the train in Little Rock, he could already feel the impact the warmer weather had on him. He guessed that it was in the low fifties, a vast improvement over Illinois. But it still wasn't the dry warmth of the San Bernardino Valley, where temperatures, even in the winter, averaged above sixty degrees and never went below forty.

Now on a military bus, Masao was weighed down by thoughts about his uncle. *Where has he been taken? How is his health? What about his store back home?* The bus made a turn at the main entrance to Camp Robinson, where the driver stopped and checked in with one of the guards, who gave him the go ahead.

The gears ground as the bus moved forward. Masao could see that this base was larger than Camp Grant and clearly a facility for military basic training. In fact, this sprawling installation boasted over forty-eight thousand square acres in 1942, with over sixty-seven hundred buildings, including fifty-two hundred hutments, or soldiers' quarters.

Housed at Camp Robinson was the Medical Replacement Training Center, or MRTC. This program provided the critical training for medics who would be shipped out to battlefields. Since Masao had been through basic medic training at Camp Grant, this was his assignment. He wasn't quite as enthusiastic about being a medic as he might have been. What really excited him was the combat training that was in a heightened state at this facility.

The base was bustling with activity in every direction as far as Masao could see. Camp Robinson hosted the Branch Immaterial Replacement Training Center, or BIRTC. Regardless of their specialty, soldiers would be trained at this center in basic infantry skills to prepare them for combat. At the height of war preparations, the BIRTC would continuously run at the capacity of sixteen thousand soldiers at a time. Masao was eager with anticipation as he experienced the sounds and sights of soldiers in training.

The bus stopped and the soldiers exited. The benefit of being the only Asian on the bus had been that he'd had a seat all to himself; the downside, he'd had nobody to talk to. He hoped that there would be other Nisei here, but as he got off the bus and looked around, he knew he would be alone.

FEBRUARY 1942—WEST COAST

Meanwhile, the nation was in a panic, especially along the West Coast. Caucasians feared the possibility that their Japanese neighbors, people they had known for years, were actually the enemy. The media fueled hysteria, and the US government was equally leery of Japanese residents. Many Issei men, like Tatsuo, had already been arrested and taken away to ensure security. But that alone didn't ease the minds of many.

Newspapers were bombarding the West Coast with alarm. Headlines were laced with racist remarks that consisted of various emotional statements calling for the immediate removal of every Japanese person. There was little humanity shown. In fact, the more brazen the statement, the bigger audience it drew. The famous columnists of the time, such as Westbrook Pegler and Walter Lippmann, fueled the fire of public frenzy with writings that suggested certain fifth column activity along the West Coast, even though government reports had emphasized there was no such activity to fear.

Executive Order 9066 gave the War Relocation Authority and military commanders the discretion to create military areas and secure them as they saw fit. The decision to sign it didn't come easy to President Roosevelt, who had faced enormous public and political pressure from both sides. Powerful men opposed the notion of the relocation of Japanese from the West Coast. James H. Rowe, assistant to the US attorney general, wrote a message to the president urging him to consider the constitutional rights of Japanese Americans. Indeed, the attorney general himself, Francis Biddle, addressed the president directly in an attempt to steer him away from the massive evacuation.

Reasonable voices were no match for the incendiary propaganda, though. Key military personnel were insistent that the West Coast was the next target of the Japanese, and they wanted to secure the area quickly. Politicians, eager to please their constituents, jumped on the hateful bandwagon. The newspaper columnists were in heaven; they had the platform to spew abhorrence for Japanese souls far and wide and they did so, repeatedly and loudly. The language in public was becoming more vitriolic as wrath unfolded. Some Caucasian folks who lived along the West Coast recognized the additional golden opportunity of eliminating some of their competition in farming and commerce by way of evacuation—one more reason to make noise about moving the Japanese out.

On February 19, 1942, President Roosevelt made it official when he signed Executive Order 9066. Military commanders wasted no time in establishing military areas and deciding who would be evacuated first. Six days later, on February 25, the military arrived at Terminal Island, in Los Angeles, en masse. The people of Terminal Island, it had been decided, would be the first community to be moved. Signs were posted and the word got out; they had exactly forty-eight hours to take care of business and evacuate the area.

MARCH 18, 1942—THE PRESIDIO, SAN FRANCISCO

More officers arrived on the base, now the main nerve center for the War Relocation Authority. Intense discussions took place in top-secret security clearance conferences regarding who should be evacuated from the coastal regions. The voices that carried fear about sabotage and espionage were louder than any levelheaded voice.

"Immediate evacuation of all persons of Japanese lineage, aliens and citizens alike." An officer was reading from an order to the generals and administrators who sat around a large conference table.

"Citizens, sir?" Another officer said, requesting clarification.

General DeWitt snapped at the officer, indicating he had little, if any, tolerance for anyone of Japanese ancestry.

"If they have even one drop of Japanese blood, they need to go," another administrator barked out.

"We'll have the signs ready to post in a week, sir. Assembly centers are in place and ready to house evacuees," a young officer eagerly reported. "Our vulnerable areas have already been secured."

General DeWitt nodded in approval at this. Just then, a brave officer posed a question that nobody had thought of.

"Sir, what about our guys here on base?" He was referring to the dedicated Nisei soldiers who were, at that very moment, just down the road in building 640 on Crissey Field studying the Japanese language, learning how to interrogate and interpret, and ready to engage in military efforts on behalf of the US Army. These soldiers were the first class of the Military Intelligence Service Language School and had been on base since November, 1941. A highly secret operation, only officers with the highest security clearance were privy to the existence of the MIS operation. There was an uneasy feeling in the room; possible enemies were among them on base.

"When will they complete the program?" a lieutenant asked.

"April, sir. They graduate in April."

The lieutenant looked at DeWitt and understood the look on the general's face. There was only one decision that would be acceptable.

"Move 'em out. They can't stay here. The day after graduation, they're gone."

MARCH 1942—FORT MISSOULA, MONTANA

Fort Missoula had been turned over to the Department of Justice and was being used as an alien detention center. The Immigration and Naturalization Service, or INS, operated out of this location and conducted loyalty hearings of all enemy aliens who were detained between 1941 and 1944. Fort Missoula would be known as a separate camp from the relocation centers that would house most of the evacuated Japanese and was, in reality, a processing facility before men were sent to Department of Justice prisons.

During this period, there were some twelve hundred Italians, one thousand Japanese, and twenty-three Germans who were considered resident aliens. The Italian men were mostly merchant seamen and others who had been employees of an Italian luxury liner that had been seized in the Panama Canal. Most, if not all of these men, were simply in the wrong place at the wrong time.

Tatsuo had been sent to Fort Missoula on a train. An armed guard was stationed on every train car, where little movement and less conversation was allowed. The shades were always down, day and night. The men, all considered enemies, couldn't open the shades to peek out for a moment, not even to check to see where they were or what direction they were headed. They were not allowed to ask such questions, either.

At Fort Missoula, Tatsuo endured hours of grilling at loyalty hearings in front of as many as five military or INS officers. These hearings were conducted to determine whether the men in custody were to be sent to relocation centers or an actual prison. Tatsuo was hoping for a relocation center.

"Do you believe the emperor is the God of Japan?" they had asked him in one of the hearings.

"No. I believe he is the emperor." Tatsuo had been told to respond in Japanese through an interpreter, who happened to be Korean. He wasn't sure the interpreter was getting everything right but understood enough English to be fairly confident. He also wondered why, if this was a loyalty hearing, these people weren't insisting on English-only answers. He certainly knew enough English to respond in English. He wasn't sure what the expectation was, but since he wanted to follow the path that would get him out of custody, he followed their instructions and spoke Japanese.

"About this war, about the attack by the Japanese that brought the United States into war, who do you want to win this war? The United States? Or Japan?"

"I came to the United States when I was just sixteen years old. I have lived here longer than I lived in Japan, for twenty-two years now. Most of the man I am is due to how I have been raised in the United States, not due to Japan. I am very appreciative of everything I have learned while living here."

"You haven't answered the question, Mr. Abe," one of the officers spat at him. The interpreter didn't accentuate the disdain, but Tatsuo felt it.

He didn't know how to rationalize what he was feeling. Japan was his country; his citizenship was still attached to Japan. But since he had moved to the States in 1920, he had rarely visited Japan. He loved his life in San Bernardino and desperately wanted to return to that life as soon as possible. If he estranged himself from Japan in this hearing, which was being recorded, would he ever be allowed to return to Japan? If he estranged himself from the United States, what would happen to him, to his family?

"Mr. Abe, please answer the question," another officer was insisting.

"I am not interested in this war. I don't care who wins. I just want peace. As soon as possible, I want peace." He thought the answer would satisfy them, but it did not alleviate their concerns.

To make matters worse, the man he left in charge of his store was pressuring Yukie and Tatsuo into relinquishing ownership. Yukie had been allowed to send letters to Tatsuo and had forwarded correspondence regarding the store, not wanting to make any decisions about the business by herself.

"Tatsuo, we need to decide on this quickly," the acting manager of Star Cash Grocery had written. "Customers are dwindling. Nobody wants to buy their goods from a Japanese store. Anything Japanese is very bad. I urge you to change the store to my name as soon as possible in order to save it." The latest of a series of letters suggested that Tatsuo sign the store over, legally, to him.

Tatsuo's house was in Masao's name. It would be safe. But the store—it was a different question.

"There is nothing in the store name that indicates it has Japanese owners. I don't understand how changing the ownership will help," Tatsuo had challenged, but there was an answer for that as well.

"Tatsuo, everyone knows that Star Cash Grocery is owned by Tatsuo Abe. Everyone knows it's owned by a Japanese man. That's why nobody is shopping here any longer. What we need to do, quickly, is change the name of the ownership, and change the name of the store. Every other merchant in Little Japan has done this in an attempt to save their property. I am trying to help you, Tatsuo. Don't be a fool."

Tatsuo had a funny feeling about it, but he eventually succumbed and arranged to have the store put in the manager's name. He was helpless to do anything else since his future was still undetermined. And he assumed he wouldn't be returning to San Bernardino any time soon. As he mailed the final paperwork that would solidify the deal, he wondered if Star Cash Grocery would ever again be the store it once was.

CHAPTER SIX

LIFE OF LONELINESS

This would be the first Christmas without Doris. Masao had assured everyone that he would attend the traditional Christmas Eve dinner, even though he hadn't joined the family for Thanksgiving. The plan was set: Alan's brother, Pat, would pick Masao up.

"He's not going to come," I said in the car as we were on our way.

"He'll be there," Alan insisted. I looked out the window at the frost along the highway. It had been a cold winter already, cold and depressing.

"I don't think so. Maybe we should come up with a plan." My suggestion only irritated Alan.

We were among the first to arrive. I nervously nibbled on vegetables while I waited for Pat to show up with Masao. Alan detected what was going on in my mind.

"He'll be here, just be patient. Jeez . . . you're worse than I am." With that, I switched from vegetables to the candy tray.

Eventually Pat's family showed up. They funneled into the house, all eight of them, but no Masao. I was jumping out of my skin to question everyone, but it wasn't my place. I would have to let Alan take the lead on the inquisition. He asked his niece, Katharine, what had happened.

"He was just sitting there in the dark," she reported.

"And you just left him there?" Alan asked with as much objectivity as he could muster. I could tell, though, he was immensely bothered by the vision of his father sitting alone, in the dark, on Christmas Eve.

Katharine's three little children ran around her and she needed to tend to them, so Pat's wife, Stephanie, jumped in to explain. "You know, Alan, he just needs to be left alone tonight. He's pretty lonely and I think he just wants to be alone with his thoughts."

"We weren't going to carry him out of his apartment. He would have been kicking and screaming if we'd done that," Katharine added.

It all made sense. And it didn't.

Alan looked at me. I looked at him. He didn't have to say a word—I was already grabbing my things.

On the way to Masao's, Alan drove fast, weaving in and out of cars, a notable difference from his usual granny-like driving. I was glad, though. I wanted to get to Masao.

We knocked and walked in and, sure enough, it was dark.

"Dad?" Alan called out as he flipped on the light.

Masao was surprised to see us. "Ohhh. You didn't go to Taryn's place?" he asked.

"We were there, but we were worried about you. Come on, let's go. We can go together," Alan suggested.

"Ah. No need. I don't want to go." Masao dug in his heels. I understood. It would be just another reminder that he was alone in the world. But Alan persisted.

"The whole family is there. We're all waiting for you. Come on, let's go." Masao waved him off as he picked up his TV remote

"How about we go casino," I butted in, phrasing the question the way Masao would. That caught his attention.

"Oh, I go casino." Masao was delighted with the idea.

Alan looked at me with wonder. I shrugged. I knew what made Masao happy—it was forgetting about his hurting heart. Although Alan hated to gamble and hated the casino in general, he was happy to be going this time; happy that his dad wouldn't be spending the night alone in the dark. As I helped Masao with his coat, Alan looked on, unsure how it was that I knew his dad so well.

"I'm glad to spend Christmas Eve with you," I said softly to Masao, who smiled at me.

The following February, the three of us went to Hawai'i in remembrance of Doris's passing. One morning, I met one of his war buddies, Saburo Nakamura, who went by Naki, and who had served in the South Pacific with Masao. I was delighted to meet someone from Masao's past.

We met at a breakfast place near Fort DeRussy, an innocuous-looking facility situated on a beautiful park on Waikiki Beach. It was battery operated and manned by the Sixteenth Coast Artillery, one of several batteries that guarded the coast of O'ahu in 1941. These forts were equipped with anti-aircraft guns, some of which had brought down enemy planes on the morning of December 7. Now a museum, it showcases the various heroes who have emerged in wars and battles since 1924, when it was established.

My immediate impression of Naki was that he was a warm, congenial, gentle man, much like Masao. He was quick to smile and seemed humble in ways that I would never understand.

Watching the two men banter at breakfast was heartwarming. It was as if they had shed their elder bodies and were back in the thick of the 1940s, a couple of twenty-somethings who had survived the horrors of war. The inside jokes were rampant; Alan and I had no chance of appreciating the humor but laughed along anyway just because it was entertaining to see these guys and their youthful energy. There wasn't a lot of room in the conversation for me to insert questions, so I just enjoyed their company.

When we left the restaurant, we walked Naki to his car. Masao's physique was still very trim, if not too thin, but Naki had grown some in the waistline, and that seemed to make his stride a little uneven. Masao, from the wheelchair being pushed by Alan, had the audacity to give Naki a hard time.

"Goddamn, Naki, you walk like an old man," he spouted. But Naki was also a little hard of hearing, and Masao's really great line, literally, fell on deaf ears. Or maybe that was Naki's way of being polite, since Alan and I were there. It was illuminating to see Masao in this light, turning back into the soldier he had once been, reliving his younger days with one of the few men in the world who understood World War II the way he did.

Masao wanted to show me some of the places on the island that were important to him. We drove by the condo unit that he and Doris had stayed in for months at a time, we ate at Zippy's many times because they had good *saimin,* and we ate at the Prince Court buffet because it was one of Doris's favorite places. And, of course, we visited Doris where she was interred at the Punchbowl almost every day.

Masao and Saburo "Naki" Nakamura in February 2012

The National Memorial Cemetery of the Pacific, or the Punchbowl as most people know it, has a rich history, as do many sites in Hawai'i. The Hawaiian name for the area is Puowaina, or Hill of Sacrifice. The crater was formed by volcanic activity some seventy-five thousand years ago. Puowaina has seen evolution in full. Human sacrifices were performed there very early on. It was used as a rifle range at one point, and during WWII, tunnels were dug throughout the rim of the crater to shore up the batteries below.

Names on the grave markers and on columbarium units are a testament to the melting pot the United States has become. The ethnicities of men and women who served our great country are represented there: Hawaiian, Japanese, Irish, Jewish, Italian, Latinx, Pacific Islander, and others. Doris's niche was located in the columbarium. I would fix roses and arrange them at the foot. Masao would sit with his private thoughts about his beloved Doris for several moments with his head down, his hand shielding his eyes. I was never sure whether he was crying or avoiding the sun, but I suspected the former. After he had finished his private and silent conversation with Doris, he would come back to us.

Masao was content in Honolulu. Being there seemed to stir memories for him. I was delighted because he was always in the mood to tell stories, and I loved learning more about his days from the 1940s.

1942—HONOLULU

The United Service Organization (USO) was expanding rapidly and becoming busy due to the enormous influx of soldiers on the island. Doris found herself a job with one of the USO offices that was housed in the Japanese school she had attended as a young girl.

As a woman, it was a little easier for her to blend in and her American first name helped. While some Japanese families had actually changed their surnames to either Hawaiian surnames or European-sounding names, Doris's dad refused to make such leaps. And so, Doris Okada found her way to a job that suited her and also helped war efforts.

Japanese American men on the island, second- and third-generation, had a much tougher time. They were immediately considered suspect by military and civilians alike. The Hawai'i Territorial Guard, many of them ROTC students without full military training, proudly followed orders and stood guard at key points on the island. Close to 75 percent of the guardsmen were of Japanese descent, and when the Pentagon realized that in January of 1942, orders came down to release all territorial guardsmen who were of Japanese origin, no matter how long their families had lived in Hawai'i. Many Nisei men considered their release from the guard the most painful form of societal rejection.

The former ROTC cadets, though, weren't about to give up and petitioned Lieutenant General Delos Emmons, who had been appointed as the military governor, to let the ROTC serve in some defense capacity. Emmons was benevolent toward Japanese Americans and often brought a reasonable voice to outlandish allegations brought forth by other commanders. Emmons agreed to allow the ROTC cadets to serve in the defense effort that would become known as the Varsity Victory Volunteers. These men handled some of the most difficult manual labor the army was assigned. And they did it with pride. The same men would eventually be allowed to enlist in the military, and they did so in droves. Over ninety-five hundred Japanese American men from Hawai'i tried to enlist in the military. Only twenty-seven hundred were accepted.

At the USO office, Doris kept busy. She worked long hours, often putting in more than the required forty-five hours per week. Men would flirt with her as they came by the office for various needs. They saw her as a demure and subservient *wahine*, there to fill their masculine needs, but they were wrong. She was friendly, but she shut them down if they went too far.

One day a handsome Nisei walked into the office. He was dressed in volunteer clothes, and she knew right away this was a guy who had done the hardest labor the army could hand out, hoping to be allowed to enlist.

"May I help you?" Doris asked as she met him at the counter.

"Hi, uh, me and some of my buddies were wondering if volunteers were allowed to attend the dance this weekend."

He seemed like a guy who had been condescended to by soldiers, looked down on, even laughed at, in his attempt to prove himself loyal, like so many other Nisei and Sansei men.

Doris glanced out to the front of the building and saw a group of other Nisei guys, all in the same dirty condition, waiting patiently. "Sorry. No. Those functions are strictly for military men. Volunteers can't get in." She hated to deliver the bad news to him.

"Okay, thanks. It was worth asking," his voice was low.

"What's your name?" Doris asked. It came from out of nowhere. The girls in the office almost fell off their chairs. Never had the attractive, sought-after Doris shown any interest in the men who had come through the office. The young man stopped and turned toward her.

"Oh, I beg your pardon, I should have introduced myself. I'm George." He held out his hand to shake hers, then pulled it back. "Ah, sorry, I'm still grimy from work."

"It's okay, I don't mind," and she held out her hand to shake his. She liked the feel of him, and she liked his eyes. They were honest.

"I'm Doris. Nice to meet you, George. You have the same name as my father." George nodded at this and smiled. "Say, George, if you're looking for a little fun, there's a gathering this weekend up in Manoa, a bunch of friends of mine are getting together for a barbeque. You interested?"

George was quick with his answer. "Sure. Can I bring some of my buddies?"

"Why not?" As Doris wrote down directions, he gazed at her. He liked the shape of her face and that she wasn't afraid to be forward.

From that moment on, George and Doris became an item. They relied on each other for strength when they felt overwhelmed by rumors or racist remarks. They spent time together and, as much as they could, traveled around Oʻahu discovering wonderful spots to have a picnic or neck. One of their favorite places to picnic, though, was right there in Waikiki, just adjacent to Fort DeRussy. They would sit together in the soft sand as long as they could, often watching the sunset before rushing to get home by curfew. They found ways to maintain bits of normal Hawaiian life in the midst of confusion.

APRIL 1942—FORT MISSOULA, MONTANA

"Abe." The guard stood at his detention unit with papers in hand.

Tatsuo walked over to the door.

"You're being moved to a different location. Pack up."

Tatsuo packed, hoping that his loyalty hearing had earned him the chance to be reunited with Yukie. With his suitcase in hand, he boarded the train that would take him to yet another unknown destination.

The train ride took days, and the prisoners were allowed off only once every four hours to use facilities. The shades were drawn the entire time. Prisoners had no clue where they were going, or for how long.

Eventually the train slowed, and the prisoners were let off. Tatsuo would learn that he was in Louisiana at a military facility called Camp Livingston. He would be detained here for weeks until he would be sent to another facility, a prison, in Santa Fe, New Mexico.

That's what you do with prisoners of war, he thought, *you keep them moving and mixed up so they don't have a chance to congregate.* What the US military didn't understand, though, was that these particular prisoners hadn't had a reason to unite until they became prisoners of war.

Being considered an enemy wasn't what bothered Tatsuo. It was being away from his family, from his little girl that he missed, and his new little baby that Yukie might have to deliver all on her own. He missed his grocery store and his way of life in California. He thought himself a fool for turning the grocery store over to his manager. He thought himself a fool for sending all his hard-earned money to Japan. From what he had heard, Japanese banks had folded. Assets had been seized and were being used by the Japanese government to further military efforts. He had nothing—less than nothing. How would he manage once he was released, *if* he were released?

As he and the other prisoners were escorted to their new detention cells behind barbed wire, he thought about Yukie. She was now four months pregnant and must be tired. He wondered what his daughter, Kathleen, looked like now and if she was close to crawling. His heart ached as he realized all the wonderful things he was missing with his little girl. He wondered whether or not his nephew, Masao, had been shipped out to Europe yet. And he worried about Star Cash Grocery and what had become of it.

APRIL 1942—WEST COAST

By the end of March, the Selective Service was notified to no longer accept any persons of Japanese descent for service within any branch of the armed forces, whether they were citizens or not. The War Department also declared that any current soldier of Japanese extraction would not be sent overseas. The Military Intelligence

Service Language School, including one of its leaders, Captain Rasmussen, became increasingly frustrated with the mixed signals within the military. What was the point of training all the Nisei soldiers for interrogation and interpretation if they were not going to be deployed to the South Pacific because they were not allowed to leave the shores of the United States?

To complicate matters for the MIS, word had arrived that they were no longer welcome on the Presidio. Once the current class completed the program at the end of April, they were to vacate. The Western Defense Command was eager to proclaim the West Coast completely clear of any and all Japanese, including military men. This was a confusing and complicated time, a part of American history that is hard to comprehend in the mind or understand in the heart. Occurring from the very same location, the Presidio, one arm of the military was in charge of the massive ethnic evacuation along the West Coast. Meanwhile, under another arm of the same military branch, Captain Rasmussen was frantically trying to recruit Nisei soldiers stationed along the West Coast for his next class of the MIS. The location of the MIS Language School was yet to be determined, and it was unclear if the graduates of the program would even be utilized as intended, but Rasmussen persevered.

Citizens along the West Coast had mixed feelings about the evacuation of Japanese people. Milton Eisenhower, brother to General Eisenhower and director of the War Relocation Authority, was outwardly supportive of the massive evacuation along the West Coast. Inwardly, though, he struggled with this process, stating at one point that history would prove it a mistake. He resigned within months of accepting the position of director.

Vitriol for the Japanese was everywhere. "Slap the Jap" posters were sold for a mere twenty-five cents to anyone who needed a reminder that the Japanese were treacherous, faithless, untrustworthy, inhuman, depraved, soulless, and disloyal, among other scurrilous traits. Storefronts and public facilities were festooned with signs that told "Japs" to "Keep Out—You Rats." Merchants had advertisements indicating their loyalty to America by expressing hatred toward the Japanese: "We Don't Want Any Japs Back Here . . . EVER!" Headlines in newspapers announced the "Ouster of All Japs." In some areas, people of Chinese blood wore buttons to distinguish themselves from Japanese, not wanting to be associated. Every hateful act, such as spitting on them, and every vile and racist comment aimed at them, along with the anger that could be directed at them—all of it was deemed acceptable.

Young and old alike, all the Japanese in California, Oregon, and Washington were tagged and funneled through assembly centers before finally being sent to one of the relocation camps, flanked with barbed wire and surrounded by armed guards. They were forced to leave behind many precious items and family treasures.

At the Presidio, Captain Rasmussen was busy on three points: graduating his first class of MIS interpreters, recruiting his next class, and determining a new location for the MIS Language School to appease the Western Defense Command leaders, namely Lieutenant General DeWitt. To find a new location, Captain Rasmussen was included in a meeting in Salt Lake City that was attended by the governors and other representatives of eleven Western states. On the agenda was the consideration of geographic areas that were appropriate for the relocation facilities, as well as the location of the MIS facility. This meeting did not go well.

"If you bring Japanese into my state, I promise you they will be hanging from every tree," one governor fumed during the meeting. There was such hostility that Captain Rasmussen wondered if there was any state that would accept the MIS. None of these eleven states wanted to be burdened with any program that involved Japanese personnel, evacuees, or prisoners of war.

After the debacle of a meeting in Salt Lake City, Captain Rasmussen kept scouting for a new location for the language school. Eventually, he met with the governor of Minnesota, who was willing to accommodate this military effort. There was a glitch, though. There was only one army base in Minnesota, Fort Snelling in the Minneapolis–St. Paul area, and this base was already operating at full capacity. There was simply no space to house a language school. But the governor was very eager to help and suggested using a former Civilian Conservation Corps facility that was located in Savage, a small town about ten miles away from Fort Snelling. It was being used to house indigent men, but the governor offered to relocate them to free up the space. Captain Rasmussen was delighted, and on April 7, the move was approved by the War Department.

Rasmussen returned to the Presidio to work out his other frustrations; namely, how to get the military at large to understand and appreciate the strategic tool they had in the Nisei soldiers who had just gone through five months of interrogation and interpretation training. He had successfully located the whereabouts of 150 Nisei and had them lined up for the second class of the MIS, which would now be facilitated at Camp Savage, Minnesota. But he worried about what would come of the soldiers who were ready to deploy.

Publicly, and to the ranks of the military, the message was that no Japanese military men would leave the shores of the United States. Among only the highest-ranking officers, the top-secret missions involving American soldiers of Japanese descent were understood as necessary, and on rare occasions, accepted. With that philosophy in place, on May 1, 1942, there was a small graduation ceremony for the forty Nisei who had successfully completed the language school. Soon after, approximately twenty soldiers of the MIS Language School were shipped out to destinations unknown. The remaining soldiers and officers packed up and headed for Minnesota.

JUNE 1942—SAN BERNARDINO

As June approached, Yukie couldn't deny the evacuation signs that were posted on telephone poles all over town. Now six months pregnant, she packed what she could and boxed everything else up. She hoped that, at the very least, the house would be intact upon her return. As she packed, she wondered if Tatsuo would be with her when their second child arrived in September. She didn't care where they were, she just wanted to be with her husband again.

The defense preparations and the massive evacuation let the Western Defense Command claim success and assure the citizens along the West Coast that the Japanese among them were no longer a threat. They had all been moved off the coast. Citizens were warned to be on the lookout and report anyone who appeared to be Japanese, even if they were wearing a military uniform. The homes, farms, and businesses that had been occupied and run by Japanese had been vacated, taken over, or looted. The fear-mongers had won.

JUNE 1942—SAN FRANCISCO

In the still of night, the SS *Maui* entered through the Golden Gate Strait, beneath the magnificent Golden Gate Bridge and under the watchful eye of soldiers who filled the pillboxes embedded in the bluffs on either side of the strait. The SS *Maui* docked at a port in Oakland, where over fourteen hundred Nisei, members of the Hawai'i Territorial Guard, opened secret orders, learning that they were now part of the Hundredth Infantry Battalion. These men disembarked and quickly filled three waiting trains, which were blacked out with shades drawn. The trains immediately left for Camp McCoy, Wisconsin. They would take different routes to arrive at the same destination, another ploy to keep the passengers hidden from the general public and from other military personnel.

The public was never notified. Soldiers of lesser rank were not privy. There would be many times that Nisei soldiers were transported in secrecy and only the highest-ranking officers would be aware. By late June, the Nisei soldiers at Camp McCoy were training as the newly designated Hundredth Infantry Battalion—Separate. The "Separate" designation indicated that the battalion had no home; it would be an orphan unit until it could attach to a division many months later.

At the same time, the new MIS Language School class of 150 Nisei soldiers entered the first phase of training at Camp Savage. Meanwhile, at Camp Robinson, Masao wondered if he would ever see another Nisei. He was lonely, and he craved rice. He resigned himself to the fact that neither of these desires would be satisfied any time soon.

SUMMER 1942—CAMP JOSEPH T. ROBINSON, LITTLE ROCK, ARKANSAS

Because Masao had undergone medic training, he was assigned to the dental clinic. With the influx of thousands of soldiers, the clinic chairs in the waiting room were filled. The dentist, Dr. Major Hall, worked on cases as fast as he could.

"Soldier, when was the last time you brushed your teeth?" Major Hall asked a patient one day.

"I don't remember," the soldier responded with instruments in his mouth. Masao cringed and instinctively reached for a mask to put on. Major Hall nodded, indicating the mask was a good idea. They were both mortified by the tooth decay they encountered on a daily basis.

The two had a great working relationship, and Masao never felt any hint of dislike or racism coming from Major Hall. It was the one place on base and in Little Rock that Masao felt unguarded. Still, he wanted something more. He wanted to be in combat training. He regularly applied for different military positions and was regularly rejected.

"What happened to the Tenth Army Division?" Major Hall asked Masao while working on a patient one day. Major Hall knew of Masao's desire to be on the battlefield and not only empathized with him but encouraged him. The Tenth Army Division had a ski unit, and Masao had some experience skiing. He had been excited to apply.

"Application rejected," Masao answered flatly as he handed a different tool over. The major pondered this while he worked.

"Did they give a reason?"

"No. No reason. I can't imagine it would matter that I'm Japanese in the mountains in Italy. But . . ."

"It's a tough situation, Abe. Don't give up," Major Hall suggested after a few minutes. But Masao was beginning to realize that the American military didn't know what to do with him. To the US Army, he felt as if he was nothing more than a threat—a threat that must be watched.

Masao's uncanny ability to find the best food in town led him to a diner in Little Rock. He would end up there whenever he was on leave or given a one-day pass. Since he was always alone, he had to figure out a way to keep the wolves at bay when it came to his heritage. There weren't many Asians in Little Rock, and Japanese Americans were almost nonexistent.

The waitress, Meg, brought a T-bone steak dinner and set it in front of Masao, who sat at the counter one day. He immediately cut into it and savored the warm, thick protein as he chewed.

"For a little guy, you sure do eat a lot," Meg said with a smile.

"We can't get good food like this on base," he answered with his mouth full. She brought him a cup of coffee. He had become a regular, and she knew what he wanted even before he asked.

"Thank you." Masao smiled and reached for the sugar as he stuffed another bite of steak in his mouth. Down the counter, a man stared daggers at him.

"You there. Soldier." The man said loudly. Other patrons looked over.

His mouth full, Masao motioned for him to wait a minute. But the man didn't want to wait.

"Where're you from, anyway?" he demanded. The other diners looked at Masao. They also wanted to know. He stood out. He was the only person of color in the diner.

"He's an Indian. From southern California. The Chappo tribe, right?" Meg answered for him.

Chappo. It's what all the Latinx customers called Tatsuo. Masao had capitalized on this and turned the nickname into a tribal title that saved him the agony of explaining his Japanese identity. Masao nodded to Meg, letting her know she had it right and stuffed another piece of meat into his mouth so he didn't have to talk.

"Christ Almighty. I guess they'll let anyone wear a uniform these days. At least you ain't a Jap," the man stammered and turned away.

"Good Lord, Buford. The Army ain't gonna let the Japanese join. What are you thinking?" Meg laughed as she topped off Masao's cup with hot coffee.

Masao focused on his food. He felt vindicated, and not. He was, unfortunately, getting used to routine verbal assaults on his race. Nobody liked the Japanese. Nobody. On base, he was living in isolation among the troops. Soldiers in his quarters would make small talk with him, but he always ate alone. It made him appreciate Major Hall even more. But Masao would be losing his only ally.

"Can you take me with you?" Masao pleaded in pure desperation when Major Hall announced his new orders. "As an assistant?"

"It doesn't work like that, Abe." Major Hall would be shipping out for Europe. "You'll get your orders, just be patient."

The dentist who replaced Major Hall wasn't talkative. It was all business. Masao wasn't sure if the guy was racist or just cold, but he no longer enjoyed working at the clinic and kept looking for opportunities in the army.

One morning, Masao heard a sound coming from outside. He scanned out the window, diverting his attention from his job. Soldiers were marching, and in his imagination he was with them, feet moving in perfect unison.

"Abe. Abe." The new dentist, Dr. Vance, needed a tool. Masao handed it over and returned his attention to the formation of soldiers.

"What outfit is that?" Masao asked to no one in particular. Dr. Vance glanced out the window, then looked at Masao. He could see what was going on; he could see the longing in Masao's eyes.

"Those guys are paratroopers. They ran three miles in their boots before you got out of bed this morning," Dr. Vance condescended. But that didn't stop Masao from finding out how to apply.

Masao faithfully waited for orders that never came. All he received was a rejection letter from his paratrooper application.

His military career appeared dismal at best.

Anticipation filled the air at Camp Robinson. Masao was making his area perfect: bed—made, foot locker—clean, floor—swept. At 0800 they were to be lined up on either side of the road that President Roosevelt would be chauffeured along. The president would be making inspection at precisely 0830. The entire town of Little Rock had heard the news and had made signs to greet the president all along the railroad route.

"I can't believe we're actually going to meet the president," said the PFC in the bed next to Masao. He was excited for the event.

"He's not going to shake the hands of ten thousand guys, you know?" Masao tried to calm his comrade, but it was no use. He was equally as excited. At last he would feel like he was a part of the military he served; he would feel like a soldier among soldiers. He felt lucky to witness such a historical event.

"Who cares, at least we'll get to see him." The PFC smoothed out the last wrinkle on his bed. Just then a first sergeant marched into their quarters. There were salutes all around. The first sergeant went straight to Masao and handed him a paper.

"Good news, corporal. A one-day pass. You don't have to stand for inspection."

Masao took the pass but was confused. The first sergeant was packaging the one-day pass as a gift. But this was no gift. Masao was hoping it was all a mistake.

"Go hide yourself," the first sergeant said, pounding in the final nail. Then he spun on his heel and marched out.

Masao stood with his one-day pass in his hand, stunned. The sergeant's words echoed in his ears. Nearby soldiers looked on briefly before they continued about their business. Not one of them came to the comfort of Masao. Not one of them cared if the "Jap" among them was excluded from the presidential visit. Masao tried to conceal the humiliation he felt. He glanced at the PFC beside him, who looked away sheepishly.

While President Roosevelt made inspection of the thousands of troops at Camp Joseph T. Robinson, Masao, one of the few Japanese Americans on base at the time, sat at the counter of the diner in Little Rock.

"You're not involved in all the hoopla over at the base?" Meg asked as she poured coffee.

"Nah. No need," was all Masao could reply.

★ ★ ★

In the summer of 2011, we were at dinner at one of the downtown Las Vegas casinos. We were just finishing our salads when Masao cringed a little bit.

"It's my leg," he reported.

"Did you bring your medicine?" Alan asked him. Masao nodded. His medicine, as it turned out, was Aleve. "Maybe you should soak in the bathtub tonight," Alan suggested.

I liked the sound of that. It had been years since Masao was able to soak in a tub. His apartment only had a shower, but even if he had had a bathtub, he was far too frail to try to navigate that process by himself. Since baths were part of Japanese culture and tradition, it was something that Masao missed.

"Ah. No need," Masao waved him off. I could see what this was, though. He didn't want to be trouble for anyone, not even Alan.

"That's a really good idea, Mas. A nice hot bath, it would probably make your leg feel better." I encouraged him, trying to describe it in a way that would convince him. It felt like we were trying to persuade a toddler.

"Maybe," he succumbed, and that meant "yes" in my book.

Masao resisted but eventually gave in to our demands. The bathrooms at the Golden Nugget Rush Tower were spacious; there was plenty of room for Alan to assist him in and out of the bathtub. Alan would gently wash his back for him and stay with him while he soaked, then help him dry off and get into his pajamas. Masao would sleep like a baby those nights. I couldn't think of a more loving way for one human being to care for another. It became a tradition during our stays.

The next morning at breakfast, Masao was refreshed and wanted to chat. "You know, during the war when I was still at Camp Joseph T. Robinson, in Japan, things got *really* bad."

"Do you mean for your parents?"

He nodded. "For my parents, yes. For everyone, a-no?"

Masao and Alan in Vegas

APRIL 1943—SENOUE, FUKUSHIMA-KEN, JAPAN

The Japanese military was stretched thin. They had invaded countries all over the Pacific Rim and were now being challenged by the United States in the South Pacific. Japanese strongholds were falling one by one. Not only was the military running short of men to serve, they were running short of equipment. The government put on a front that Japan was winning the war, but there were plenty of signs that just the opposite was true.

In the Abe home, Yasoshichi and Tomie had only one son left at home. Jiro, their second son, had died from the same appendicitis affliction that had taken their Yuriko some seven years earlier. Only their youngest remained. He was in his early teens, and his parents already feared for his future. They hadn't heard directly from Masao since Japan had attacked Pearl Harbor. They heard about him, indirectly, through Tatsuo, who was having struggles of his own. At this point, nobody knew if Masao was still in the States, in Europe, or in the South Pacific fighting face to face against the Japanese military.

The loss of two children had been almost too much for Tomie to bear. She felt certain that her beloved Masao, the child she had abandoned when he was just nine, would not make it out of this horrific war alive. Her worry was only magnified by the absence of any news from him directly.

Families such as the Abes had a self-sustaining source of food. They had expanded their farm and grew vegetables that they canned and stored. Other families weren't so fortunate and made a living by any means possible, sometimes resorting to illegal behavior. Life was bleak at best throughout Japan.

★ ★ ★

"I couldn't communicate with my mom. She couldn't read English," Masao recalled as he sipped his coffee. The waitress brought our food and set it down, but Masao hardly noticed.

"And I didn't want to risk writing in Japanese *kanji*." I pushed the ketchup over to him for his Portuguese sausage. He put the ketchup on his egg instead, but he didn't eat. He was still with his mother.

"It must have been hard for my mom. She lost two children, a-no?" He shook his head out of sheer empathy. "Things were bad in Japan."

And then, he seemed to notice his food and picked up his silverware to eat. His eyes told me there was more, and I wanted to hear it.

"How did you communicate with anyone in your family, Mas? Your mom, your dad, your uncle . . ."

"I could only write to my Uncle Tatsuo. But I didn't want him to worry. He had enough problems of his own."

SUMMER 1943–CAMP JOSEPH T. ROBINSON, LITTLE ROCK, ARKANSAS

Masao had succumbed to the notion that he might begin and end his military career at the Camp Robinson dental clinic. The current appointed dentist was a guy named Major Duncan. He originated from the San Francisco area and seemed to have an unusual empathy for Japanese people. He talked with fondness about the Japantown in the Bay Area and had developed a liking for Japanese food. As such, he sympathized with Masao's rice cravings, as well as Masao's desire to move up in the ranks and find a place in action.

"What is Kibei?" Dr. Duncan asked Masao while working on a cavity-ridden mouth of yet another private who didn't brush his teeth.

"It's a term used to describe people like me. American-born, but educated in Japan."

"Ehhh?" The private with a mouthful of instruments jerked when he heard the word Japan.

"Relax, private," Dr. Duncan insisted, and pushed him back down in the dental chair. His patient tried to relax but kept an eye on Masao as though the enemy himself were in the room and loaded with grenades. Masao felt it and wished he had cloaked his answer with coded words that Dr. Duncan would have understood.

"Why?" Masao handed a different tool to the doctor, noticing the heavy, gross plaque that needed to be chipped off. "And we might need a chain saw to get this mortar off."

Duncan chuckled at Masao's humor. "I saw a posting at HQ. Some language school in Minnesota looking for Kibei. Have you seen that?"

"Never. And I check that board all the time." Masao was floored.

"Thanks." Dr. Duncan took another tool that Masao anticipated he might need. "Well, you might want to check it out. It looks like it's been there a while."

Immediately after work, Masao was at the bulletin board filled with announcements and opportunities. He hadn't been there in weeks; he had tired of all the rejection notices and needed a break from it. He scanned the board for the notice Dr. Duncan talked about, but he couldn't find it. He was about ready to give up when he spotted it on a small piece of paper that had yellowed over time. *How did I miss that?* But this posting was intended to be inconspicuous, almost hidden, so it didn't attract the wrong kind of attention.

The next day, on a one-day pass, Masao sat at Meg's counter eating a steak. He pulled the notice from his pocket and read it again. He wasn't sure what the position was or what the language school was all about, but he knew he had to pursue it. He wanted to be with others like himself; he needed it. When he got back to base, he submitted his application for the fourth class of the Military Intelligence Service Language School at Camp Savage, Minnesota.

The Eighty-First Infantry Division ten-man Interrogation/
Interpretation Team
FRONT ROW: Masao Abe, 321st; Shiuso Chojin, HQ; Shiro Sakaki, 323rd
BACK ROW: Saburo Nakamura, 322nd; Kei Kitahara, 323rd; Robert Sakai,
HQ; Tomio Ichikawa, 322nd; James Kai, HQ and team leader; Hiroki
Takahashi, HQ. Not pictured: Frank Kabota, 321st

CHAPTER SEVEN

FINDING HIS WAY

"Mas?" I called out as I went in his apartment. He was sitting in his recliner watching the Japanese channel. He was in sweats, a sure sign that he wasn't feeling well, either physically or emotionally.

"Hey, Sandie." He turned down the TV a little bit.

"Are you feeling okay?"

"Oh. So-so."

He didn't look okay. I noticed some newspapers had been knocked off his dining room table. I was almost afraid to ask. "What happened here?" I said in a light-hearted tone as I picked up the mess. He looked over and shook his head.

"I took a little tumble this morning," he said casually. This was a man who did not want any sympathy and trusted that I wouldn't go that direction.

"Are you okay?" I asked as objectively as I could.

"Oh, yeah. Just feel like an old fool. Can't even trust myself to get around a small apartment. Sad case."

I looked behind the table in the corner and there it was—his cane. It had been out of reach for him. In one morning, it had become a tool he could no longer trust. Then I noticed Doris's walker was closer to his chair than usual. I carefully picked up the cane and placed it by the table, within his reach. *It's got to be so hard,* I thought, *getting to the point that falling down is the scariest thing you can think of.* He must have dragged himself up; it probably took several minutes and utterly exhausted him. I sat down and watched TV with him. There were no subtitles on the Japanese station, but I didn't care. I was figuring out how to approach this situation with him.

"You want to go casino?" I asked.

"Nah. No need." Translation: I'm scared I will fall and it will be embarrassing more than anything.

"How about dinner somewhere?"

"Nah. It's okay." Again, he wasn't going to risk going out in public feeling so vulnerable.

"I'll go get something, then."

"Nah. I have food here." He motioned to the refrigerator. I got up and strolled around his apartment while I figured things out. I stopped at his wall of pictures and looked at the one of his war buddies, all dressed in their finest, cleaned up and shaven, posing as a team for the photographer. I noticed Naki and how young they were. Their whole lives in front of them, if they could survive the war.

"Is this Naki?" I asked him, pointing to Naki in the photo. My strategy worked, he perked up and took interest.

"Yep, Naki. Which one am I?" He was testing me. I could pick Mas out in any picture.

"That's easy, this one," and I pointed to a guy I knew wasn't him.

"No. I'm—I'm the one sitting." He was getting up to show me, wheeling over with the walker. "This one," he pointed himself out.

"I know. I'm teasing you." He chuckled as we both admired the young men in the photo. I looked at the photo again. "Who are the other guys?"

"We were a ten-man team, attached to the Eighty-First. That was a long time ago, boy."

"There are only nine guys in this picture," I pointed out.

"Yep. A guy named Frank, he wasn't there. He didn't like to socialize with the rest of us," he said as he rolled himself back to his recliner and sat down with a sigh. He suddenly looked bored and restless.

"I'd love to hear about this team."

He glanced at me and pondered my request. "How about we go casino? I tell you on the way." Two minutes ago, the casino had been out of the question.

"Of course, but one condition." I looked at him the way a mother would look at her child.

"What's that?" He was curious.

"We take the walker," I said, patting Doris's walker.

"Nah. It's too big for the car," he argued.

"It is *not* too big for the car. But nice try."

He looked dejected, not really wanting to admit that it had come to this—that he needed the walker, that the cane was no longer strong enough to support his progressively weak legs.

"Come on, let's not take any chances. If you take a spill on my watch, I'll never hear the end of it from Alan." That made him chuckle. He nodded and took hold of the walker, leaving his cane behind.

"We were ten guys who were on the same IIT team," he started out before we even got out of the garage. IIT meant, I knew from before, Interpretation/Interrogation Team.

"Was this at Camp Savage?"

"That's right. Camp Savage."

JULY 1943-CAMP SAVAGE, MINNESOTA

Masao stepped off the train at Camp Savage in July 1943. The first thing he noticed was that the camp was small and filled with Nisei. It felt good to be around others like himself. He had been so isolated at Camp Robinson.

The fourth MIS Language School class began almost immediately. Masao's instructor was Captain John A. Burden, fresh from the battlefield. Masao sat at a desk along with the other thirty Nisei assigned to this particular classroom. Captain Burden rolled out a map. He stood with a pointer in hand.

"Good morning," he greeted the Nisei after the formal salutes. "I'll be your instructor at the outset. I was a part of the first graduating class from the Presidio. I've been stationed in various places in the South Pacific, trying like heck to figure out the best way to utilize the brave men of the MIS."

He looked around at the Nisei, who were paying full attention to his every word.

"We learned a lot from Guadalcanal," Burden continued. "Point one. How many of you think that you'll be involved in the torture of prisoners?"

The Nisei soldiers looked confused. A few raised their hands.

"Compassionate and humane treatment is the better approach. Japanese prisoners open up and reveal information and intelligence when they are treated with humanity. At first, we had only Caucasian officers fielding intelligence on the line, but we've also learned that Japanese prisoners feel more at ease when they see faces like their own."

Masao nodded slightly and took some notes on this point. He was relieved that he wouldn't have to torture anyone.

"Point two," Burden continued. "Before Guadalcanal, the military had Nisei soldiers driving trucks around for Christ's sake, and manning interpretation far at the rear. Not anymore, though. Some of you will be on the front." He let his words resonate with that last statement.

Masao felt a surge of energy shoot through him. At last he would be able to utilize his training from both the Japanese and the US military. It would all be useful in the line of active duty.

"Other soldiers don't know about the MIS operation, nor will they," Captain Burden continued matter-of-factly. This caught Masao's attention. He wondered how the operation all fit together if the American soldiers were unaware. *This could get ugly.* "A lot of them will think you are all Chinese who speak Japanese." This drew soft laughter.

"One general—this is a true story now. One general asked a Nisei if he was Chinese. The Nisei told him, 'No, sir.' The general asked if he was Filipino. The Nisei said, 'No, sir.' The general asked if he was one of the code talkers. The Nisei said, 'No, sir.' The general said, 'Well you can't be—.' And the Nisei said, 'Yes, sir.' And the general had the Nisei taken off the line, back to the rear, and eventually out of the sensitive zone."

The reality of Captain Burden's story settled on the soldiers. A couple of them glanced at each other. Masao didn't know anyone just yet, so he just looked down and pretended to scribble more notes. *What the hell am I getting myself into*, he thought as he adjusted his glasses.

"It's only been recently that our higher-ranking officers saw the benefit of taking prisoners. We've uncovered a lot of intelligence at the hands of the MIS—guys like you who are out there, risking their lives, as we speak. We need you to do the same. And we know you will."

Masao felt better. This Captain Burden seemed like a good fellow, the kind of guy you could trust. *I'll probably die out there trying to get intelligence, likely at the hands of some radical like Kunio, but at least a few people will appreciate why.*

From the time of its inception to when Masao joined the Military Intelligence Service, the operation had experienced many challenges, mostly at the hands of its own military. The first three classes of Military Intelligence Service Language School soldiers were scattered throughout the Pacific Rim in one of three capacities. First, they would be assigned to groups that served at one of the large intelligence centers located around the Pacific Rim. This was by far the most common route for MIS graduates. The three main intelligence centers were in Hawai'i, Australia, and New Delhi. These intelligence centers were manned by the Nisei linguists who listened to Japanese radio chatter and news channels for intelligence-related information and also scoured Japanese documents pertaining to military strategies and strongholds.

The second route for MIS graduates was to be recycled back into the language school. Soldiers were appointed to a position in the operation at Camp Savage, either as an instructor, an administrator, or office personnel. As the MIS operation grew, more graduates were needed to instruct or to facilitate instruction in some way.

The third course was for graduates to be part of a small team and attach to combat units, working either on the front lines embedded in units, or for division headquarters behind the lines to conduct detailed interrogation that could not occur on the front line. This facet of the MIS operation took many months before it became effective.

The first graduates of the Presidio MIS Language School had been split up. About half went to Camp Savage to continue the efforts of the school. The other half were dispersed throughout the Pacific Rim. Five were sent to Alaska, eight to Australia, three to Fiji, and six to New Caledonia.

Things hadn't gone as intended for this first round of graduates; the notion of this type of intelligence work was dramatically underappreciated. The MIS Nisei were often given tasks that were menial and well beneath their skill level. To make matters more complicated, the MIS operation was still top secret. On the battlefield, hatred toward Japanese continued to rise.

One Nisei was sent to the South Pacific attached to an infantry battalion. This Nisei spoke and read perfect Japanese, having spent years in Japan. There was little intelligence work to do at his location on Bora Bora, however. There were no captured prisoners to interrogate or any documents to translate. He was eventually assigned to drive a truck.

The Nisei soldiers who had been deployed to New Caledonia arrived at the dock and were immediately told to cover themselves, cloaked in secrecy, while en route to the base. Their presence in New Caledonia, a colony of France and a hub of US military activity, had to remain top secret. At first, these Nisei were assigned guard duty around division headquarters and sometimes had innocuous documents to translate. In the coming months, though, they would interrogate downed Japanese pilots. In one case, the Japanese pilots were so badly burned that all they could utter was "Kill me." When the Nisei reported the limited interrogation, they were admonished by commanding admirals.

"Goddamn you. What in the hell did you go to school for anyway? You damn bastards," one admiral was reported to have said in a public berating of the Nisei soldiers.

Three other MIS graduates had been attached to the Thirty-Seventh Division that was shipping out for Fiji. The MIS Nisei were sent to join the Thirty-Seventh Division in Pennsylvania. They arrived only to find that the division had already left for the West Coast, the very place they had just traveled from. Adding insult to injury, once the Nisei arrived on base, they were arrested for being absent without leave. They eventually convinced the military police of their identities and were allowed to return to San Francisco just in time to catch up with the Thirty-Seventh before they shipped out to Fiji.

There were two Caucasian graduates of the Military Intelligence Service Language School from that first class on the Presidio:

Captain John A. Burden and Captain David W. Swift. Both had lived in Japan and spoke excellent Japanese. The first round of trained MIS linguists, including Captain Burden, was allowed to support the marines on Guadalcanal and elsewhere only from a distance. They were not included in battle strategies. They were never sent to the front lines. The founders of the MIS and the captains on the field became increasingly frustrated that the skilled and trained MIS soldiers, who were waiting for orders and eager to serve, were simply being overlooked. The MIS operation was not working as it had been intended.

The second class of MIS linguists graduated from Camp Savage, and they were also sent to various places along the Pacific Rim. It was much the same for them. Eventually, it became evident that communication between the front lines and the MIS soldiers who possessed a wealth of interpretation expertise had been faulty. Commanders on the field didn't know who to contact or how to arrange for linguists. Finally, Captain Burden was summoned to attach to a marine division on Guadalcanal.

When the marines raided Guadalcanal, they had interpreters in the way of Japanese-speaking officers who were Caucasian. But the prisoners they had in custody spoke too fast for these Caucasian officers to garner any information. Not only that, Japanese prisoners were few and far between; most of them never had a chance of making it back to headquarters alive. There was simply too much American anger toward the enemy. The story went that Imperial soldiers had ambushed and then executed wounded and helpless marines in horrific ways. This story spread like wildfire, and as a result it became common for Japanese prisoners to somehow "die" on the way to headquarters.

Upon arrival on Guadalcanal, Burden discovered that the culture had been to take no prisoners. "The only good Jap is a dead Jap" was a phrase he heard often. Burden heard one commander issuing orders to "kill the sons of bitches." Documents found in enemy camps were often overlooked or just destroyed; soldiers were more interested in gathering souvenirs than they were in securing documents. There seemed to be little understanding on the front lines that Japanese prisoners might contain valuable intelligence that could assist the Allied Forces with strategies to secure islands currently held by the Japanese.

Captain Burden continually voiced his concerns. Eventually, Burden convinced the commanders to offer incentives to marines to bring prisoners back alive. The tactic worked. The linguists, all Caucasian, worked around the clock as prisoners and documents were escorted back to division headquarters. To the surprise of the commanders and marines, Japanese prisoners were cooperative, sometimes even asking fellow prisoners the answer to questions they themselves did not know. The intelligence the Japanese prisoners revealed was astounding, including positions of troops, casualties, locations of command posts, the morale of soldiers, and other bits of intelligence that proved extremely useful.

Burden's experience on Guadalcanal convinced him of two things: the MIS operation was crucial to effective military strategy in the Pacific, and positioning interpreters far to the rear was not effective. He wanted the Nisei linguists on the battlefield, where they could produce the quickest results. He wanted the Nisei on the front lines.

Meanwhile the Nisei linguists stationed on various island posts were still performing menial tasks. Captain Burden arranged for two Nisei to join the offensive on Guadalcanal. When the Nisei first arrived, they were mistaken for Chinese-Americans. But after they produced noteworthy intelligence, they were accepted as part of the war effort by the small circle of military personnel who were involved with the interrogation process. The Nisei, and the presence of them on Guadalcanal, was never made known to the ranks.

It was the same situation in other campaigns in the South Pacific. Commanders were reluctant, at best, to bring the likes of Nisei linguists to the front and preferred to keep them at a distance. Eventually, the Nisei were brought forward, a few at a time, and embedded closer to the action where the immediate interpretation led to swift results on the battlefield.

In January 1943 President Roosevelt made the official announcement that all citizens would be considered for military recruitment. Considering that Nisei soldiers were already on the ground around the South Pacific, and that the Hundredth Infantry Battalion had been activated and was in its seventh month of training, this was just a formality.

There had been several homogeneous battalions formed with other ethnicities: Filipino, African American, Chinese, Native American, and others. In April of 1943, the 442nd Regimental Combat Team was formed at Camp Shelby, Mississippi, and was designated as an all-Nisei unit.

While the one hand of the government was clearing all Japanese out of the West Coast, the other hand of the government was quietly using Nisei men in various branches of the military and shipping them out to strategic, if not highly sensitive, locations. President Roosevelt was a genius in this sense. Seemingly benevolent to the needs of his voters, he cleansed the West Coast of any Japanese while, at the very same time, shrewdly capitalizing on the loyalty and honor of the many Nisei and Sansei who wanted to prove their worth. While the Nisei linguists were not yet fully embedded on the front lines, the operation was gaining steam and heading in that direction.

It was because of the character and perseverance of the men in that first MIS Language School class from the Presidio that other operations were allowed to develop, including subsequent MIS classes, as well as the Hundredth Battalion and the 442nd.

The graduates of the second and third MIS Language School classes would follow in the footsteps of their alumni and scatter throughout the Pacific Rim, while the Hundredth Battalion would eventually attach to the 442nd and head to Italy, where they would prove themselves more than valiant.

Through instruction, Masao and other MIS soldiers learned about the challenges the operation had endured. They were cautioned about the dangers that awaited them if they were to be embedded on the front lines. Dangers that would be directed at them from the enemy, and the possibility that they would be under threat from their own side of enemy lines as well.

At Camp Savage, there was little time to develop close ties with anyone. The daily routine of the MIS Language School was the study of Japanese *kanji*—all day long. Wednesdays were reserved for military training and tactics. Oftentimes soldiers would march for five to ten miles as a mere warm up. Exams were given every Saturday. These exams would place students in a level system that had been established by the school. Soldiers would banter about what class they had been assigned to—smart or stupid.

Saturday nights and Sundays were the only blocks of free time, and poker games would inevitably break out in various barracks. Masao was always around for poker games and soon had buddies that had formed a coalition, a type of brotherhood Masao had longed for.

As Masao endured the routine, week after week, he started noticing soldiers who were Japanese American, but seemed to be standoffish. It became almost unnerving the way these guys would just hover and watch the others, especially during poker nights.

"Hey, George," Masao said in a low voice one evening just before the poker club gathered. His buddy, George Inagaki, had become a trusted friend. George leaned in to hear Masao. "Those guys, like David over there. What's he doing? He never joins us, he just watches. I've seen others too," Masao whispered, gesturing toward David who was loitering nearby.

"Maybe he's CIC. Counter Intelligence. Those guys are here to keep an eye on us, I've heard," George explained.

Masao's eyes widened; he shook his head. "Jesus. We can't win."

The MIS operation was gaining more and more steam and making direct contributions to the progression of American and Allied troops in the south, southwest, and now the central Pacific regions. Masao and his friends understood that they might end up face to face with the Japanese enemy. They also understood that they would be seen as the enemy, not just by Imperial Japanese soldiers, but by Allied soldiers. Some of the missions the MIS soldiers would embark upon would be the most dangerous in all of World War II, simply because of their ethnicity and where they would inevitably serve.

In the spring of 1944, the Nisei were in class as usual when in marched a new face. Everyone stood at attention. Once at ease, the new instructor gave surprising information.

"Soldiers, you're near completion of the course. The next stage of your training will be infantry. At Camp Blanding."

While the instructor rambled on, Masao wrote a note to George. "Where the hell is Camp Blanding?" George shrugged. It turned out to be located about fifty miles southwest of Jacksonville, Florida, where it had housed two complete infantry divisions.

Trains were waiting for the soldiers as they packed up. Once again, the cars had the shades drawn and soldiers on board were warned about the dangers of alerting the public at large to their presence.

At Camp Blanding the MIS soldiers were trained in the necessary combat and infantry skills, but they were trained in separate locations from the other GIs. Masao wasn't sure if their presence on base was ever even noticed, much less acknowledged. Whatever the case, the infantry training that he and other MIS soldiers had endured meant one thing: they were heading to the battlefield.

MAY 19, 1944—CAMP SAVAGE, MINNESOTA

Back at Camp Savage, soldiers graduated from the MIS program in the spring of 1944. The Nisei had gone through a nine-month rigorous training, had succeeded in passing courses, combat training, and had passed a loyalty screening. Masao had also been promoted to staff sergeant; he now wore a new uniform that carried the stripes of his new rank.

"You have two weeks leave. Report back here at 0800 on June 2. Your orders will be waiting for you at that time," the commanding officer stated at the end of the ceremony.

Back in the barracks, Masao hastily packed a duffel bag.

"Where are you off to?" George asked him.

Masao desperately wanted to see his Uncle Tatsuo, who had now been moved to a Department of Justice prison in Santa Fe, New Mexico. He wasn't sure what obstacles he might encounter traveling alone and hoped his US Army uniform would deter any problems.

"I've got to get to my uncle out west."

Without saying a word, George dug in his foot locker for some hidden cash. He handed a wad of it to Masao. It was over a hundred dollars.

"Here. Take it, Masao," George insisted.

Masao was astonished but waved him off. "Thanks, George, but no. I have no way of paying you back."

George continued to hold the money out for Masao and looked into his eyes. He saw that Masao was a very proud man, someone who had the utmost integrity. It would be hard for him to accept any help at all. "Masao, consider this a gift. Besides, this is really just money I've won off you over the last six months. Look at it that way."

Masao smiled, accepted the money in one hand, and shook his good friend George's hand with the other.

"Thank you." Masao's voice was sincere and honest. The train whistled in the distance.

"You gotta go." George picked up Masao's duffel bag and handed it to him. Masao sprinted for the door, then stopped and turned.

"Thank you, George."

MAY 1944—SANTA FE, NEW MEXICO

He took the train to Santa Fe, then hitchhiked to the prison that was just outside the city. The truck he had ridden in from the train station pulled up across the street from it. Masao got out.

"Gracias," Masao said to the Mexican driver. Masao stood there in awe as he stared at the prison surrounded by high cement walls. Guards in towers were stationed at all four corners, thirty-caliber machine guns pointed down and in. He was horrified. This was a place that looked like it housed the most ruthless murderers and rapists. Inside, though, were nothing more than farmers, business-men, and fisherman who had been deemed dangerous enemies.

Two teenagers from across the street noticed Masao and their words snapped him out of his stunned gaze.

"Traitor!" shouted one of the teenagers. Before Masao could com-prehend this little punk's words, the other one sounded off.

"*You* should be in there *too*."

"Go back to Japan, you ugly *Jap*," the first one yelled before they ran off feeling vindicated and having a whopper of a story to tell their family and friends—how they faced the enemy himself and let him have it.

Masao shook this off and approached the guard station. The guard looked up. At first he was shocked to see a Japanese man in front of him, but then he noticed the uniform, the stripes.

"Sir. Can I help you?"

"I'm here to visit my uncle."

"Your uncle, sir?"

"Yes. Tatsuo Abe. I believe he is being held here."

The guard looked through papers while Masao fixated on the machine guns in the towers.

"Sign here," the guard said. His voice had changed. A minute before, he was talking to a soldier of the US military. Now he was talking to the relative of an inmate. Masao felt it.

"There's a visiting shed over there. Go outside and wait," the guard directed.

"Thank you." Masao stepped away and waited. Another guard came over and opened the shed. But for two chairs, this makeshift visiting room was empty. He was never allowed inside the prison itself. Thirty minutes later, Tatsuo was escorted in. He was a shell of the man he had once been, weak and pale. Masao immediately stood up and went to his uncle, who smiled when he saw Masao.

"Uncle."

"Masao. Boy, you look swell in that uniform."

They shook hands warmly. Tatsuo motioned that they should sit. The escorting guard was suspicious; he looked at Masao in his uniform with disdain. Masao focused on Tatsuo.

"You don't look so good, uncle. They aren't feeding you in here?"

"They feed us. But the food is horrible. No rice," Tatsuo said as he looked at the guard to make his point.

"I can't believe you are a prisoner." Masao was scanning Tatsuo up and down, noticing the bones sticking out on every limb.

"I guess I'm the enemy," he chuckled. "So, you finally going to Europe?"

"No. South Pacific. To fight Japan."

"Japan! You'll die for sure. Better for you to go fight the Germans." The guard took delight in Tatsuo's assessment of Masao's fate. This didn't go unnoticed by Masao.

"Japan, Germany. It's no difference."

"Japan is winning the war, Masao. You have less chance of survival against Japan."

"Where do you hear that?"

"Well, in here. Everybody says so." Tatsuo insisted.

"In here? Uncle, these Issei guys just want Japan to win. Japan's not winning." Masao laughed at his uncle's lack of information. "Japan is getting pushed back into itself."

"Japan wins. United States wins. I guess it doesn't matter. Me and my family, we've already lost. The store—gone. All the money I sent to Japan—gone." Tatsuo resigned himself to the worst possible scenario.

"What happened to the store?"

"I put it in my manager's name. Foolish, I think. No?"

"Probably so."

The guard took note of this. He had not heard this angle of the Japanese internment/imprisonment before.

"I'm sorry about all of this." Masao looked at Tatsuo, his beloved uncle and the rock of a man he had depended on.

"Not your fault." Tatsuo glanced at the guard before he continued. "So—what if you face one of your cousins or schoolmates in battle? You gonna shoot?"

"*Heck yeah*, I'm gonna shoot. If someone's shooting at me, I'm going to shoot back."

"I guess you have to, no?" Tatsuo nodded. He understood. It was kill or be killed. There was a moment of anguish before Tatsuo spoke about what truly ailed his heart. "They tell me the only way I can ever see Yukie and my daughters is to return to Japan. I haven't even met my new daughter." He was becoming emotional. Masao didn't want the guard to have the satisfaction of seeing a strong man like Tatsuo broken.

"What name did you give your new daughter?"

"Anna. Her name is Anna."

"Pretty name. That's a pretty name, uncle," Masao reassured Tatsuo. "Uncle. Stay here, in America. I have a feeling it will get better."

"They don't want us here, Masao. I just can't bear to think of my little girls living like this." Tatsuo was near his breaking point, but he refused to give in to the looming tears.

Masao needed to say something to pull him back from the brink. "Uncle, I will check on them. Poston, no?"

"Poston, yes. Thank you, Masao."

"One more thing," Masao's voice was firm but soft. "I have taken out life insurance on myself. Ten thousand dollars. You're the beneficiary. It's in my will and it's final." Tatsuo was flabbergasted and speechless. "If I don't make it back, you have a way to start over again in San Bernardino."

"I don't know what to say. You honor your family in every possible way."

They visited for the full hour they were allowed before Masao began his journey west, to Poston, Arizona. On the train, he was hoping that Yukie had it better than Tatsuo. He couldn't shake how his uncle had changed. He couldn't let go of the injustice of it all. The glares from white folks were becoming more and more noticeable and irritating. They had no idea the turmoil that he and other Japanese Americans had churning inside of them at all hours of the day. It seemed there was little empathy for anyone Japanese, American or not.

MAY 1944—POSTON, ARIZONA

As Masao walked toward the Poston Internment Camp, his heart ached. He saw rows and rows of barracks out in the desert; it was in the middle of nowhere. Barbed wire surrounded the facility and guards were posted at strategic points. He approached the main entrance that was flanked with guard stations. These guards were different from the ones at the Santa Fe prison; these had come to know and even like the thousands of Japanese Americans who lived there. And they had grown used to seeing military Nisei come for visits.

"Good morning, sir. Are you here to visit a relative?" The guard asked in a cheery voice. It was music to Masao's ears. At least they were pleasant here.

"I am. Yukie Abe, my aunt. I believe she is here."

Within minutes Masao was escorted to Yukie's "home," her cordoned-off section of a barrack.

"Ahhh. Masao!" She put her toddler down and went to Masao to hug him. "You wear that uniform well," she admired her nephew as she picked up little Anna. "This is your cousin, Masao." Little Anna pointed a finger at Masao, and he gently took it and wiggled it between two of his fingers.

"How are you doing here, Yukie?" Masao looked around, noticing the newspapers that were stuffed in the cracks on the floor and in the walls. Her little area was the size of a bedroom.

"We make do. Did you see Tatsuo?" She asked with a great sense of hope in her voice. "They are pressuring him to go back Japan. They say it only way he can see us again. Is this true?"

Masao sat his aunt down on the bed as a means of calming her. He picked up a toy and handed it to Kathleen, who was still clinging to Yukie's dress.

"I have no way of knowing, Yukie. But they can't keep you here forever. Encourage him to stay in the States. I think it's best. Don't you?"

Yukie nodded and held little Anna close. The sound and voices of other families in their rooms was ever present. Nobody was overly loud, but the low murmur never went away.

Yukie pressed her lips together, biting her inner mouth to stop the tears from coming. "It's not good place to raise children. And it's not good they don't know father."

Masao nodded. He agreed with everything she said. It was hard for him to have two worlds on this clear collision course inside his heart and mind. Nothing made sense and everything made sense.

"They have you. And you are strong. You'll be back with Tatsuo in San Bernardino before you know it."

Yukie tried to be strong. But instead she leaned into Masao and wept.

SUMMER 1944—CAMP SAVAGE TO SEATTLE

"Christ almighty, why'd they want us back here so soon? I could have spent more time with my aunt or gone to San Bernardino to check on my uncle's affairs," Masao said one night while resting in his bunk, frustrated with the slow pace of the military and the issue of orders.

"I could have spent more time with my wife," George added with a sigh.

"I need a girl," Masao said, sharing his private thoughts. "A nice Japanese girl who is smart, independent, and knows how to make great sashimi." His thoughts drifted back to Japan, to Miyoko. "I had a girl in Japan, before I came back to the United States. I wonder what's become of her."

"Ah. If she's in Japan, she's aged twenty years in ten, Abe. Resources are scarce. Hope must be dim. Only military leaders are living well," George speculated.

"By now she's met someone else, no? Maybe she ended up with my classmate, Kunio, the radical. Kunio. Hmm." Thoughts drifted through his mind and out his mouth. He knew they were safe with George. "He must be an officer by now."

"Maybe you'll meet him on the battlefield. What's he made of?"

Masao thought about this as a breeze came through the open window and wafted across his face. "He's made of anger. The most dangerous kind of soldier."

"Nah. The most dangerous kind of soldier is one who has been trained well and acts with honor."

Masao rolled over onto his side, propping his head on his hand so he could look at George in the next bed over. George rested with his eyes closed, probably thinking about his wife.

"It won't matter anyway," Masao lit up a cigarette. "Our own guys will be aiming for us first."

It would be days before they received orders; Masao would get his first. "They want me on the train tonight. 2100." Masao read from the paper he had been issued.

"Does it say where?"

Masao shook his head. "Nope."

They waited a while longer to see if George would receive similar orders, but nothing came. At 2030 they shook hands. Masao picked up his duffel bag and looked at George.

"I'll never forget you, George. Thanks again, for everything."

"You bet. And good luck out there."

Masao nodded. "Same to you."

With that, Masao left the barracks. George and Masao would never see each other again, and Masao never forgot George and his kindness.

Masao was on his assigned train car early, along with a dozen other Nisei who were all in the same mental state as Masao—excited and anxious at the same time. Masao had seen all of these guys on base but didn't know any of them. A younger soldier with a fresh face boarded and Masao recognized him as Saburo Nakamura.

"Abe, right?"

Masao nodded and they shook hands. Saburo sat beside him after he hurled his duffel bag on the shelf above.

"Saburo?" Masao was trying to remember his name.

"I go by Naki. I don't know how I got that name, but it sure has stuck with me." Naki smiled as he talked. Masao noticed his sincere presence and almost sweet face. *He's going to be a weapon on the battlefield*, Masao thought. *No enemy in the world could feel threatened by this guy. They'll tell this interrogator anything he wants to hear.*

"Long trip ahead of us, don't you think?" Naki asked as he looked around to take inventory of the other passengers.

"Probably so," Masao agreed as he watched more soldiers get on.

Just then, a Caucasian soldier boarded with a clipboard. "At ease, soldiers. Wave goodbye to the good life you're leaving behind, then close your shades for the duration. This will be a long journey. There will be stops along the way—don't worry. The USO has been generous with all our troops, including our guys from Savage. You have eight minutes if you need to use the facilities before departing. One last thing, the shades are drawn for a reason. Leave them down the entire journey. Nobody sees in, nobody sees out. Godspeed."

And then he saluted and jumped off the train to head to the next car. Masao and Naki looked at each other.

"We can't even look at the scenery," Masao commented. Naki shrugged.

The train chugged through the flat land of Minnesota and into North Dakota. Just before sunrise, it stopped. A Caucasian soldier boarded their car.

"Soldiers, listen up. You will debark here for forty-five minutes. Use the facilities. The wonderful USO ladies have coffee and snacks for you. Wash up if you want. It's 0545. We depart at 0630."

Off the train Masao looked around. The countryside was flat and deserted. The USO had a tent set up and tables were lined up with various food items and hot coffee. He helped himself to coffee and a breakfast roll, then glanced at the lady behind the table.

"Do we pay somewhere?"

"No, soldier. We're here to support our troops!" she reported with delight.

"Well, thank you." Masao tipped his hat to her.

"You're welcome. Take some for the road if you want." That sounded like a good idea to Masao, and he helped himself to another roll.

"Where are we, anyway?"

"You're in Bismarck, North Dakota!" Her enthusiasm was annoying for a soldier on little sleep who knew not his destiny.

"North Dakota." Masao looked around. *This must be a sad place to live*, he pondered to himself. *Dry and desolate.*

"The town is over that-a-way." The lady pointed off in the distance as though she could sense what Masao was thinking. "We're the capital of North Dakota!" She had far too much energy for him.

"Thank you for supporting us." He nodded, and then he headed over to where other soldiers were smoking. The soldiers in the group were having a debate about where they were going and when they would arrive.

"We've got to be in Wyoming or Utah, somewhere like that," one of the soldiers was saying.

"Wyoming and Utah are states that have trees and mountains. Do you see any trees around here?"

Another soldier chimed in. "I think we're in Nebraska."

Masao, forever the gambler, decided to capitalize on this and ratchet it up a notch.

"Let's get a little pool going," he proposed to the group at large.

"Okay, Abe. I say we're headed for Los Angeles." A guy that went by Jack, even though his name was Masaru, threw out the first bet.

Masao nodded and looked around. "Okay, Jack's in. Anyone else?"

"I'm in. I say the Bay Area, maybe Oakland," another soldier added.

"Bay Area."

"I say Portland," said another soldier, switching it up.

"I'm going with Jack on this one. Los Angeles." The last soldier besides Masao and Naki made his bet.

Naki studied Masao. He knew Masao was up to something. "What's your bet, Abe?" Naki asked shrewdly. Masao knew that Naki knew he had the inside scoop. It was a brilliant move on Naki's part.

"Ah. You should put your bet in first. You're smarter. You were in the smart class at Savage. I was in the stupid class." Masao wasn't going to take the bait, and it was true. Masao hadn't been in the top tier for whatever reason; it had been a mystery to him. But the match was on. No matter what other soldiers would bet, this was really between Masao and Naki.

"All the more reason to allow you the first wager," Naki came back in a quiet voice that carried great weight. "After all, we all know that Abe should have been in the top class. You were robbed of that, so I wouldn't dream of robbing you of the first wager."

Boy, he's good, Masao thought. Naki waited patiently to see what Masao's next move would be.

"I think we're still in the north. It's dry like Nebraska, but not humid," he bullshitted. He had no idea about humidity in Nebraska.

"I'm going to say we're headed more north. Seattle. Tomorrow night at the earliest."

The other soldiers laughed at this and gave him a hard time about his lousy bet.

"Two more days on this train? I don't think so, Masao," Jack lobbied. "We'll be in some port by tomorrow morning."

"Seattle isn't even on the radar for the army," another soldier claimed.

But Naki knew Masao was on to something. And after the heckling stopped, he made his wager. "I'll go with Abe's theory. Seattle. As for the time, I think it will also be tomorrow night. Abe, let's pick times. I say between 2200 and midnight."

Holy shit. This Naki has just beat me at my own game, thought Masao. His cigarette nearly fell out of his mouth. Naki saw this and the slightest smile appeared on his face. Then Masao grinned. He liked this Naki.

"I'll say this," Masao started out, "I hope to have you at my side on the line." Naki smiled at the compliment—probably the greatest compliment you could ever give a fellow soldier. "Okay, Naki. I say tomorrow night between 2000 and 2200."

"Five minutes," a soldier called out from the train. The gamblers agreed on five dollars each for the pool as they headed for the train.

Back in their seats, Masao eyed Naki. "Goddamn, Naki. Those other guys can't gamble for shit. But I could lose it all if I don't keep my eye on you."

Naki just smiled and closed his eyes for a nap.

The next morning Masao woke up before anyone else. From the feel of the train, they were either on a decline or on flat terrain. He dared to open the window shade enough to see out. The sun was about to come up and provided just enough light for him to see that they were crossing land that looked like wheat fields. *We could be anywhere.*

After another hour the train slowed and stopped. A soldier soon hopped onto their car and made the usual instructional announcement, with one exception.

"You'll have over three hours at this stop, soldiers. Do not leave the USO-designated area. This facility has showers. However, there are only two shower stalls for over forty men. Be swift in there. The USO has generously provided towels and toiletries. It's 0840. Be back on board at 1200."

It was a long three hours. This stop, like all the other stops, was far away from any city, town, or civilization. Only the kind USO workers were privy to the Nisei soldiers en route to the coast. On the train, a deck of cards made its way out. Masao was thrilled to join, but he lost half his money to Naki. After a few hours they felt the train start to move and, soon after that, the unmistakable grind of the train crawling up a steep grade. The soldiers looked at each other, trying to figure out what mountain range stood between them and the coast.

"Sierra Nevadas?" Jack posed the first question.

"Could be." Naki threw down an ace that gave him a royal flush. He cleaned up again. And now, Masao figured, Naki was baiting Jack. His concurrence with Jack's prediction about the mountains only beefed up Jack's confidence. As the train pulled itself up the grade, it jolted, making it hard to shuffle the cards. Naki was the new dealer and dealt cards to the remaining players.

"Want to double down, Jack? On the pool?" And there it was. Naki was going in for the kill. *Boy, is he good*, Masao thought. Masao folded his hand immediately and waited to see if the fish would bite on Naki's well-placed bait. They would. Everyone doubled their bet. Everyone was sure they had picked right. Everyone but Masao; he was beginning to doubt himself and wished he had paid more attention to his third-grade teacher in San Bernardino when she talked about mountain ranges.

This one thought took him back there, to San Bernardino. He longed for the days when things weren't complicated, when things made sense. When it wasn't a crime to be Japanese and when he didn't have to hide himself. He started to think about his Uncle Tatsuo, his Aunt Yukie, his parents in Japan, the house in San Bernardino. The wonder turned into worry, and he wished he could just gaze out the window, if only to take his mind off his concerns.

"Abe." Naki nudged him.

"You in or out, Abe?" Jack was like a shark circling prey. Masao was annoyed by this Nisei hiding behind a white name.

"I'm in."

Naki studied Masao. He knew what had just happened. He knew that Masao had gone down the vortex of Japanese American strain and distress.

"Good. We're all in then," Naki said out loud, then nudged Masao ever so lightly. "Thought I lost you there," he said so nobody else could hear.

Hours passed before the train started to descend. This would be it. It wouldn't be long before a winner would be declared and claim the pot of money. Surely, they were close to the port. Then the train slowed and stopped. They all thought they must have reached their final destination, but something was wrong. There were no sounds of a train station, of other trains. They waited. The train huffed and spewed steam as it stood still on the tracks. Masao checked his watch. It was seven p.m.

"Why are they waiting?" Naki asked.

"Waiting until dark," Masao said, clearing up the mystery, "so nobody sees us get off the train." The severity of that thought seemed to bother Naki. It was incomprehensible to realize that the military would go that far to keep soldiers, American citizens, a secret. But he knew that Masao was right. Naki looked down.

"Nothing to be ashamed of, Naki, it's just the way it is." Masao, a few years older than Naki, may not have had the academic smarts of his new buddy, but he had more wisdom. He had overcome more challenges and could frame this unfair military approach in objective terms.

"The air is cool." He nudged Naki with his elbow. "We're in the north. There's an outside chance it's the Bay Area, but more than likely, you and I are right. Seattle."

Naki looked over at Masao and finally smiled. "Now it's just between you and me, old boy."

"That's right," Masao affirmed. "Thought I lost you there . . ."

After a long while, a Caucasian soldier boarded their car and walked down the aisle, checking each shade and making sure it was shut.

"Final approach, gentlemen," he called out.

When the train was underway it moved along more slowly than its regular speed, as though cautious in its approach to wherever it was going. The soldiers on board were quiet, straining to hear anything that would give them a clue as to their whereabouts. It wasn't because of the bet; it had become nerve-wracking trying to figure out where they were going. Finally, the train slowed, then crept along before coming to a halt.

"We're here," Masao assessed.

Naki nodded in agreement, glancing at his watch. "It's ten o'clock sharp. If we're in Seattle, looks like we're splitting the pot." Naki showed him his watch as proof.

All Masao could do was chuckle.

It was a stealth-like operation in the darkness. The Nisei soldiers quietly disembarked the train and loaded a nearby bus. There were Caucasian soldiers lined up like traffic cones to direct the Nisei soldiers where to go. Buses waited for them not more than fifty feet from the train platform. There were no detours, not even for the bathroom. The entire operation was shrouded in secrecy.

As Masao stepped off the train he spotted Smith Tower just a few blocks to the north and knew right away—they were in Seattle. Soldiers weren't permitted to talk at all during the short walk to the bus, but he and Naki exchanged glances and Masao nodded over what was unmistakable: they had won the bet.

On the bus, the windows were covered. Naki and Masao sat together silently. A soldier stepped on the bus with a clipboard and walked down the aisle to check off names.

"Listen up soldiers. You're en route to Fort Lawton. It's approximately a forty-minute ride. From there, you'll be assigned to barracks. Some of you ship out as early as tomorrow morning, so be prepared." He saluted and left. The door closed, the gears ground, and the bus started its trek to Fort Lawton.

Fort Lawton, located on a bluff just north of downtown Seattle, was the closest military facility for housing the Nisei soldiers until they shipped out. The next morning Masao woke up early, well before reveille. He just had a feeling that he would be getting orders to ship out, and he was right. Some of the Nisei would remain at Fort Lawton for several days while others, like Masao, would be plucked the morning after they arrived. He and nine other Nisei, including Naki, were ordered to report to the pick-up location on base, where a bus was waiting.

The bus took them to a pier down the bluff from Fort Lawton, where they were loaded onto a military transport vessel that already held a thousand soldiers. They were quickly ushered below deck before any of the other soldiers noticed their presence.

These ten men would form an Interrogation/Interpretation Team, or IIT, and would be attached to the Eighty-First Infantry Division, known as the Wildcats. The team would be split up. Four men would remain attached to division headquarters, two men would attach to the 321st Regimental Combat Team, two to the 322nd, and two to the 323rd.

All of this was still unknown to Masao and his comrades, who had been escorted to the belly of the vessel, undetected.

★ ★ ★

"There were ten of us. Four were attached to division headquarters. That was James Kai, Bob Sakai, Shiuso Chojin, and one other, geeee, now, why can't I remember his name. He's still living somewhere in California, I think, gee, what's his name now . . ." Masao was thinking hard. I could tell that it bugged him that the names weren't just rolling off his tongue. At the same time, I was so impressed that his memory of events seventy years before was so sharp.

"Ah. Hiro, Hiroki Takahashi, that's it. Four guys, attached to division headquarters. Then, a guy named Frank Kubota and I, we were attached to the 321st. The 322nd had, uh, let's see now, Tomio Ichikawa and Saburo Nakamura, and the 323rd had Shiro Sakaki and Kei Kitahara. James Kai was our team leader. He was a *really* sharp guy." Masao looked at me to make sure I was listening and recording the names of his war buddies. It was important to Masao that their significant contributions during World War II were known and remembered.

"And Bob Sakai," Masao continued, "he was attached to division headquarters. He was a smart guy too, boy. He went to, ah, what's the name now, Harvard. He went to Harvard after the war." Masao always admired those who had gone to college, an opportunity that had escaped him. He was so smart in so many ways but didn't appreciate that about himself.

"Did any of those other guys know about Japan like you did?"

"I think three of us had lived in Japan. Me. A guy name Hiro Takahashi, and Chojin, Shiuso Chojin. Funny story about Chojin." He grinned as he remembered this story. "The Caucasian army guys, they were always trying to give us names they could remember. So they came up with Jonesy for Chojin. Heh! Jonesy." He chuckled.

"Did you call him Jonesy?"

"Nope. Never. His name was Shiuso. We all called him by his last name, Chojin." And he chuckled again. Masao's name would have been easy to whitewash, I thought. Abe, with a short, accented *a* and short *e*, pronounced "Ah-bay," could easily be turned into Abe with a long *a*, pronounced "Aaabe" like in Abe Lincoln.

Names. They were probably the least of the worries of the men on this team. During the voyage from Seattle to their next destination, the ten guys formed a camaraderie unlike any other during World War II. These ten, the only ten Nisei in an infantry division comprised of twenty-five thousand soldiers, would become beacons for each other.

Once they landed in the battle zone, they would also be isolated targets.

JULY 10, 1944—EIGHTY-FIRST "WILDCAT" INFANTRY DIVISION, SAN FRANCISCO

While Masao and his new comrades sailed, their future was being planned in San Francisco. On shore and ready to board a military transport vessel in San Francisco Bay was a young Counter Intelligence Communications (CIC) officer by the name of William Aimone. He was recently married, fresh, and a non-commissioned officer.

Captain Aimone had earned his officer status by coming through the ranks. He was drafted in August 1941 and after Pearl Harbor was offered the opportunity to become one of the first of 150 special agents of the army's CIC. He jumped at the chance. As part of the CIC training, he was instructed, in part, by top former FBI, CIA, and other "super-snoopers" as to the tricks of the spy trade. Special agents, like Aimone, had even undergone covert surveillance of rabbit spies, trailing them around cities such as Chicago and reporting their whereabouts and activities. The mission of the CIC was specific: catch enemy spies or saboteurs who were after the nation's weapons, plans, and/or codes.

Aimone was eventually assigned to central command headquarters in specific states where he would conduct extensive background checks on army personnel who had access to top secret activities. This meant questioning family, friends, employers, schools, and any social connections to be sure that there were no questionable character traits of the army personnel who had access to national security information.

In September 1943, Aimone learned he would be transferred to the South Pacific. He would be attached to an infantry division and would be the commanding officer of the division's CIC detachment that consisted of several special agents. That infantry division would be the Eighty-First.

On board the transport vessel in San Francisco Bay, he was summoned to the private cabin of the commanding general of the Eighty-First "Wildcat" Division. Aimone entered the private cabin office and was directed to wait. Moments later, in walked Major General Paul Mueller, the general in charge of the entire Eighty-First. General Mueller was in his early forties and was a no-bullshit kind of a guy, one who got things handled efficiently and effectively. Captain Aimone stood at attention and almost broke out into a sweat when the Major General himself walked in.

"At ease, captain," Mueller said, wanting to get down to business. "You're the only officer in the Eighty-First with an intelligence classification," Mueller stated firmly, assessing Aimone head to toe. Aimone was glad he had given his uniform a fresh press early that morning. Mueller continued as he methodically paced the small room, "I have an important job for you."

"Yes, sir."

"The War Department has sent us a team of Jap soldiers. I don't know why we got stuck with 'em but I don't trust 'em. Not a one."

"American, sir?"

"Supposedly. The War Department says they're going to be our secret weapon. Top secret, they say. I don't know how the hell we are supposed to run things in the South Pacific when we have to watch these guys. But who am I to question the War Department."

Aimone's eyes were wide. He was trying to digest everything that was coming at him. *He wants me to put these guys under surveillance.*

Mueller continued to sputter out his thoughts, forming his plan almost on the spot. "They're all sergeants, like your CIC men, but they came without a commanding officer, of course. They're attached to the G-2 Intelligence Division, same as your detachment." Mueller paused before delivering the punch line. "I want you to take them under your command. You're their CO, effective immediately."

A hundred questions cluttered Aimone's brain. "What is their assignment, sir?"

"Good question, captain. I'll tell you this much," Mueller said as he walked to a map detailing military strategy—what island would be hit first and by what units. He studied the map as he completed his thought. "We're going into enemy territory. An enemy that those American Japs can communicate with easily. It's your head if those soldiers are spies and give us any trouble. So get on the job and find out what they're here for because I don't have a *goddamn* clue." Mueller glanced over at Aimone, who was now standing near the map. "On the other hand," he said, "if the War Department has their head on straight, which I doubt, but if they do, and these guys happen to be clean, find out what they can do to help us with this war."

Aimone nodded. "Yes, sir."

General Mueller looked him in the eye and deliberately paused before he spoke again. "One more thing."

"Sir?"

"They're going to have the biggest goddamn target on their chest of anyone out there. Spies or not, I figure we need to keep 'em safe." Mueller pointed to the map he stood by. "Our guys are trained to kill. I'd hate to see them take out a useful weapon." Mueller's eyes gave him away; he wanted to believe that these Japs weren't trustworthy. It would have made everything a lot more manageable for him. But there was something inside the general that knew how useful Japanese-speaking soldiers could be on the battlefield.

Mueller nodded, then left as swiftly as he had arrived. Aimone, a sweaty mess beneath his pressed and starched uniform, exhaled deeply and wiped his forehead. After he collected himself, he wandered over to the porthole where he could see the long lines of soldiers, almost all of them Caucasian, loading the ship.

Aimone's ten-man team, on a different vessel, soon learned that they were headed for Hawaiʻi. The seven-day voyage was grueling for the soldiers who didn't fare well on the sea. For Masao, the only grueling part of the voyage was losing every last dime in poker and having to borrow from Naki, who had won loads. The Nisei soldiers interacted with other soldiers, most of whom took them for Chinese. But the trip wasn't without problems. Soldiers of lesser rank would sometimes treat the Nisei as though they were nothing. On one occasion in the galley, the mess sergeant challenged Masao.

"You there. You need to pick up the dishes from the table," the mess sergeant blurted out. It was unheard of for a staff sergeant to pick up after privates or PFCs.

"Excuse me?" Masao couldn't believe his ears, and yet he could. He tried to remain neutral about this, even though inside he started to fume.

"You heard me. You can't leave the table in shambles." He was referring to other soldiers' food splatter and utensils that had been left behind.

"I'll tell you what," Masao chose his words carefully. "When I see other staff sergeants picking up after soldiers, then I will too. But until then, I'll just pick up after myself."

The mess sergeant glared at Masao. But Naki, who had noticed and had been lingering nearby, came close to Masao. The mess sergeant sneered at them both, then disappeared to the back of the galley. Masao and Naki looked at each other.

"I hope this isn't a sign of times to come," Naki commented. They both knew, though, that the times ahead were going to be tough.

With the exception of the few soldiers who felt the need to pick on the Nisei soldiers, the voyage to Hawai'i was smooth sailing. Within miles of the Hawaiian coastline, the warmth of the central Pacific called men to the deck, where they soaked up sun on their leave time. When the transport vessel approached the shores of Hawai'i, excitement on the ship grew. As it came through Mamala Bay heading toward Pearl Harbor, the waters turned from a deep, sparkly azure to a beautiful glittery turquoise. The soldiers couldn't wait to hit those beaches covered with white sands and beach babes.

When the ship entered the channel between Ewa Beach and Hickam Air Force Base, the mood shifted dramatically. The men knew they were about to witness for themselves the massive destruction of the famous December 7 attack that had occurred two and a half years earlier. The captain deliberately took the vessel down battleship row, where the soldiers could see remnants of the gigantic battleships that had been sunk on that fateful day. Salvage crews had been working for two solid years, yet masts still reached out from the depths of the harbor and hulls were still visible, marking the graves of hundreds of men still encased below.

Seeing the evidence of the terrible bloodshed by the enemy they would soon face fueled the anger of the soldiers on board. Testosterone flared, and the men now wanted more than ever to move into the battle zone and reap their vengeance.

Masao felt the same—a big part of him wanting to settle the score. There was a part of him, though, that wondered where he might be right now had he stayed in Japan. Could he have been one of the fighter pilots picked for the very mission that left this swath of destruction he was looking at, or would he have already been killed in the war with China? Fate had dealt him a gentler hand. He was part of a more cautious, more calculating, and more humane military. Of that, he was proud and content. He was happy to be on the American side, even though it had its complications.

On shore, soldiers were bused to Schofield Barracks. The Nisei were on a bus with the other soldiers but were kept on board while all the Caucasian soldiers exited at Schofield.

"Gentlemen, remain on the bus. You'll be taken to your location momentarily," the young corporal directed them politely. Masao looked out the bus window at the hustle and bustle of Schofield. On the perimeter of the base, Masao noticed a thick thatch of trees that seemed to go on for acres. Huge banyan trees grew limbs that spanned out far and wide, the roots draped down and anchored to the earth. Palm trees and ferns that were the size of army tanks added to the density of the tropical forest.

The bus door closed after the last of the white soldiers disembarked, leaving only the Nisei, the bus driver, and a corporal, who happened to be Hawaiian.

"Sirs. Welcome to O'ahu. My name is Corporal Waimea, and I will be assisting you with your quarters. Your assignment, as you know, is sensitive. It's best that you have separate quarters than the general population for obvious reasons. We're traveling just one mile to the northwest, where you will be stationed for ten days. After that you'll head to Fort Hase, the marine base. I saw you admiring our jungle out yonder. Soldiers stationed on Schofield use our jungle here, but you'll have your own jungle. You'll receive the same training, plus more." The bus slowed and turned.

"We're approaching your quarters. Thank you and Godspeed."

The facility sat along the Wahiawa Reservoir in the midst of a jungle that grew around a small building, which had been converted into a barrack specifically for MIS personnel. The soldiers endured jungle training along the reservoir. They played poker, smoked, joked, and worried together. And they waited. They waited for their leave time when they could get away from each other and enjoy the sights, sounds, and *wahine* of Honolulu.

Before the transfer to Fort Hase on the east coast of O'ahu, the Nisei were given a short leave. They enthusiastically primped themselves for a night on the town and headed for Honolulu. Naki suggested Club Pago Pago as their first stop.

Meanwhile, Doris was in Honolulu, getting ready for a night out with a man named Stanley. Her old boyfriend, George, had shipped out a year after they'd met, and they'd lost contact soon after he left the island. Doris and Stanley had been together for a couple of years, now, dating on and off. Doris had just bought a new dress with her most recent paycheck. She looked absolutely stunning in it and couldn't wait to tantalize Stanley.

He was picking her up at seven and they would be hanging out with their old gang at Club Pago Pago.

★ ★ ★

"Wait, you were in Honolulu? Did you see Doris there?" I asked as I brought Masao his apple crisp from the dessert table at the casino buffet. *Maybe this is where they met, it makes perfect sense. She lived on Hawai'i and he was stationed there for a couple of weeks.*

"No. Never saw her there," he said, dashing my hopes of these two young people, who were destined to be with each other, having a chance meeting on a balmy evening while walking along a deserted beach. "I saw lots of other women there, though!" He sounded like a teenager and evidently wanted to set the record straight: he had gotten some action during his stay on O'ahu. I looked at him and smiled.

"Okay, settle down. Let's get back to Hawai'i. What happened at Club Pago Pago?"

JULY 1944—FORT HASE, HAWAI'I

The thirty or so soldiers on the city bus, including the Nisei, unloaded and walked the few blocks to Club Pago Pago. A line already formed out the door of the nightclub. The women were all dolled up and seemed to notice the new crop of soldiers approaching.

Once inside the club, the Nisei were seated at a table on the dance floor. There was no shortage of dance partners. The soldiers had a spectacular time and hated for the night to end. And even though they were in the same club and dancing on the same floor, Masao and Doris would only cross paths that evening.

After the night of heavy partying and dancing, the tired and hungover soldiers were loaded up for Fort Hase. Captain Aimone was already stationed on Hase and had a plan prepared for the Nisei upon their arrival. He had studied the mission of the ten Japanese American soldiers now assigned to him. He learned about the MIS operation, about how MIS soldiers had been utilized around the South Pacific, and he was sure he could make better use of this well-trained resource.

He had a tough decision, though; he wanted to get as many Nisei interpreters on the front line as possible but had been ordered to assure loyalty. He also had to keep them all safe. He wasn't sure it was possible to accomplish all that but had worked day and night to figure out how it might work. After weeks of research that included an extensive review of the family of each soldier, and a careful examination of their military histories and schooling, Aimone was convinced that the MIS soldiers were, indeed, loyal to the United States, even the three who had been educated in Japan. He looked forward to the day when he could hand a favorable report to General Mueller, a report that would reveal the honor of the ten-man MIS team.

Aimone waited in his temporary office at the officer's headquarters. He had sent for three soldiers, two privates and one private first class. He had carefully chosen these men.

In came three young men: Jack Dalton, a big, tall, redheaded guy; Anthony "Tony" Garcia, a shorter Latino with soft eyes; and Ruben Escola, your average all-American.

"At ease. Men, I have a special assignment for you. I can't share many of the details of this operation, but what I can tell you is that it's sensitive."

The soldiers' faces revealed the excitement they felt; they were being included in some secret military operation.

"Once we're out there," he pointed to a map in the general area of the South Pacific, "there's a good chance we'll have Japanese prisoners to interrogate. We have the trained manpower to do just that. The problem is, our guys are also Japanese. They're Americans, but their ancestry is Japanese. I'm concerned for their safety. Very concerned."

The excitement faded. Were they actually going to be babysitting some Japanese guys? Or were they going to be involved in the torture of prisoners? Neither prospect appealed to any of them.

"Questions so far?" Aimone felt their anxiety.

"Sir," Garcia started out, "when you say interrogation . . ."

"I mean interrogation, questioning. Nothing more. Our methods are humane, I assure you." He saw the soldiers relax. "Your assignment will be to protect one soldier. Staff Sergeant Masao Abe. He's on his way to Hase now. He's part of a ten-man team, each team member has three guys assigned. You are bodyguards. I don't want anything to happen to your interpreter. Not a scratch."

"Sir." Dalton raised his hand slightly. Aimone nodded for him to proceed. "Are we being pulled out of our unit?" Dalton was a soldier who wanted to be in the middle of the action.

"No. You're all still with your unit, the 321st. Sergeant Abe will be attached to your unit as well. Don't worry, boys, you'll see the action. We want these interpreters embedded right on the front line. That's why we need the protection. And I mean around the clock protection."

"Sir." Dalton had another question. "What do we do if we get a prisoner? Take him to the rear?"

Aimone replied, "We'll have military police assigned to each platoon. They will bring any prisoner back to division headquarters. Your job is to protect Sergeant Abe. He knows his job, he's been in training for months. You worry about watching him. Like I said, not a scratch."

AUGUST 12, 1944—GUADALCANAL, SOLOMON ISLANDS

On a transport vessel heading west, Masao was assigned to quarters with his bodyguards. By night three, there had been so much vomiting that Masao had had enough. The bunks were four high, one stacked right on the other, and when soldiers on the top bunk got sick it spilled down to the bottom bunks. It was hot and that made the sour stink even more unbearable. Masao couldn't stand the stench for another minute. Also, the constant sound of gut-wrenching puking made it impossible to get any sleep. He grabbed his pillow and blanket and headed out of his quarters.

In the cargo hold, Masao found a place under one of the jeeps and made himself a little bed all by himself. He slept like a baby.

When Dalton woke up and saw Masao's bunk empty, he flung himself out of bed to find Garcia. "Where's Abe?" he whispered.

"He's not in his bunk?"

Dalton pointed to Masao's empty bunk.

"We've gotta find him. Get Escola."

"I'm going to kill that little son of a bitch for making me lose sleep," Dalton huffed as he found Escola and woke him up. The three searched the decks for Masao, to no avail. Not in the latrine, not in the galley, not on deck anywhere.

"Jesus, where could he be?" Garcia asked. "I hope he didn't go overboard." The thought made the three nervous.

"Maybe he's in the cargo hold," Dalton thought out loud.

"Why would he be down there?" Escola asked as he looked in another bunk room.

"I don't know. But I hope he's not sabotaging gear."

"Let's not jump to conclusions, Jack. Jesus Christ," said Garcia.

The search intensified as the three made their way down to the cargo hold. They traversed the area, darting in between landing craft, trucks, and jeeps.

"Abe. Abe—you in here?" Dalton called out, not giving thought to address Masao as sergeant, not a single concern to address him as "sir," as a private first class should.

"Over here," Masao called out. The three followed his voice, but it took them a few minutes to spot him. He was peeking out from under his jeep bedroom.

"What in the hell are you doing down here?" Dalton barked.

"The stench from all the vomit is killing me. Three nights is enough. I'm not spending another thirty up there. This is my new bunk. Like it or not." Dalton, Garcia, and Escola looked at each other, then more closely examined Masao's "bunk."

"There are other jeeps, you know," Masao pointed out. A short while later, each of the four had established their own bunk area in the cargo hold.

Weeks passed before they spotted Guadalcanal in the distance. It had been taken back from the Japanese months earlier. Charged with a blend of excitement and anxiety, soldiers stood on deck watching the island become bigger and feeling their freedom and worry-free nights slip away.

"All hands. All hands. Now hear this. We anchor at Guadalcanal at 1300 for a dry run. All hands. All hands. We anchor at 1300," announced a voice over the loudspeaker. They knew what to do and sprang into action.

As they neared the shore, the Jacob's ladders were tightened for soldiers to scale down.

Landing craft deployed from the cargo hold through huge doors at the mouth of the ship. When the orders came, they scrambled down the rope ladders and jumped into the nearest landing craft to head for shore. Masao, surrounded by his reluctant bodyguards, felt self-assured. He glanced around and took pride in his military. All the men, many younger than he was and a few older, radiated confidence. The ride to shore was bumpy, and eventually they felt the craft come to a sliding halt. The doors of the craft opened with a crash, and the soldiers piled off, heading through the shallow water for shore as ordered.

On shore the seasoned and fatigued marines, battle scarring their faces, looked with detestation at the army soldiers in their clean uniforms, their shaved faces, and full bellies. Every US Army soldier felt it. It sank in and their enthusiasm vanished. This was real. In a matter of weeks, if not days, and if they were still alive, they would have the same expressions, the same loathing for inexperienced soldiers who came on shore clean and smiling.

There was a dramatically different mood on board after the dry run. Soldiers, at the very least, were apprehensive. Most were afraid.

CHAPTER EIGHT

BATTLE

Alan and I had made the decision to take Masao to Vegas for Thanksgiving. Once there, we followed our usual routine and sat at the Grotto restaurant one evening. I was devouring a strawberry cassata that I spotted on the extravagant dessert cart. Masao would have a bite of mine every so often, but I made Alan get his own dessert. I was turning into my own worst nightmare, blowing money like I had it to spend and eating huge desserts as though my body could afford it. Rather than focus on what a gluttonous gambler I had become, I remembered where Masao had left off when we last talked about the war.

"Hey, Mas," I said in between bites. He looked up as he sipped his coffee. "Last time we talked you guys had just completed your dry run on Guadalcanal."

"That's right. Dry run. Yep."

"What happened after that?" Alan waited to hear his dad's war story too. We both loved it when Masao went back to the 1940s and pulled up history for us to hear.

"Heh! After that, we went into *battle*." He looked at me to see if I was focused. I nodded that I was. "On Angaur. An island."

"Find out where that is," I motioned for Alan to get out his phone and look it up.

"And, gee. Things got tough after that," Masao reflected.

"Were you scared?" I asked, then realized what a really stupid question it was. Alan looked at me like I was an idiot.

"Heck *yeah*. I was scared shitless."

SEPTEMBER 17, 1944–ANGAUR, PALAU

Masao, in full battle gear, looked off the bow as he waited, packed in with all the other soldiers. They watched navy destroyers pummel the island with shell fire, bombarding it heavily before sending in ground troops. Fighter planes attacked from overhead. Masao wondered if the Japanese had a chance against all this firepower, then he thought about Kunio and that radical will of his. Surely, there would be many soldiers who had that same sense of superiority, even in the face of certain doom.

"*Move out!*" Soldiers, in rows eight wide, hurled themselves onto Jacob's ladders and climbed down to hovering landing craft. Masao climbed down the rope fixture with ease, glancing at smoke rising from the tiny island.

"Whose idea was this?" he said, his private thoughts erupting from his lips. Garcia, who was just next to him, heard.

"I don't know, amigo."

They both jumped into the landing craft followed by Dalton and Escola. In a flurry, the landing craft deployed along with several others, forming a ring at sea and awaiting orders to go ashore. On board it was a choppy ride; soldiers struggled to keep their balance. One soldier got sick, likely more from nerves than the motion. Relentless explosions continued in the distance. The craft rolled and rocked in the swells. Tension was mounting with every passing second.

"Maybe they'll all be dead by the time we get there," Garcia hoped. Masao nodded, looking at the soldier who was puking again.

"Wave Three, commence to Blue Beach," a voice on the commander's radio announced. The landing craft broke from the

Amphibious assault on Angaur, September 17, 1944

ring and headed to a beach in the distance. Fear escalated rapidly. Masao's heart was pounding faster and harder than ever before. To make matters worse, somehow he and Garcia had been shuffled to the very front of the craft.

"How'd we end up in the front?" Garcia said. Masao thought that Garcia must be the type of guy who talks when he's nervous.

The tempo of the naval gunfire intensified. Fires burned all over the island. Black smoke billowed into the clear sky; debris and chunks of trees fell with a splash in the surf. A beautiful paradise was quickly being demolished. The landing craft that carried Masao and other soldiers was a thousand yards from shore now. Landing Craft Infantry (gun boats specifically designed to clear the way for landing soldiers) and mortar boats took position in front. As dozens

of these boats neared the beach, naval air fire concentrated on the shore, clearing the way for ground troops.

On the beach, army tanks now dragged themselves out of the surf onto land, taking position to protect the dismounting men. The landing craft approached the beach, facing relentless rapid fire and mortar rounds by the enemy. With a loud bang, the ramp of the craft released, making way for the men to jump off. The radioman was just to the side of Masao and leaped, immediately sinking to his neck. Masao abruptly stopped.

"Christ, the water's too deep!" Masao shouted.

The radioman stood up, and Masao could see that he had fallen. The water was only a couple feet deep. The radioman called back, "My knees buckled. I'm so damn scared." Masao noticed that his face looked like a little boy.

Crafts landing ashore during the amphibious assault on Angaur

Masao jumped off the craft in unison with Garcia. He looked around for Dalton and Escola. They were right behind him.

"*Let's go, let's go, let's go!*" Dalton was shouting out of sheer fear. The four of them ran as fast as the surf would let them. Fifteen feet from the beach now, Masao heard the unmistakable whistle of a mortar just above their heads.

"Christ almighty—*run*," he shouted to nobody in particular. A grenade landed twenty feet in back of the four, thrusting them forward. Masao looked back to see the faces of men as their bodies exploded. His first inclination was to go back to see if any were alive, but Garcia grabbed his arm.

"*Mi Dios.*"

On the beach, code-named Blue Beach, the four slammed their bodies down against a sandy ridge, cutting their hands on the sharp coral. Other soldiers lined up beside them. Machine-gun fire hit all around. Shards of coral scattered in all directions, spraying the men with razor-like fragments.

Masao looked back to the surf as the landing craft's ramp went up, and it retreated back to the sea, leaving the men to fend for themselves. Bodies littered the beach. *This can't be real*, he thought. He looked at Garcia, who was terrified. To his other side, Dalton had his eyes closed. *Maybe he's praying*, Masao thought. Escola, on the other side of Dalton, clutched his gun, his eyes squinting to avoid fragmented coral from injuring them.

Navy fighter planes screeched overhead. Tanks advanced off the beach from all directions. Masao watched Tech Sergeant Dan Cooper, the leader in charge of the company he was assigned to, scurry down the coral ridge. The sergeant grabbed the radio and tried to communicate in the midst of the explosions. Masao waited and watched, his hands glued in a firing position on his rifle.

After what seemed like an hour, the incoming machine-gun fire ceased. The grenades stopped. Masao looked around and saw several amtracs advance off the beach, armored bulldozers forging the way through the dense foliage. Sergeant Cooper crawled over to his squad. They huddled around him.

"We got lucky," he yelled over the gunfire and the tanks' menacing grinding. "Our planes knocked out most of their mortars. There's still dozens buried in, we don't know how deep. We're going to push our way inland as far as we can until we meet up with the 322nd. It could be a while. They're having a hell of a time on Red Beach. They haven't even made it on shore yet."

Masao thought about Naki attached to the 322nd as he watched Cooper pull out his map to check coordinates, then scan his unit. "Where's my radioman?"

"Over there, sir." Garcia pointed down the ridge.

"Don't call me sir," Cooper stated as he motioned for the radio-man, "unless it's your intention to get me shot. Not sir. Not Sarge. Not commander. Call me Coop."

"Sorry, si—Coop."

Cooper rolled over and scanned the terrain with his binoculars. "That way," he pointed. "Stay close by the amtracs. *Let's move.*"

The soldiers hustled over the ridge and hovered behind an amtrac. Twenty yards in, sniper fire took down a soldier at the front. They heard the yell as he went down and they all instinctively dropped for cover.

"Man down!" someone called out. Soldiers scrambled to move the wounded soldier to the rear. A trail of blood followed as he was dragged by Masao.

"He's not going to make it," Masao heard himself say. *Fifty feet into battle and he's gone.* The enormity of the thought weighed on him.

"Over there. Let's get the little ape," another soldier hollered, eager for revenge. The racial slur pierced Masao's ears; he watched the soldiers go in for the kill. They threw a grenade at a cave open-ing from where the sniper had shot.

"Don't let the little weasel come out alive," another soldier shouted. A soldier armed with a flamethrower went out first, shoot-ing liquid fire directly into the cave. The Japanese soldier ran out on fire, screaming and writhing in pain. Machine-gun fire imme-diately put him out of his misery. His lifeless body continued to burn. It was a horrific sight for any human to witness. Masao knew it would get worse. Much worse. He looked around at his unit. But for Garcia, all of his US Army comrades were white.

"Yeah! Take that you little Nip," the flamethrower soldier bel-lowed as though he had scored a touchdown in a high school football game. While the soldiers celebrated their first kill, medics ran by Masao with yet another wounded US soldier from the front, from a different squad entirely. Masao gripped his rifle a little tighter.

Soldiers who drew back to the amtrac gave Masao a steely look. *I'm never going to make it out of here*, he thought.

The platoon inched forward. It wasn't long before a routine developed: find caves, employ the flamethrower, and gun down the burning soldiers who ran out on fire. The 110-degree heat was oppressive and guys were soon shedding their shirts. The constant sound of explosions was unnerving at first but became normal. Enemy bodies started to clutter their path—they were burned beyond recognition and still smoldering.

Now two hundred yards from the beach, a narrow swath had been etched in the tropical landscape. It was barely enough for tanks and troops to maneuver, but it sufficed. Sergeant Cooper dropped back to the middle of the platoon to meet up with Masao and his bodyguards. Acutely aware of Masao's mission, the safety of this Nisei interpreter on his shoulders, and the realization that the other soldiers in his platoon were out for blood, he couldn't help but be uneasy.

"Abe. I'm inclined to have you fall back to combat intelligence. We can bring POWs back for you to interrogate, at least until division headquarters gets set up."

But Masao didn't want to be seen as soft. He felt the need to prove himself as a soldier. "It might be better if I keep pushing the line with the squad. These guys aren't coming out alive anyway." From the front of the line, heavy incoming machine-gun fire followed by another satchel charge shook the ground. A mortar shell landed fifty yards behind them, killing medics and a wounded soldier.

"They're everywhere. You two—" Cooper shouted and pointed at Dalton and Garcia who were ducking behind an amtrac. "*Cover him.*"

Dawn was barely breaking when Masao opened his eyes the next day. He vaguely remembered trying to dig a foxhole, but the ground was made of hard clay. No soldier had success with digging, so they'd barricaded themselves with small boulders instead. He'd maybe slept an hour, the sounds of constant artillery and brilliance of the continuous flares making it impossible to get rest. Plus, he was scared, like other soldiers were.

He heard the sound of tractors that had been working through the night; it must have been a hundred yards up from their location. Just then, Dalton jerked awake.

"*Wake up!*" shouted Sergeant Cooper. "General Mueller landed at division HQ pissed that we're behind schedule. Grab your gear, let's move out." Moments later, Masao and his bodyguards took their positions behind an amtrac. Soldiers armed with flamethrowers and mortar gear ran by them, heading for the front of the squadron.

"It's time for another Nip barbeque," the flamethrower said as he looked right into Masao's eyes when he trotted by. The word *Nip* hung in the air. Masao didn't have time to react, though, because suddenly, there was an enormous explosion, shaking the ground in all directions. Soldiers crouched as the amtrac halted and the driver popped out of the top. Masao looked a half mile to the north, where billows of black smoke rose up, darkening the sunrise.

"Holy *Christ*. What kind of bombs do they have?" Garcia sputtered as he hovered next to Escola. The four remained squatted behind the amtrac, waiting for orders.

"They hit the ammo dump on Red Beach," a soldier called out.

"The little rats aren't going to back down without a fight," Dalton shook his head with his thought.

"Of course not, Jack. Neither would our guys. Do you think these things through before you say them?" Garcia said, as he wondered if the real battle would be in their group of four.

It was hours of plodding through the jungle in the sweltering heat. Suddenly there was excitement from the front.

"Enemy spotted. He's surrendering," an exuberant soldier called back. A Japanese soldier waving a makeshift white flag barely emerged from his foxhole at fifty yards. The expression on his face was clear: he was terrified.

"*Abe!*" Cooper shouted. Masao, Dalton, Garcia, and Escola ran to the front of the platoon. Other soldiers took position around them.

"Let's get a little closer," Cooper motioned. They warily walked toward the Japanese soldier.

"Tell him to come out with his hands up," Cooper ordered.

"*Come out with your hands up,*" Masao shouted to the prisoner in Japanese. His white flag still waving, the soldier slowly came out. He was skin and bones. His ribs protruded from his chest. Sergeant Cooper motioned for the group of six to close in on the foxhole, vigilantly. The Japanese soldier looked at Masao, they nodded, ever so slightly, to each other.

"Abe, tell him to—"

Before he could finish, sniper fire hit the Japanese soldier in the back of his head—exploding it. Brain matter sprayed the soldiers. They automatically hit the ground.

"*Cover us!*" Cooper yelled back to the platoon as he scanned the area. "Where'd it come from?"

"We're never going to get prisoners at this rate. Their own guys aren't going to let them surrender," Garcia whispered to Dalton.

"That wasn't Jap fire," Dalton stated. "Otherwise, why didn't they shoot more of us?"

Still on their bellies, Cooper thought through his next move. "We've gotta go in there."

"In where?" Dalton asked, not believing what he was about to hear.

"There." Cooper motioned to the foxhole. "Abe, get ready, we're going in. Garcia, you're with us."

Cooper, Masao, and Garcia shimmied on their bellies toward the foxhole, passing the dead soldier on the way. The opening of the hole had remnants of camouflage netting. It was dark inside. They hovered on the edge in squatting positions, guns drawn. Masao felt his legs shake and thought that his pounding heart was a sure giveaway to Cooper that he was scared to death.

"Holler in there, Abe. Tell 'em their comrade is dead. To come out with their hands up," Cooper ordered.

Masao cupped his hands around his mouth. "Come out with your hands up. Your comrade is dead!" *Goddamn my voice sounds weak.*

It was silent.

"It could be a trap," Garcia cautioned. Masao understood what Garcia was getting at. But Cooper had his orders: gain intelligence. That couldn't happen if everything was blown to pieces.

"I don't think so. I think the guy was solo here." Cooper stood. "I'll go in first." Cooper, gun still drawn, dropped inside the dim hole. Masao followed with his sidearm service pistol ready to shoot. Garcia was close behind Masao.

Inside, the soldier's meager existence spoke volumes about the shape of the Japanese military on Angaur. Empty cans of rations had been licked clean; water canteen, drained; two rifles and no ammo. Masao noticed some papers and books and collected those. Cooper explored the back of the hole to see if there were tunnels leading to other locations, but it was walled in.

"Anything useful, Abe?" Cooper asked, motioning to the books.

"I don't think so, sir. But I'll have a look outside."

Garcia took the rifles and Cooper led the way out. Outside, Masao scanned the papers while Cooper waited.

"Letters to his wife," he reported. "He had two little girls." He looked at Cooper. "One was learning the piano. He wondered if they still had the piano." He continued to flip through pages of letters, then switched to the books. "These are just novels," he said, leafing through to make sure he wasn't missing anything on the inside. "Just novels."

"Okay, secure those for HQ. Let's move on." Cooper was heading back to the platoon.

Masao followed, and while he felt like a soldier's soldier by completing his first dangerous mission on the battlefield, he also felt the lingering weight of inhumanity.

The nights were only slightly less hot than the days. Cooper's platoon hunkered down on the line taking turns getting shut-eye. Flares went up every few minutes to light up the area. Any movement would be shot at, so when a flare went up, soldiers kept still. Machine-gun fire and mortar shells exploded from distances in all directions. Sergeant Cooper walked through the line. His soldiers littered the area with their tired bodies.

"Stay alert. They'll be trying to infiltrate the line," he warned in a whisper as he waded through. Soldiers who were on lookout, worn from the hypervigilance it took to constantly scan the surrounding jungle, struggled to stay awake. Masao sat next to Garcia while Dalton and Escola slept. He watched another flare go up. Garcia nudged him.

"Hey, see that?" Garcia whispered.

"What?" Masao tensed up and looked around, thinking the enemy was approaching.

"*Alacrán*. Scorpion. Very dangerous." Garcia pointed to a black scorpion crawling along. "I'm going to kill it. If it stings you, it's going to hurt like hell."

"Okay," Masao nodded. Garcia grabbed a rock and was ready to go in when a shot went off. The scorpion was obliterated by Dalton, who had woken up and noticed the arachnid.

"Jesus, Jack," Garcia shouted in a whisper. But the charge from the bullet had made them a direct target in the darkness of the night. Suddenly, there was rapid machine-gun fire coming at them from fifty yards out, spraying bullets all around them. The four hugged the ground. Realizing his grave error, Dalton grabbed his Browning automatic rifle, stood up, and ran toward where the shots were coming from, shooting his weapon and spraying the area. Garcia, Escola, and Masao followed, the three shooting relentlessly with whatever weapon they had. The incoming fire stopped and the four hit the ground together, now well outside line camp.

"Do you think we got 'em?" Dalton whispered.

"I don't know. Shut up so we can listen," Masao whispered back. On the ground, they searched the darkness for any movement, listening with intense concentration.

"Between the enemy and these damn scorpions, this is going to be a long night," Garcia said in a low voice to Masao, who nodded in agreement. Another flare went up. They spotted no movement but didn't stop their intense scrutiny of the area.

As dawn barely broke, all four were still hugging the ground, alert. They slowly felt safe enough to stand. They looked at each other, not sure what to do next—fall back to line camp or go in to see if they were successful in defending their line camp. Meanwhile, soldiers had branched out to search the perimeter for the four who had gone missing in the night.

"Come on," Masao motioned for them to go forward.

"You're crazy. Let's get back, they'll be looking for us," Escola reasoned.

"Escola's right," Garcia urged. Masao looked at Dalton. His eyes asked, *What's your stand?* Dalton wasn't about to chicken out. He nodded at Masao.

"I'll lead." Dalton started to cut through the brush.

"He's right," Garcia said as he held Masao's arm so he couldn't take the lead. "We have our orders too, Abe." The four lumbered through the thick brush until they came upon two dead Imperial soldiers whose bodies were ripped apart by their barrage the previous night. They stood there for a few minutes, feeling the weight of the moment, of taking lives in the true spirit of war. The enemy shot first, after all.

Masao perused the bloody sight, noticing a pack on one of the dead soldiers. He went in to take a closer look.

"What are you doing?" Dalton's question was more like an accusation.

"I'm supposed to find intelligence, but I also want to see what kind of rations they have." He opened the soldier's pack and pulled out a tin can. He wiped the blood off and read the Japanese writing.

"What is it? A bomb?" Escola was dubious.

Masao shook his head, "No. Teriyaki beef. My favorite." He tucked it in his uniform and took the pack of Japanese cigarettes too. He was looking through their uniforms for any papers of significance when Sergeant Cooper marched up.

"I don't know which one of you imbeciles attracted the fire last night, but I don't *ever* want to see a stunt like that again. Understand?"

"Yes, sir," the four answered together, standing at attention.

"Abe, you are here on a unique mission. Your orders are to stay embedded in the platoon until you're called for interrogation. Don't make me regret the decision to pull you along. I'll have you back at CIC before you know it."

"Yes, sir, uh, Coop."

"If I might—" Dalton started to speak, but Cooper cut him off.

"No, you might not. Abe—stay in the middle. You three—your orders are to cover him. *Do I make myself clear?*"

The soldiers nodded as Cooper marched off in a huff.

"We got 'em good, though," Escola congratulated the group. The four followed Cooper at a distance, their voices low so Cooper couldn't detect their giddiness.

"I'm pretty sure I had the kill shots," Garcia claimed.

"Shut up, Tony. We all know it was me who killed the bastards, so let's just leave it at that," Dalton was sarcastic, but Masao wondered if he was the type of soldier who liked to take credit.

"What are you talking about. You were shooting up in the air. My grandma has better aim," Garcia shot back.

And while Masao enjoyed the banter among his team of four, he didn't feel quite part of the team. He didn't feel the camaraderie. He wasn't sure he ever would.

★ ★ ★

Back in Vegas, it was midnight and Masao was going strong. Alan had given up and gone to the room an hour earlier.

"Those guys, heh! They would congratulate themselves after something like that." He remembered the incident like it was yesterday. "I didn't feel so good about it. No need to celebrate when someone dies." His voice had changed with his afterthought. I glanced over and noticed that he was making ten-dollar bets.

In between button pushes he looked over at me, noticing my tired, red eyes. "You want a coffee?"

"No, I'm fine. Keep playing. You're doing good." I smiled, pointing to his winnings on the machine.

"Heh! I finally found a good one." He was right. His luck came and went, but mostly went. After a few button pushes, a thought occurred to him.

"You know, we took Angaur in just a few days, maybe a week or so." I nodded that I was listening. "We went in one way, and, ah, the 322nd, they went in a different way. And then we met up at a point. That was a good day."

SEPTEMBER, 1944–ANGAUR, PALAU

Cooper's platoon moved along with the amtracs, following tractors as they cleared the way. Suddenly, voices called out from the distance, American voices.

"Hold your fire. 322nd approaching. *Hold your fire.*"

The 321st and 322nd Regimental Combat Teams had successfully completed their assignment. Soldiers were allowed to relax for a brief time. Masao and Naki sat together under a tree.

"Have you taken any prisoners?" Naki asked Masao in between drags off a Japanese cigarette.

"Just killing everyone we see," Masao answered as he watched Garcia and Escola use palm leaves to fan themselves.

Naki looked off in the distance. Masao felt a heaviness coming from his friend. He examined Naki, noticing that his face looked strained. He nudged him.

"You okay?"

Naki looked at Masao. There was a long, anguished pause before he spoke. "I've seen . . ." his voice trailed off. He was unable to put words to the horror his mind had been replaying over and over, scenes that had permeated his thoughts, destined to remain there forever. Naki didn't have to complete his sentence. Masao looked into his friend's eyes. He understood the essence of the situation, as well as the scar it had left on Naki's psyche and heart.

"I wonder if we're going to make it out of here alive." Naki's voice was faint. Masao looked over at Dalton, who was bullshitting with other white soldiers. Masao knew some of his comrades, and perhaps even his bodyguards, were suspicious of him and his fellow Nisei soldiers.

"The odds aren't too good." Masao succumbed to that reality as he put his cigarette out in the sand.

After a few hours, the 322nd was ordered back out. Masao and Naki bid farewell, wondering if they would ever see each other again. Masao, still attached to Cooper's squad, waited for orders. He found a nice spot in the shade with Garcia and Escola. Dalton came from out of nowhere and joined them. Masao lit up.

"Did you hear about the guy in the 322nd?" Masao asked to nobody in particular. Dalton was uninterested.

"What happened?" Garcia glanced at Masao.

"Stung by a scorpion. Right on the balls," Masao announced. Dalton took note.

"I knew the scorpions were going to be trouble," Garcia said.

"His nuts, they swelled up to the size of melons." Masao was going for the shock factor. It worked. Dalton cringed.

"Jesus. That's just—Jesus," Dalton uttered. The four sat there thinking of the poor guy with aching testicles.

"Is that one of those Japanese cigarettes, Abe?" Garcia asked. Masao nodded, offered one to Garcia, then to Escola, who declined, then to Dalton, who reluctantly took one.

They sat in silence smoking the strong tobacco.

"Round up, fellas," Cooper hollered. They grabbed their gear and joined the company. "We're being shipped out to an island six miles north. Peleliu. We'll be attached to the First Marine Division. Four thousand marines already downed in just one week. They estimate over eleven thousand Jap soldiers still occupy the island. It sounds like a goddamn hell hole. Red Beach—1700." He looked around at his guys. "Soldiers, brace yourselves. Angaur was a cakewalk."

SEPTEMBER 1944—PELELIU, PALAU

Soldiers stood on deck as the transport ship approached Peleliu. They were alarmed by the destruction. Not a tree stood on the beach and surrounding hills—all had been torched, leaving only charred stumps.

On shore, the sickly sweet smell of death was immediately noticeable. A First Marine Division gunnery sergeant, his face reflecting utter hell, saluted Cooper and the other tech sergeants as they approached, followed by their soldiers.

"Get used to the stench. Over here." The gunnery sergeant waved them over to a makeshift headquarters. A map was laid out on a crude excuse for a table.

"What's left of the First Marines are up in this area here, near what we call the Five Brothers. The Seventh Marines are here. Your men will fan out and meet up here, at the base of these hills throughout this area here." He spoke quickly as he pointed at different areas. Masao lingered on the beach nearby with the rest of Cooper's outfit. The sound of a bulldozer a hundred yards away caught his attention. He strained to see what it was doing and realized it was scooping up swollen bodies and dumping them into a mass grave. Back in the huddle where the map was being studied, the army sergeants heard the bulldozer as well.

"Get used to that too. Enemy bodies. We figure they had over ten thousand when we got here, and we've taken out at least half, but they keep pouring in from somewhere. No telling how many are here now." He pointed to the map again. "Recon says East Road on the way to Five Brothers is secured along here. But we're finding out that recon is full of shit. Either that or these Japs have one hell of a labyrinth of tunnels throughout these hills. They're still locked in heavy on this mountain, Umurbrogol. They own it. But not for long. At any rate, you'll encounter pockets of resistance at every turn. Sometimes it's just a lone guy, sometimes it's a whole squad. Watch yourselves."

"What kind of artillery are we dealing with?" a sergeant asked.

"Everything. You name it, they've got it. They seem to have an endless *goddamn* supply," the gunnery sergeant spewed out as he glanced around. Then he noticed Masao.

"What's this?" He motioned toward Masao as he demanded an answer.

Cooper spoke up. "Sir, he's with intelligence. Interpreter."

"You've got to be kidding me. What the *hell* do we need to interpret? I hope you ain't planning to take any of these pricks alive after what they've done to my guys out there. Hell, what they've done to all our guys on every *goddamn* island we've taken back."

"Sometimes there are documents." Cooper again voiced reason.

"Documents my ass. Just like the army to cavort with the enemy. Jesus Christ."

"Sir, uh—where, exactly, is headquarters?" Tech Sergeant Thompson asked.

"You're standing in it—exactly," the gunnery sergeant responded with a grimace, waiting for any of these army guys to challenge what the marines had accomplished. "Welcome to purgatory."

★ ★ ★

The holidays had been tough for Masao. He hadn't gone to any events with his family, and he seemed more depressed than usual. When he became depressed and lonely, he would sink deeper than normal and stay there longer. The second anniversary of Doris's death was approaching in February and magnifying his sadness. Alan had planned a trip to Hawai'i to honor her with Masao, his brother Mike, and sister-in-law Kathie. Until then, I kept my routine with Masao sacred—nothing interfered with our weekly visits. It was a relief when the five of us went to Hawai'i; the trip seemed to lift his spirits.

We spent our first day in Honolulu visiting Doris at the Punchbowl and eating a lot of food. It was a beautiful evening, and we were tired from traveling. The next day we would see Naki, something I was looking forward to. Masao was sitting on the balcony, taking in the activity of the tourists below on Lewers Street, a great little area in Waikiki. I spotted him out there watching the sun set and decided to join him. I brought two sweet iced teas and handed one to him as I sat down.

"Thank you," he said as he sipped. "Beautiful night, a-no?"

"It sure is." There was wonderful Hawaiian street music playing in the distance, the sultry voices drifting up to our balcony and soothing the air around us.

"One time, during the war, we caught a prisoner. Our first prisoner, in fact," Masao said, pausing for a moment as he formulated his thoughts.

I shifted my body and turned toward him.

"I was with an outfit, and the tech sergeant was a guy named, ah, Cooper I think. He was a good guy, a great soldier. Anyway, it had been days in that jungle. It was hot, *really* hot, boy. Jeez. And we were already tired and hungry. But nothing like those Japanese guys. They really had it bad."

Masao looked at me to see if I was awake and listening. I felt flustered because I didn't have my tape recorder or anything to take notes on. I nodded and squelched the urge to run for paper and a pen and, instead, just listened.

SEPTEMBER 1944—PELELIU, PALAU

Cooper's squad navigated the dense brush in the sweltering jungle in an area known as the Badlands. Suddenly, sniper fire came at them from a cave at close range. The soldiers dropped to the ground and returned machine-gun fire in the direction of the sniper bullets. Masao was on his belly, along with Garcia and Dalton. The sniper fire stopped just as abruptly as it started.

"Hold your fire." Sergeant Cooper commanded. They all waited. Nothing. They shimmied closer to the cave opening.

"*Dalton.* Fire a round."

Dalton sprayed the cave opening with his Browning. No fire returned. Cooper motioned for Masao to come forward. Masao shimmied up to the front.

"Okay, do your thing," Cooper ordered. Masao nodded.

Masao called out in Japanese, "Come out. You will not be harmed."

A voice from inside the cave called back in Japanese, "I'm out of ammunition. I am unarmed. Don't shoot. Please."

"What's he say?" Cooper inquired.

"He says he has no more ammo."

Cooper surveyed the area. He was suspicious. "What do you think?"

Masao shrugged. "He would probably still be firing at us if he could."

"Okay, get him out here."

"*Come out. You won't be harmed. Keep your hands up.*" Masao called out loudly in Japanese.

Out came the terrified Japanese soldier. The American soldiers almost gasped at the sight. He was in the same poor condition as the other surrendering solider on Angaur. His uniform was tattered and dirty. Two soldiers quickly ran in and patted him down while two others went into the cave.

"Poor devil," Cooper said, motioning to Masao as he took in the pitiful sight. "Okay, ask him where his CP is."

Masao looked at the soldier, wondering whether he knew him. Maybe they went to school together in Japan, or maybe he was a distant relative. It would be hard to tell with the guy's body so emaciated.

"My commanding officer wants to know where your command post is," Masao said in perfect Japanese.

He still had his hands up, nervous about his fate with these American soldiers. "It used to be over that ridge. But you guys got too close, so they moved it." His voice was weak.

"It used to be over that ridge, but they moved it." Masao reported to Cooper, who was still examining the soldier's withered body.

"When?" Cooper wanted to know.

"When?" Masao asked the soldier.

"Maybe eight days ago. I'm not sure. Time has been lost to me." The Japanese soldier reported.

"Eight days ago, he's not sure. He's lost track of time."

Sergeant Cooper examined the soldier. His face softened and he sounded almost empathetic. "The guy's been without supplies for a week. Left here to die." The US soldiers came out of the cave with books and papers. Sergeant Cooper looked through them and handed them to Masao. "Look through this stuff, see if there's anything useful. Okay, let's get him back to camp."

Line camp wasn't much of a camp—more like a few holes and a makeshift galley. Masao instructed the prisoner to sit.

"Sit here. Don't move from this area. Some of these guys are trigger happy," Masao told the prisoner. Masao sat and read through the prisoner's books and papers. A mess sergeant by the name of McCoy walked over with a plate of hot food and a cup of water and handed it to the Japanese prisoner. Masao couldn't believe his eyes.

"Hey. Hey, McCoy. What gives? What about me? How come this guy gets hot meals and we don't?" Masao asked as he watched the prisoner scarf his food. McCoy refilled the prisoner's water cup as he looked at Masao. Clearly, McCoy was a humane guy. It didn't matter what uniform a soldier was wearing; starving was starving.

"Don't bitch. You guys eat three meals a day. This guy here hasn't eaten a full meal in days, weeks maybe." Masao looked at the Japanese prisoner. He took out his K ration and bit off a chunk of the dry biscuit.

"This is bullshit, if you ask me," Masao scoffed.

"Well, no one's asking you." McCoy huffed off. Masao was figuring out how to steal some of the prisoner's meal. The prisoner felt it; he turned away and hovered over his plate to eat in private.

Sergeant Cooper came to the area with a crumpled map. "I'd like to get a closer look at their CP, or what's left of it. Ask him if he remembers how to get there."

Masao nodded and turned toward the prisoner. "We want to go to your CP. Do you remember where it was?" Masao asked. The prisoner, with his mouth full, nodded. Cooper laid out the map on the ground. The Japanese soldier scanned the map and pointed to an area.

"Way over there, huh. Okay. It'll be easier to get to it by road; we'll need a rig from HQ." Cooper seemed annoyed as he thought out loud.

Soldiers in general hated to go back to headquarters, but squad sergeants hated it most. The only military that hung out at headquarters were a bunch of higher-ups who didn't know the first thing about ground combat, but they made most of the decisions for guys on the line. Cooper probably hated headquarters more than anyone, but he wanted to check out the command post. It was the first one they'd heard of and he didn't want to let anything go untouched.

Back at headquarters it was evident how much better officers had it. Hot coffee was brewing, heartier food was abundant, and fresh water was plentiful. Officers that filled headquarters were typically commissioned, having earned their rank off the battlefield. As Cooper's squad hovered just outside the protected encampment, their sergeant went inside to get approval for the use of the military vehicle, the jeep.

Jeeps were built for this terrain. They were rugged, sturdy, and could navigate anything. Sergeant Cooper was in the passenger seat alongside the driver, who was also a radioman.

A short distance from headquarters, Cooper muttered, "Dealing with goddamn HQ. What a snafu."

Garcia looked at Dalton and mouthed "snafu?"

Dalton answered, "Situation normal, all fouled up."

"When it's HQ you're dealing with, it's all *fucked* up," Cooper corrected Dalton. The soldiers look at each other and grinned. They liked Cooper's style.

The first part of the route had been easy to travel. Cooper had the map open, and the prisoner would point to different roads they needed to follow. Eventually, they ended up at the foot of a steep hill. The road looked more like a trail with huge gouges cut every which way. It seemed like an impossible climb. Cooper looked at Masao.

"Where to?"

"Which way do we go?" Masao asked the prisoner.

"Up that hill. It's on the other side."

"It's on the other side of this hill," Masao reported.

"Okay, let's take 'er up," Cooper ordered the driver, who put the jeep in first gear. Up the jeep started, gears grinding as the driver shifted up and down. The drive shaft groaned, and the tires dropped in and out of the deep grooves, but slowly and steadily they climbed. Then, the hill took a steeper grade, and the prisoner waved his arms frantically. Cooper noticed.

"Whoa. Stop!" Cooper ordered the driver. "What's his deal, Abe? Are there land mines?"

"What's going on? Are there mines?" Masao asked the prisoner.

"No. No land mines. We—" the Japanese prisoner began to answer, but Masao interrupted to ease Cooper's mind.

"No land mines," he said, and to the prisoner, "Continue."

"We must get out of the car and push it over the top. It won't make it up this steep part." The prisoner was making all sorts of hand gestures as he spoke. The soldiers in the jeep looked on, bewildered.

Masao listened, but was confused. "The car, it will tip over," the prisoner insisted, concerned about their fate.

"What's he say?" Cooper wanted to know. The jeep hung there in limbo on the hill while the interpretation ensued. Masao was timid to give the interpretation for fear of being laughed at.

"He says that the jeep won't make it. That we should get out and push."

"Get out and push! Is the guy nuts? Let's go." The jeep made more whirring noises but easily made it to the top, after tossing the guys around. At the top of the hill, the Japanese prisoner was astonished. He looked around in amazement at the feat of the jeep and was awestruck by the four-wheel drive ability. He said something in Japanese and Masao chuckled.

"What's he say?" Cooper asked.

"He said, 'No wonder we're losing this war.'" Masao chuckled again. The entire jeep enjoyed the remark as they rolled down the other side of the hill toward the abandoned Japanese command post.

There was an unnerving feel to the deserted CP. The jeep rolled in slowly. They all got out and looked around. The Japanese prisoner motioned to a weathered, makeshift hut. "That used to be the ammo hold," he told Masao.

Masao nodded to Cooper. "Ammo hold." Cooper motioned to Garcia to check it out.

Garcia went in with his gun drawn and came out within seconds. "Nothing."

"They cleaned up before they moved." Cooper looked around. "There's nothing here."

"Sir," the radioman called over to Cooper, "HQ on the horn. They've uncovered some intelligence."

"What do they have?" Cooper was generally skeptical of anything HQ came up with.

"One of their officers said their payroll was near this command post. In a pond."

Cooper glanced around and noticed a muddy swamp. "Maybe there."

The soldiers dug with their helmets as makeshift shovels, and the prisoner was right in there with them. Masao wondered if it might have been Hiro Takahashi, one of the Nisei interpreters assigned to HQ, who had uncovered the intelligence. Hiro, like Masao, had grown up in Japan and likely spoke the most fluent Japanese among the four Nisei soldiers at HQ.

The Japanese prisoner chatted while they dug in the mud and Masao kept interpreting to ease Cooper's mind. "He doesn't know why they kept money for army payroll. They were supposed to die here. He's got a point. Who's the payroll for? Soldiers have been ordered to fight to the death, not to let the Allied Forces advance through the island, even if they have to die defending it."

"Probably for their officers," Cooper figured. "It's always about officers. Doesn't matter what side you're on."

Dalton hit something with the stick he was using for a shovel. "We've got something here," he announced. Sure enough, out came a box, heavy and muddy. They struggled to get it on land. Inside were thousands of yen, and documents.

Back at headquarters, officers saw the jeep approach and walked toward the edge of HQ. "Any good intelligence?" one of them asked as the jeep came to a stop.

"It's their payroll, sir, and a few documents that may be of use." Cooper wanted to get this over with so he could get away from headquarters.

The officer's eyes lit up as the soldiers heaved the box out and opened it. "Anything in the documents, Abe?"

"Probably, sir. They're military."

"I'll have one of the CIC guys take a look." The officer was entranced by the money. "Go get Sakai for me, will ya?" He motioned for Masao to get one of the Nisei interpreters assigned to headquarters. Masao did as ordered, then he sat down next to the prisoner.

"What will happen to me now?" the prisoner's face reflected his anxiety. They both watched officers as they examined the Japanese money, handing a token bill to each of the soldiers who had retrieved the payroll from the pond, careful not to dispense more than just one bill to each.

"You will be taken to one of the POW camps. But probably more interrogation here first."

The prisoner's eyes widened. "Torture, no? Or worse?" He was afraid of the answer.

Masao watched other officers gather around the payroll box. "No. No torture. The guys who will interrogate you are Nisei, like me. They won't hurt you," Masao assured him. The Japanese soldier looked over and saw one officer who appeared more greedy and self-indulgent than the others.

"Officers. They're all the same, no?" the prisoner assessed. Their eyes connected for just the briefest of moments, but in that instant—a thousand thoughts. Masao wondered how it was that fate had dealt him a better hand than this guy. Had one variable in his life been different, he could have been sitting on the other side, starving and scared to death. Had his father not sent him back to the States when he did, had the Japanese military changed the age of conscription, had the Japanese government not let him out of the country, had his little sister not died . . .

Those thoughts stuck with Masao as he gathered his gear, along with the rest of Cooper's platoon, and headed back out, away from the protection and luxury of headquarters.

"Get yourselves dug in," Cooper ordered as he walked along the primitive line camp that had been assembled. Masao and his three bodyguards had found a natural indentation in the ground and used it for their dugout. At the first sign of darkness, the flares started. Masao was just about to doze off when he heard something.

"Heeey—yeww!" someone called out from a distance. The voice had a distinct accent.

Dalton jerked his head up. "What was that?" he whispered.

"Shhh . . . ," Masao cautioned him. "Be quiet, don't move." Their bodies clenched up, their ears strained to listen, their eyes scanned the darkness. Finally, another flare went up. Dalton slowly reached for his rifle. The weapon weighed thirty pounds, so it was a struggle for him to maneuver it quietly.

"*Shhhh!*" Garcia motioned for him to halt.

"*Hey Yann-kee*—you go-ing to *die* tonight *Yann-kee*," the voice hollered out.

"Where's it coming from?" Garcia was wildly surveying the dense foliage. Dalton steadied his rifle in firing position. It seemed like years before another flare went up. Masao shifted his position so he could examine a different perimeter. His heart was pounding; sweat trickled down his cheek.

"I *see* you Yann-kee," the voice jeered.

"I don't know," Dalton answered Garcia in a hushed whisper. "It seems to be, what, a hundred yards away? What do you think?"

"Maybe. He could be up in that hill, over yonder." Escola pointed to a small hill jutting up from the forest.

"Yann-kee's gonna *die*," the voice taunted, followed by an evil-sounding laugh.

"It's not getting any closer," Masao assessed.

"What?" Dalton whispered.

"The voice. It's the same voice over and over, and it's not getting any closer to us. It's one guy, and he's staying in his cave."

Dalton nodded. "You could be right." Everyone was hyper alert for several minutes, watching flares go up, straining their eyes to see any hint of the enemy approaching. It was eerily quiet for several moments.

"Now I'm nervous," Masao whispered. He readied his sidearm and motioned for Escola to do the same. Another flare went up.

★ ★ ★

"Some of them must have been very confident, a-no? To do that," Masao said as he remembered those horrible and frightening nights. We were at Zippy's with Naki, and the two veterans had been reminiscing about the war all throughout breakfast.

"Yeah, because we were losing a lot of guys on that island, a lot of marines died there. Right, Abe?" Naki added.

"That's right. And the Japanese soldiers just kept coming in from somewhere, thousands of them. Nobody could ever figure out how their military was getting so many guys. Replacement soldiers. They just kept coming."

"And those bodies." Naki appeared physically sick. His face cringed and contorted as he looked at Masao, who immediately understood what he was talking about. Naki couldn't finish his thought, so Masao finished it for him.

"There were bodies all over that island, enemy bodies. We picked up our guys, a-no? We took our guys to a special place to be buried. But enemy bodies, you saw them everywhere. Hundreds."

"A military cemetery was made for our guys. Right, Abe?"

"That's right. But their guys. It was a different story. And sometimes," Masao continued. His attention shifted toward Alan and me, his eyes wide as he remembered his thought, "their bodies would swell up, you know, because of the heat."

I swallowed hard.

"And, sometimes, a soldier would go by and stick them with a knife, or bayonet, and their bodies would explode." He used his hands to illustrate what an exploding body looked like. Naki nodded, agreeing with Masao's memory.

"And every so often—" Masao continued. I put my hand up, palm out, to shield myself from his words. "Sometimes, their bodies would just explode on their own. Guts and bodily fluids would spray for feet." There was no amusement in Masao's voice. This was just part of the hell that was Peleliu.

"That stench. It would get into your, uh, uniform. It would get into your, your nostrils, and it would just stay there for days." Naki added more details. His face was that of a young man, reliving just one of the horrible aspects of the war.

Then the two soldiers at the table went silent, lost in their thoughts back in 1944 on that island out in the middle of the ocean. An island that had turned from a paradise into a hellhole and had become a graveyard for thousands. Masao made a "tsk" sound with his mouth, as he often did when he told stories or considered unthinkable situations.

"One time," Naki began. He had that look on his face, the same look Masao had when a memory was crystal clear in his mind. The same look Masao wore when a memory had to come out, had to be heard, maybe even recorded somehow. "I was—just landed on the island. What was that island, Abe?"

"Uh, Angaur? The first island?"

"No, no. The other one, what's the name, now?"

"Peleliu, no?"

"Yeah, Peleliu. And, uh, your team—you were already there. But we just arrived. And, I was attached to the 322nd Regimental Combat Team."

"322nd, that's right," Masao nodded.

The mood at the table was serious. "And there was this one lieutenant. He wasn't supposed to be with us, you know? But he knew
we had a live cave. He knew there was some action and he, you know,
wanted to be a part of it, I think."

EARLY OCTOBER 1944—PELELIU, PALAU

Naki, with his bodyguards close by, huddled around a cave nestled
in the side of a hill. The rest of the outfit stood at the perimeter,
scanning the brush for movement. Naki had maintained a steady
conversation with the Imperial soldier, who was holed up inside
the cave, and had persuaded him to surrender. But now, it seemed,
there was a glitch of some sort with headquarters. Their tech sergeant was on the radio some distance away in an ongoing negotia-
tion about what to do with this enemy prisoner.

One of Naki's bodyguards nudged him and pointed toward the
cave. "Do you think he's alone?"

Naki nodded. "And out of ammo. I think we'd all be dead if he
had any grenades left."

The bodyguard nodded in agreement, then nodded toward the
tech sergeant who had hung up the radio and was on his way to the
cave site with a scowl on his face. "Looks like trouble."

The tech sergeant stomped over. "We gotta wait, boys. The son of
a bitch lieutenant wants to *oversee* the operation."

Twenty minutes later, a lieutenant in a clean uniform arrived,
surrounded by an entourage of protection, and carrying a rifle with
a dark wood butt. "Okay, what do we got?" the lieutenant spouted.

"Sir, Nakamura here has been in contact. We think he's alone
and without ammunition."

"Very well. Nakkiworra, is it? Go ahead and do your thing. Let's
get him out here."

Naki nodded as he inched forward to the cave opening. "Soldier, are you still there?" he called out in Japanese.

"Yes," the Japanese soldier answered back. His voice was laced with fear.

"Okay, here's what I want you to do. Take off your uniform except for your underwear. Tell me when you have that done." Naki looked at the lieutenant. "I'm telling him to take off his uniform."

The lieutenant nodded. He looked at Naki as though Naki, himself, were from the Imperial Army and had somehow managed to slip into an American uniform.

Naki felt it and suddenly an uncomfortable feeling swept over him. He looked at his bodyguards, guys he had come to trust. They felt it too; he could see it in their eyes. The presence of this lieutenant poisoned the air around them. But one small nod from the bodyguard standing next to Naki eased his heart.

"Okay, I'm in my underwear," the Japanese soldier called from inside the cave.

"Okay. Now I want you to come out with your hands above your head. Nobody will hurt you. Just come out slowly and with your hands above your head. Okay?"

"Okay," the weak and petrified voice answered back.

Naki nodded toward his tech sergeant, "He's coming out."

As soon as Naki could see the enemy come into the light, he continued coaxing him out, "Just stop there for a moment and let your eyes adjust," he said when he noticed the soldier squinting in the sun. "It's okay, we're not going to hurt you. Keep coming out."

Inch by inch, the enemy soldier made his way out of the cave. He stood there in his underwear with his hands up, and his skeletal body trembled.

Naki looked at his tech sergeant for instructions when, out of nowhere, the lieutenant raised his rifle and shot the prisoner in the head at almost point-blank range. The blast of his rifle reverberated throughout the area. Blood spattered the shocked faces of Naki and his bodyguards. Naki watched with disbelief as the prisoner's limp body fell backward onto the jagged rocks. He felt his bodyguard step back and wondered if this was the end.

Am I next?

"Jesus," the tech sergeant said under his breath and then bit his tongue. The look on the faces of guys in the outfit were all the same: astonished and mortified. Naki looked down at the Japanese soldier and watched blood ooze onto the rocks. His neck looked broken by the fall.

The lieutenant didn't seem fazed in the least by the disturbed reaction of the platoon. He lowered his rifle, looked around for anyone to dare him, glanced a steely glare at Naki, and then gave a slight nod of self-approval at a job well done. As if it were part of his routine, he searched the ground for a stone, spun his rifle around and

Saburo Nakamura (front left), 322nd RCT, interrogating a Japanese medical officer on Angaur, 1944

Hiroki Takahashi, Eighty-First Infantry Division HQ, checks out an enemy cave on Peleliu, 1944

carved a notch in the butt using the sharp stone as a carving tool. Naki noticed that this was his seventeenth notch. *He's keeping track of all the enemies he's killing.* The lieutenant gave one last look at the man he had just killed, the trophy he'd just scored, and marched off.

Naki found himself alone at the cave opening, looking down at the soldier who had followed his instructions, who had trusted that he wouldn't be harmed, who wasn't armed, who wasn't even dressed in his uniform. He felt a tap on his arm.

"Let's go, Naki," his bodyguard said as he pulled Naki to the safety of the platoon.

★ ★ ★

Back at Zippy's, we were in a world of our own at the table. Naki's memory was heartrending; its heaviness lingered at the table, even while busy waitresses bustled by.

"It was just—murder, you know?" Naki looked around the table. The feeling of injustice was intense; the responsibility Naki felt and had carried for almost seventy years was palpable. "He only came out of that cave, you know, because I persuaded him to come out. I felt like I was part of it. But I didn't know that was going to happen that way. He wasn't killed in a battle or anything like that. It was just—murder."

It was quiet while we all digested this ugly piece of history.

"Not your fault, Naki. There were guys like that, a-no?" Masao comforted Naki. "Did you tell me that before?"

"No, I never told anybody about this. Nobody, not even my wife. It's too . . ." Naki didn't have words to describe what he felt, but the look on his face was pure shame. "Besides, I don't have anyone to corroborate my story, you know? Who would have believed me?"

Masao nodded. "I would have believed you."

After our Hawai'i trip, we returned to our regular routine. It was springtime and I was on my way to Masao's place. He had slept until eleven that morning, then turned on the TV to the Japanese channel. After watching a while, he had decided to make himself a fried egg sandwich. A decent cook, he always had the thick-sliced Japanese bread on hand, as well as eggs, tomato, and lettuce. A fried egg sandwich was something he enjoyed often. He started the toast while he fried his egg, scrambled style. When his egg was done and the toast not, he'd put the egg aside and gone back to his recliner to watch TV.

But the toast burned black. Smoke billowed into his room and set off the fire alarm. Masao, a little hard of hearing, was enjoying a show that really captured his attention—obviously, because he didn't notice the smoke or hear the alarm. Meanwhile the facility management was notified of the fire alarm, as was the local fire department.

Masao watched TV, having forgotten about his toast by then and oblivious to the impending intrusion.

"Huh?" Masao uttered when four firemen bolted into his apartment.

"Sir, are you okay?" one of the firemen asked. The others searched the apartment, and the problem in the kitchen was quickly discovered.

"What's going on?" Masao asked, confused and feeling embarrassed—another old codger who could no longer be trusted to live on his own.

"Your toast, sir, it set off the alarm."

"Ohhhhh, my toast." Masao smiled. "It was for my fried egg sandwich." He was now up and rolling himself into the kitchen to make his own inspection. It was true. His popped toast was black and smoldering. He glanced at the firemen surrounding him. "You guys sure did respond quickly!"

The firemen smiled at him.

Masao wanted to offer something for their trouble. "I make you a fried egg sandwich. You want one?"

Masao recounted his morning excitement to me while we were on our way to the casino. His stories, even contemporary ones, were always entertaining. While part of him was embarrassed to cause so much trouble for the firefighters, the lighter part of him chuckled at himself. He was in a chatty mood that day and his thoughts eventually took him back to our visit with Naki when the two of them were telling war stories. Remembering Naki seemed to spark more of Masao's memories from the battlefield during World War II, and I was happy to see the soldier in him emerge once again.

EARLY OCTOBER 1944—PELELIU, PALAU

Cooper's squad had been pushing hard toward Umurbrogol, a peak on the island that was actually a conglomeration of coral hills. The Japanese navy had dominated this part of the island and had held it fiercely, with new troops coming in from somewhere to continue fighting off Allied Forces. Recon had been working day and night to try to identify where the supply line for the Japanese military was, but they had come up empty-handed. The dead bodies from both sides continued to pile up.

Dusk was closing in and Cooper wanted his guys back at line camp where flares would be going up. "Hold your fire. Coming through," Cooper shouted as they approached the primitive camp that was supposed to provide some sort of secure shelter and food for the tired soldiers.

"Grab a bite and get yourselves dug in," Cooper ordered. Masao attempted to dig through the tough clay with his helmet. A medic approached him, a soldier Masao had never seen before.

"Hey, Sarge. John Galligan." He held out his hand to shake. Masao took it, confused by the hospitality. "Here." Galligan handed Masao a tin cup full of steaming-hot water.

What's all the hospitality about? Masao held the tin cup.

"For coffee or something. You got one of those little packets of instant coffee from your rations? Or just let it cool and drink it. It's safe. It's been boiled." Galligan nodded and then disappeared as quickly as he had arrived in Masao's space.

Masao searched his pockets for an instant coffee packet and finally found one in a beaten-up package. He ripped it open with his teeth, careful not to spill a drop of the precious, clean water, then sprinkled it into the tin cup. He swirled the mixture, then took it in, closing his eyes to get the full effect.

He imagined that he was back in San Bernardino on a crisp, autumn morning, when coffee tasted its best, or in that wonderful diner in Chicago before Pearl Harbor had ever been a blip on the radar. He imagined that he was anywhere but the South Pacific, where he was dirty and hadn't seen a shower in weeks, where he was hot and exhausted and most of the time scared for his life. He sipped the coffee that, in any of those other scenarios, would have tasted horrible. But in this moment, it tasted like the finest coffee in the world.

★ ★ ★

"Every time I was at a line camp, that guy, Galligan, would bring me hot water. He was really nice to me, boy," Masao remembered with fondness and gratitude.

"How often were you at line camp? Every night?" I was struggling to understand how the battlefield worked.

"No, not every night. Sometimes we would advance on the line, a-no? And then just have to set up camp when it got dark. Those were tough nights, boy. Really tough." He gazed out the window of the car. It was as if he was watching himself in his mind's eye, replaying history, one frame at a time.

"Heh! My bodyguards and I, we used to pass the time whispering back and forth on those nights. We should have been watching for the enemy, a-no? But we would get bored. Heh!"

OCTOBER 1944—PELELIU, PALAU

Cooper's squad was ordered to stay out for the night—it was too far for them to fall back. They had stopped advancing at the foot of a hill that had supposedly been secured. There was a high degree of likelihood that intricate caves had been tunneled throughout the hill, even though recon had assured them the caves were clear. Cooper was a shrewd soldier, though, and knew how to protect his squad in even the riskiest situations.

Masao and his bodyguards were ordered to get some shut-eye before taking over perimeter watch. It had rained all day and the men were soggy and hot at the same time. Still, they tried. They found a tree to lean against and lowered their heads with helmets on, weapons readied. The rain stopped and the jungle became eerily quiet.

"Apple pie," Dalton whispered in the darkness out of nowhere.

"Are you sleep talking again, old boy?" Garcia nudged him.

"It's funny what you miss. Right now, I miss my grandma's apple pie. She makes it every Thanksgiving and Christmas." Dalton's face revealed his longing for the sweet taste of his grandmother's apple pie.

There was only the sound of raindrops falling from palm leaves. The skies opened up and the moon shone through clouds that had been so relentlessly pouring rain.

"I miss my girl, Lupe. But now that you mention it, I sure wish I had some of my mom's tamales. She takes days to make her tamales, wrapped in banana leaves. God, those are good. When I get home, I'm going to have her make me a batch. Maybe two batches." Garcia could smell his mom's fresh tamales baking on the open wood fire stove they had in the backyard. He breathed in through his nose, imagining he was there with his family.

Masao listened as he scanned the terrain.

After a few moments, Escola contributed. "I have a little girl. She's three. She has curly red hair and a beautiful smile." Escola smiled as he thought about his daughter's face. "I have no idea where she got the red hair. There's no red hair on my side. But I know my wife didn't cheat. So it's got to be in the gene pool somewhere. But my little girl . . . her smile . . . makes me melt. I miss that. I miss melting when I see her smile." The other guys looked at Escola and realized he had it the worst. Escola was a man of few words but, evidently, had the most to say. His eyes filled with tears. The men looked away to give him his privacy.

"What about you, Sarge? What's the first thing you're going to do when you get home?" Garcia asked Masao.

"Huh. You know, I don't think I have a home anymore," he said.

"What are you talking about?" Dalton blurted. "You must have had a home when you left, Abe."

"I was living with my uncle in California. But he was sent away. The whole family was." There wasn't a hint of self-pity in his voice.

Garcia and Escola, both from California, understood right away. They both nodded with genuine empathy. But Dalton didn't have a clue.

"What? Where'd they go?"

"Jesus, Jack. His family was sent *away*. To a camp. An *internment* camp. Everything was taken from them. Everything. Get it?" Garcia was annoyed. Masao smiled at this and nodded in agreement. Garcia had it right. Except for the part about his uncle being sent to prison, he had it right. Except for the part about the grocery store being swindled from his family, he had it right. Except for the part that he had a little cousin who had been born in a dusty barrack out in the desert, he had it right. It was close enough.

"Okay, settle down, Tony. Jesus." Dalton thought for a few minutes, trying to understand. "So, I don't get it. Where are you going to go when you are discharged?"

Garcia had just about had it with Dalton and hit him on the arm, giving him a "shut the hell up" look.

"What did I say?"

"It's okay, Tony," Masao gently eased Garcia's heart. "Jack, I honestly don't know where I'm going to go when I get discharged. I have no idea." He paused for a moment. "If I make it out, I'll find a new home."

Cooper's squad had spent days on the line. The constant sound of mortar explosions indicated that they were very close to the action. They were finally falling back to line camp to replenish their ammo and catch a quick break. The marines were close by and a few lingered in the area.

"Coming through. Coming through. Hold your fire," Cooper announced as they came within forty yards, waiting for the signal to move forward. The exhausted soldiers hiked into the primal-looking line camp, eager to get their hands on some K rations. Out of nowhere, a marine major jumped in front of them, flailing his side arm. The squad sprang into action surrounding Masao, who was startled and stepped back into the loose huddle.

"Hey—Hey! There's a *Jap*," the major shouted as he wildly pointed his sidearm directly at Masao. Things got tense in a hurry. The major took aim, ready to fire. Garcia quickly stepped in front of Masao as a human shield.

"Major, he's with us, sir."

"He's a *Jap*. Don't you see? Move out of the way or I'll kill you both." His eyes were jittery and unfocused as he motioned for Garcia to move.

"You shut up, major. You're not going to touch him." Cooper secured the major's sidearm with little struggle. The major looked confused and unstable, unable to digest that his own soldiers would turn against him.

"Sir. He's United States. He's an American soldier." Cooper wanted to avoid further escalation.

"They can't be trusted. He might be a spy," the officer protested, realizing he was outnumbered.

Cooper assessed the camp and spotted the commanding officer.

"Major, sir, let's check in with the CO." He took the major by the arm and escorted him. Garcia relaxed and looked at Masao.

"That was a close one," Masao uttered.

Cooper saluted the commanding officer while keeping an eye on the major, who was watching Masao's every movement.

"Sir. We encountered several pockets of enemy along East Road. The ridges in that area are full of Japanese soldiers. They keep coming in from somewhere." Cooper pointed to the map.

"Those goddamn little gnats. Keep your eye on him. He shouldn't be here," the nervous major paced back and forth. The commanding officer glanced at him, then at Cooper.

"Have your guys grab supplies and move out. We'll have you go along the back, this way." He pointed to the map. "See what you can find. It's frustrating as hell out there, I know that. But let's have you move out sooner than later," the CO said as he nodded toward the major.

Cooper nodded back that he understood. Masao wouldn't make it through the night in the same camp with the unstable officer, who was now mumbling to himself. "Yes, sir." He glanced over at his tired soldiers and sighed. This would be bad news for them.

His squad had scattered throughout the camp, some replenishing their ammo, some filling up their pockets with all the rations they could, not knowing when they would be back. Cooper approached Masao and his bodyguards.

"What kind of training do those marines get anyway?" Garcia asked, still in shock from the incident.

"It's got to be battle fatigue," Cooper said, watching the major skulk around. He opened up a map and laid it out on the ground. Soldiers from his squad gathered around.

"The guys in these hills here are on foot. No tanks can get in there. We're going to continue covering the back side—up this way. Get your gear ready. We move out in thirty." He avoided looking at the soldiers surrounding him, not sure he could take the disappointment on their young faces. They were badly in need of sleep.

"What about these other damn squads, Sarge?" one of his soldiers barked out, near the end of his rope and desperately needing a break.

"Soldier. These are our orders. And we're going to follow them."

While the squad prepared to move out, Masao sat and waited, lost in his thoughts. He knew why the squad had to move out and felt that weight on his shoulders. Maybe he should suggest to Cooper that another squad absorb him for a while. Maybe he and the major should just duke it out. Maybe—his thoughts were interrupted by Medic Galligan.

"Here you go, Sarge." Galligan handed Masao a cup of hot coffee, already mixed.

"Thanks, John." Masao took the cup and sipped the coffee. "That's really good."

Galligan sat down beside Masao.

"How are you holding up, Abe? They haven't given you a lot of rest."

"You too, no?"

"Just came back from taking eight more back to HQ. In fact—" Galligan ran over to grab his pack, came back, and sat down. He pulled out some bread. Bread was unheard of on the line. Masao's eyes were wide with hunger—his mouth watered at the sight of the halved loaf with thick crust.

"Ohhhhh," Masao breathed out.

"Let's chow down," Galligan said with a smile as he ripped off a piece for Masao.

"That's awful nice of you. How did you get your hands on this?"

"Well, you know how HQ hoards all the good stuff. I just helped myself when nobody was looking. I figure we deserve it as much as they do."

"Heh!" Masao nodded and ate another bite. The steady diet of crackers, dried meat, and chocolate had gotten old weeks earlier. Nothing had ever tasted as good as this bread did. He wasn't even bothered by the dirt from Galligan's pack embedded in the white center. He just brushed it off. He closed his eyes and shut out the sounds of explosions in the distance so he could bring all his senses to his taste buds. He took in a deep breath.

"John, thank you."

"You bet."

★ ★ ★

"That bread, boy, it tasted so doggone good," Masao said. A hellish battle around him—a morsel of bread. I didn't want to say a word.

I turned into the casino driveway and headed for the valet. "How about we just keep driving around so you can tell me more stories?"

"Heh! I've got to go to work." By work, he meant getting inside to gamble. He looked at me and saw the longing in my eyes. I wasn't ready to leave 1944 or Peleliu.

"Come on. I'll tell you a story about this one Japanese guy."

OCTOBER 1944—PELELIU, PALAU

It was a particularly dark night. Masao and his bodyguards were dug in, weapons loaded and ready. Flares had been going up nonstop for the last few hours—the enemy resistance seemed to reignite itself daily. Another flare went up and, suddenly, shots were fired somewhere in line camp.

"Ehhhhhhh," a voice squealed in the night. It was impossible to tell if it was an American or Japanese.

"I hope that was a Jap," Dalton whispered, steadying his rifle in firing position and searching the camp. Another flare went up and commotion stirred from behind them.

"It's coming from the supply hut," Garcia said. He squatted, ready to bolt toward the turmoil.

"Who goes there?" a voice called out in the darkness.

"That sounds like McCoy," Masao whispered, getting his sidearm in position. All at once, an explosion shook the ground and brightened the area behind the supply hut.

"*Take cover*," Masao shouted. The four dropped to their bellies. Another flare went up and they wildly scanned the area looking for the enemy, certain they were being ambushed. Things went crazy. Other soldiers didn't take any precautions and started shooting haphazardly into the night.

"What are they shooting at?" Dalton had his finger on the trigger, looking for a target, any target.

"Jack. Wait!" Masao yelled.

"Wait for orders." Escola, too, urged Dalton to hold his fire. The rapid fire continued lighting up the area with flickers of charge as bullets were fired from all directions. Finally, the commanding voice of an officer called out into the night.

"Hold your fire," one of the tech sergeants shouted. But the fire continued.

"Hold your fire, goddammit!" another voice yelled.

"That was Coop," Garcia assessed. Masao nodded. The firing stopped. Another flare went up. There was no movement. The only sounds in the dark came from soldiers as they made jittery, nervous gasps.

"I hope none of our guys bit the dust in that chaos." Dalton stated the obvious, unaware that he had been dangerously close to committing that very sin.

After a night of little sleep, the sun came up and shed light on the havoc of the previous night. Masao jerked awake; he had fallen asleep while squatting against a tree. He spotted some soldiers gathered around behind the supply hut. Rubbing his eyes, he noticed Garcia was just waking up as well.

"The supply hut is still there," he motioned. "I'm going to go take a look."

"I'll go with you." Garcia got up.

Masao and Garcia joined Mess Sergeant McCoy and other soldiers near the body of a Japanese soldier. His head was completely blown off.

"How did this guy get so close?" Garcia asked McCoy.

"Not sure. Look, he's unarmed. No weapons."

"He had a grenade," Masao pointed out.

"He had K rations in every pocket," said McCoy. "He was stealing food. He could have blown us up with his grenade, but he didn't. He blew himself up, put the goddamn thing right in his mouth. He just wanted some food. Almost made it out of here too."

"You've got too much heart for these bastards," another soldier retorted.

"Soldiers like us. Only without food or water." McCoy held on to his heart, his humanity.

Cooper joined in, looking at the dead Imperial soldier with no head. "Any intelligence?"

Masao scratched his chin. "You kiddin' me?" But he knew he had to. He stuck his hands in the blood and brain matter, searching the soldier's pockets for anything useful. The only thing he found was a pack of cigarettes and those he kept for himself.

"The concerning thing is, his cave couldn't have been too far," Cooper surmised. "How the hell did he infiltrate our line, for Christ's sake? We've got to move this camp."

★ ★ ★

The summer had turned into an unusual scorcher. Masao, a native of the desert in California, loved the heat. I walked in, and he was ready to go. He wore dressy pants and an aloha shirt but had a sweater ready, knowing the casino would be air-conditioned.

I greeted him and sat down for our usual small talk before we would leave for the casino.

"One time, we were approaching a cave . . ."

This had not happened before, his jumping right into the story. This memory must have come to him sometime in the morning, and he had probably struggled to hold onto it for a few hours, in fear that if he lost it, it would be gone forever. He wasn't going to waste any time with niceties. He wanted me to hear this.

OCTOBER 1944—PELELIU, PALAU

Line camp continued to move every night. It was clear that US soldiers were being watched closely by the enemy. The Japanese had been smart about designing the labyrinth of caves so that they had a bird's-eye view from hundreds of points on the island. Cooper's squad had just returned with some documents they had found in an abandoned foxhole. Masao was reading the worthless material before handing it off to one of the military couriers, who would take batches of documents and letters back to HQ for further analysis. Galligan had handed him a hot cup of coffee that he was just finishing.

"Cooper," the radio patrolman called out. Masao cringed. He knew this meant that they were going back out.

"Abe. Get your guys. There's another goddamn cave," Cooper called. "I don't know if there's an end to these damn caves, son of a bitch," he muttered to himself.

Masao gulped the last of his coffee. Then he had an idea and looked around for Frank, the other Nisei interpreter attached to the 321st. Frank, as it had turned out, didn't have the Japanese skills the military needed. To make matters even worse for Masao, Frank wasn't at all military material, he was more of a desk man. All the tech sergeants were aware of this and avoided taking Frank out to interpret on the line. Cooper had a lock on Masao and tried to keep him with his own squad at all times, something that pleased Masao most of the time. He liked Cooper and felt secure with his outfit, but he wanted Frank to pull his own weight.

"Where's Kubota—can't he go out?" he asked Cooper as he reloaded in the ammo hut.

"Not on your life. Besides, he's already out, left an hour ago with Thompson's squad. And you should be thanking me. All these damn tech sergeants want to attach you." Masao smiled at this, at Cooper's way of expressing himself.

After an hour of hiking they spotted the cave. When they came within twenty yards of its opening, they all crouched and hovered in the brush.

"Jesus. That's a small opening," Masao said in a low voice to Cooper.

"It's too dark in there to see what's waiting for us," Cooper said. "Come on." He motioned to Masao. The two shimmied closer. When they were within ten yards and somewhat shielded by small boulders, Cooper nodded toward the cave. It was the routine they had developed. Masao knew exactly what to do and what to say.

"Come out. You will not be harmed." Masao called out in Japanese. Silence. Masao waited a few seconds and then called out again. "Come out. Leave any weapons inside. Hold your hands up so we can see you are unarmed." There was, again, no response. Masao looked at Cooper.

"I don't hear anything. Do you?" Cooper asked. Masao listened then shook his head no.

"What do you think? It might be empty, or they're dead inside," Cooper shifted his weight, then jerked his head like he heard something. "Did you hear that?"

"No," Masao whispered.

"*Goddamn.* This jungle's playing tricks on my mind." He looked back at his squad and made a hand signal to check on the perimeter of the area.

The hand signal came back: area still secure.

"Let's throw in a grenade," Masao suggested.

"Those idiots back at HQ would shit in their clean uniforms if we destroyed intelligence," Cooper replied, even though he liked the idea. "Fire a shot in," he ordered Masao. Masao fired a shot directly into the opening. Nothing. Not a sound, not a groan.

"I think it's empty," Masao whispered.

There was a long moment while Cooper figured out his next move. The soldiers behind them looked at each other.

"We have our orders. I'm going in," he finally said. He motioned for Dalton and Garcia to come forward. Cooper approached the cave. It was silent but for occasional jungle sounds. The four hovered around the opening.

"Give 'em one more chance," Cooper ordered. Masao nodded.

"This is your last chance. Come out, or you will be killed," Masao called out in Japanese. Cooper waited another few seconds.

"Let's get this over with." And with that, Cooper squeezed through cave opening and disappeared inside. Masao was next. He went in with ease.

Once inside, Masao struggled while his eyes adjusted to the dark. Dalton came through the opening, followed by Garcia. They all stood armed and ready to shoot.

"Stand guard," Cooper called out.

The four stood in a small area at the opening of the cave. There was little light, but enough. They were astonished by what they saw.

"Oh my God," Cooper breathed out.

Twenty Japanese naval soldiers, lying on their backs, head to head, in full uniform. All still.

"Dalton, make sure they're dead," Cooper said softly.

"They look dead," Dalton protested.

"Make sure, *goddammit*." Cooper was jumpy. Dalton got out a knife.

"Jack. Not that way," Cooper directed. Dalton nodded, put his knife away, and went from body to body checking pulses.

"They're dead, all right. Cold."

At the back of the cave, seated in the middle of where the heads united, a lone Japanese naval officer sat in full dress uniform, slumped over.

"What about him?" Cooper nodded to the far end of the cave.

"Cover me." Dalton stepped in between the dead bodies, making his way to the back of the cave. Within an arm's length, he reached out to tilt the officer's head up. His fingers reached the forehead, and he used the officer's hair to pull his head to an upright position, but instead of the head tilting up, his entire scalp came off. Maggots fell out and dropped everywhere.

"*Ehhhhh,*" Dalton yelped, jumping back. "*Jesus.* He frantically brushed the maggots off his hands as he stepped between bodies, stumbling to catch his ground.

"Out of food, no water, the enemy closing in. Christ . . ." Cooper shook his head.

Outside, they sat near the cave opening and searched through documents, handing letters and books to Masao to sort by order of importance. Cooper was on the radio reporting in. "It appears to be some sort of mass suicide. A morphine overdose would be my guess. They must have stockpiled it."

"What about intelligence?" the voice on the radio asked abruptly.

"We've secured all weapons and documents. It looks like they burned the important stuff." Cooper rubbed his forehead and looked back at the cave opening.

A few yards away, Garcia and Dalton sat near Masao.

"Anything interesting?" Garcia motioned to the papers Masao was reading.

"Letters to their families," Masao answered, while reading the private thoughts of a soldier to his beloved wife.

"Hey, Sarge," Dalton looked over at Masao. This would be the first time he addressed Masao by his title instead of his last name. It got Masao's attention and he looked up from the letter.

"Hmm," Masao nodded.

"Your first name—Maseeo."

"Masao."

"It got a meaning or anything?"

"I've never thought about that before. Let's see here now." He took a stick and wrote his name in *kanji* in the dirt. Dalton watched him with interest. Masao pointed to each *kanji* as he interpreted. "It would be something like 'right man' or 'correct man.' Something like that." Masao used his foot to erase the characters.

"Correct man," Garcia pondered the translation. "That fits you."

Masao noticed a maggot on Dalton's sleeve. "You've got a . . ." He pointed.

Dalton saw it and brushed it off with a stifled squeal.

"Let's get back," Cooper called out.

"What about the cave?" a soldier asked. The protocol was to blast foxholes or caves apart so they could no longer be used. Cooper thought about it for a moment. His soldiers were all looking at him waiting for an answer. Nobody moved to ready a grenade as they normally would. Everyone had the same thoughts. It was a tomb. The soldiers had laid themselves to rest. It would be a travesty to disturb their thoughtful grave.

"There's no way out the back of it—this is the only way in or out. It's not a threat. Let's close it in a way they can remain at peace." This was a direct violation of orders, but Cooper no longer cared. It was just one way he could hold on to a bit of decency, and his guys understood. Soldiers barricaded the cave opening with boulders and rocks, making it difficult for anyone else to enter.

On their way back to line camp, Cooper received orders to fall back to HQ. Cooper muttered the entire two-mile trek, bitching about how he hated the officers and how they didn't know about advancing the line. One officer in particular had commandeered the radio from HQ and had been asking Masao all sorts of questions about the intelligence uncovered at the cave. By the time they drew near HQ, every soldier in Cooper's squad was pissed.

"Cooper, where do you want these?" Dalton motioned to the Japanese weapons they had been hauling.

"Let the MPs deal with it."

A second lieutenant eagerly approached the tired and dirty unit as they neared HQ. He directed his question at Sergeant Cooper while he looked at Masao. "No useful documents?" The first words out of the officer's mouth made Masao's blood boil.

"Sir, as I said in my report, they burned anything of importance. Just personal letters, that's all we have," Cooper answered tersely. "The mere fact that we discovered a mass suicide is indicative of a weakening enemy," Cooper reasoned.

"I'll be the judge of that, Sergeant. You just follow orders. Now, let me see the letters." Masao handed the letters to Cooper who handed them to the second lieutenant.

"Abe scanned through them on the line, out there," Cooper pointed to the battle zone.

"Well, maybe Abe needs to scan them again. More thoroughly this time. Abe, come with me." Masao and Cooper exchanged a look. Masao reluctantly followed the officer deep into the protected gut of HQ.

"Make yourself at home." The second lieutenant nodded for Masao to sit on mounted sandbags as he took a random letter from the pile of papers Cooper had handed to him. "Here, what's in this one."

Masao took the letter and glanced at it; he had already read it. "This one is about how much he missed his wife. He mentions the Yumoto Hot Springs. They must have visited there or something."

"All right, all right. Nothing about the war? What about their orders?"

"Nothing, sir. It's a love letter." The second lieutenant snatched the letter from Masao's hands and crumpled it up out of frustration. He threw it in a small burning fire. Masao watched as the words of a soldier to his love went up in smoke. He looked at the commanding officer, who was selecting the next letter to immolate.

"All right, next one. There's got to be something worthwhile in one of these." He handed another letter to Masao who opened it, his heart aching for the Imperial soldiers and their loved ones back in Japan. Had an honorable Japanese officer encountered the tomb, he most certainly would have taken these precious letters and made sure they were delivered. He would have given thought to the families of the men and provided them with the closure that they certainly craved. If the letters had been left with Cooper, the same might have happened. But now, in all likelihood, all of the letters would perish in flames.

★ ★ ★

Bon Odori is a summer festival providing a special place and time to honor ancestors who have passed on. People of all ages and ethnicities came from miles around to the Seattle Buddhist Temple to join in the festivities. The streets around the temple were decorated with colorful Japanese lanterns. Booths were set up along the sidewalks, offering crafts and delicious Japanese food. Masao made a nice comfortable seat out of his walker, and Alan and I sat on the curb and watched the parade of Japanese women in their kimonos perform a dance. Then the *taiko* drummers rolled out huge drums and played several numbers in a most choreographed and artful way. But the best part of the afternoon was watching Masao smile as he enjoyed the performances. The smell of *yakitori*, grilled chicken, permeated the air along South Main Street by the temple, and it made my stomach growl. Evidently, I wasn't the only one.

"Are you hungry?" I asked Masao.

"I could eat," he answered, happy that someone else noticed all the food.

"You guys want *yakitori*?" Alan asked. Masao and I both nodded, and that was all we needed to do. Alan would take care of the rest. I rested my arm on Masao's walker to get comfortable, held my face toward the sun, and closed my eyes to feel the warmth. Then I felt his gentle touch on my arm. I looked up at him and shielded my eyes so I could see him better.

"This reminds me of a time during the war," he said. I shifted so I could hear him better. "One time, we were on orders to advance the line, and we came to a part that had been torn up *really* bad. There had been a recent battle, a-no? A lot of dead bodies lying around, blood everywhere." He glanced at me to make sure I was listening. "And, we smelled something . . ."

OCTOBER 1944—PELELIU, PALAU

Masao was back with Cooper's squad. They hiked through burned-out brush until they entered a bowled area where there were signs of a treacherous battle: demolished terrain, torched trees, and scorched ground. Tractors were busy shoving enemy bodies into trenches while medics tended to the Allied wounded.

"No prisoners here," Cooper assessed.

"Doesn't look like it," Masao agreed. Cooper signaled for the radioman when Garcia came forward and stood next to Masao.

"Do you smell that?"

It was as if they were in a trance. "Yes, I do," Masao sniffed the air. He squinted to a spot where the smell was coming from and noticed Naki and his bodyguards cooking something over a small fire on the other side of the valley. He started walking. Seeing Naki alive was almost secondary to following his nose.

"Where you going? Hey—*Abe*," Cooper shouted as he followed.

"This won't take long." Masao motioned for his squad to come along. They arrived at the other side of the burned-out valley where Naki was cooking rice over a small fire. A hundred-pound bag sat nearby.

"Hey—Abe! Look what we found. Join us," Naki exclaimed, excited to see that his buddy was still alive. They shook hands and smiled while Masao stared at the steaming rice over the fire. Masao took his helmet off and filled it, eating it with his hand. Garcia squatted next to the fire and did the same. The rest of the squad stood around, bewildered.

"It's not like it's a sirloin steak, Abe," Dalton commented. Still, Masao and Garcia were in heaven as they stuffed their mouths.

"Please, fill up. It might be weeks before you get hot food again." Naki had appointed himself the host, inviting his guests to eat. In the middle of a war zone, cooked rice was about as good as it could get.

As Cooper's squad prepared to head out, Masao stayed with Naki until the last possible moment.

"Take care of yourself," Masao nodded at Naki as he grabbed his gear.

"You do the same." They shook hands and held on a long time before Masao joined Cooper's waiting squad.

It wasn't long before they were back in the jungle. "Did you get any of that rice to cook up later?" Cooper asked Masao. He had noticed Masao's face as he was eating the rice, content as a baby with a bottle.

"Nothing to carry it with."

"Guess not." Cooper checked his map. "You know, that's the first time I've ever had rice."

Masao was shocked. "No kidding." He studied Cooper. "Well, what'd you think?"

"Not much flavor, but it was okay, I guess. At least I feel full. I haven't felt full since we left Honolulu. Come to think of it, there was rice on my plate at a restaurant there. But I didn't try it."

"You didn't eat any of it?"

"No, I thought it looked like maggots so I didn't touch it."

"Maggots. Where in the blazes are you from?"

"Idaho. Potato country. I miss potatoes. I hope I get to eat them someday soon, Abe." Cooper checked the map as he walked. "I miss home." He looked at Masao who nodded in agreement. "Where are you from, Abe?"

"San Bernardino."

"You got a wife back there?"

"No wife. Not even a girl."

Cooper studied Masao. "I'll tell you one thing, if I had a daughter, I'd want her to be with a guy like you." This took Masao by surprise. He looked at Cooper, who didn't realize the importance of his compliment.

"Thank you, sir." The sounds of battle were ever present.

"You married with kids?" Masao asked after a bit. His question seemed to hit a nerve. He saw Cooper's face twitch.

"I'm not sure."

Masao listened and waited, not wanting to pry.

"I was married when I left. But it's been two months since I've gotten a letter from her. And the last letter I got—something wasn't right. It had all the niceties, but no feeling. She didn't even sign it 'Love, Serena.' Just 'Serena.' Like she was a buddy or something." He looked off in the distance as he talked, not wanting to attach any feeling to his words.

"Maybe you're just imagining things. Since you're far away from her. And two months isn't a long time, especially since we're out here in the middle of nowhere."

"Maybe. But the mail's been coming regular. It's the only goddamn regular thing about this place."

Masao walked beside Cooper, silently.

"No. My gut tells me that she's moved on. That the home I left won't be there when I get back."

Masao wasn't going to argue with anyone's gut feeling, especially since he so often relied on his own gut for guidance. He felt for Cooper, one of the best guys on the line. Trying to deal with a broken heart on top of the task of daily survival must have been excruciating for him. He wanted to give the guy some sort of relief.

"Hey Coop." He nudged Cooper who looked over. "You're right about one thing."

"What's that?"

"Grains of rice, they do look like maggots."

Back at the Eighty-First Infantry Division headquarters, Cooper walked with a sense of purpose toward the ammo hut. "Let's load up," he said. "Ah, shit, look what's arrived." He nodded toward a batch of new replacement officers. They were clean-cut college graduates, virgins of battle, and assumed know-it-alls.

"Try to ignore them. Let's get our gear and get the hell out of here," Cooper advised and walked faster. They passed a replacement officer who was a first lieutenant.

"Hey. Soldiers," the first lieutenant said.

Cooper kept walking and Masao followed. Neither looked at their ranking officer.

"Hey. *Soldiers!*" He had obviously been trained to be tough on soldiers of lesser rank.

Cooper stopped and turned toward the young officer. He casually looked around and then pointed to himself. "Who? Me?" Cooper challenged.

"You two. Get *back* here."

Cooper hesitated, then took a few steps closer. Masao walked in step with Cooper. "Yeah?" Cooper scowled.

"You see this bar?" the first lieutenant asked, pointing to the bar on his untarnished uniform.

"Huh. What is that, anyway?" Cooper's words were soaked with sarcasm. Masao resisted the urge to laugh.

"It's a bar," the young man said condescendingly. "When you see this bar, it means *officer.* What are you supposed to do when you see an officer?"

"What *are* we supposed to do?" Cooper was getting heated. Masao wondered if the young officer would make it to his next sentence.

"When you see this bar, you're supposed to salute. I'm a first lieutenant. You are a tech sergeant, and *you,*" he pointed his boney index finger at Masao, "I don't even know what you are." His words dripped with contempt.

"He doesn't know what you are, Abe," Cooper said light-heartedly to Masao. Then he gave the first lieutenant a steely look and leaned in toward him. "Okay, lieutenant, I want you to remember this. You see those hills up there?" Cooper nodded toward the torched landscape.

The young officer looked up. "What about 'em?"

Cooper's face intensified. "Those hills are full of the enemy. Full of Nips. And we're going to be up on that line. We're headed up there now. You'll be on the line too—maybe tomorrow, maybe a week from now. And out there," he pointed hard to make his point, "out there, you're going to see a living hell. Charred bodies. Still smoldering, some of 'em. Soldiers, our men, clinging to life and knowing they're near the end. And around every goddamn corner, snipers are waiting." He let his words sink in.

"But here's the deal—don't worry about your front side. Those guys shooting at you can't shoot for shit." Cooper pointed to the first lieutenant's bar. "I want you to watch your back. People in back of the line have much better aim than the guys in front of you. Those guys are trained to kill, and they aren't going to waste any bullets. Don't worry about the front, you watch your back."

The young first lieutenant was speechless. He wasn't sure how to decipher Cooper's message and Cooper saw that. "You're going to earn your bars out here in a different way. Understand? Lieutenant. *Sir.*" His last words nailed in his point. The first lieutenant stood mute as he watched Cooper and Masao march off.

In the ammo hunt, Cooper's frustration showed as he grabbed bullets and a few grenades.

"Salute my ass," he huffed under his breath. "I'd sooner salute that Jap who was stealing food from us a couple weeks ago." He stopped in his tracks and glanced at Masao. "No offense intended, Abe."

"None taken."

Cooper's squad had another prisoner they had taken into custody. There were no documents of any kind in his cave, and the prisoner was so thirsty and hungry that he was lethargic. Masao sat the man down, and McCoy brought over a plate of food and handed it to him. The prisoner looked confused.

"It's okay, eat it," Masao directed him in Japanese. The prisoner reluctantly took a few bites. Masao nodded. "In a few minutes, another soldier will escort you back to headquarters. You will be asked more questions there. There's nothing to worry about. You won't be tortured or killed," Masao continued. His instructions were rote at this point. McCoy handed the prisoner a canteen of water. This prompted Masao to drink from his own canteen.

"Hey, Mac, do you have any more water tablets? I feel like I'm just drinking mud," Masao asked McCoy.

"There's more coming from HQ. I'll save you a few."

Masao nodded.

Hearing the conversation from a distance, Galligan came over with a tin cup of steaming water and a coffee packet. "Here you go, Abe."

"Thanks, John. I needed this." Masao fixed his coffee, savored a sip, and looked around the empty line camp. From the looks of it, there was Cooper's squad and one other squad that appeared to be about half the size of normal. Soldiers looked dejected if not depressed.

"Where's the rest of that unit?" Masao asked. Galligan noticed what Masao was referring to.

"Ah. Benson's squad. They lost half their squad a few days ago. Ambushed."

Masao felt for the remaining soldiers. To date, they had lost only one guy in Cooper's squad and that was on the first day on Angaur.

"And then there's the soldier who went souvenir hunting."

"What's that?" Masao was confused.

"Just some dumb shit who figured he'd use this time to find a sword or something. He left an hour ago and headed up that-a-way, where it's supposedly secure. He's pretty stupid if you ask me. There's not one nook or cranny that's secure in my opinion."

Masao nodded. "He *is* a dumb shit."

In the distance the radio blared orders. *"Galligan. Wounded."*

"Guess I've got to go back to work." Galligan gathered his medic gear. Masao nodded, watching him close up a bag of supplies. But his senses heightened—something didn't feel right to him. He looked around and tried to pick up where the bad feeling might be coming from. Galligan was just about to hurry off.

"Galligan. Let's move out," the fellow medic shouted.

"Hey, John." Masao got his attention just before he left. Galligan stopped and looked at him.

"Be careful out there."

"You bet," Galligan nodded.

Within an hour Cooper received new orders. Then the rain started. It poured until the hard ground had turned to thick mud. Cooper's squad trudged quietly in the jungle. Everything was soggy as the men navigated rough terrain and swampland. The sound of the rain filled the space around them and muffled the sounds of explosions in the distance.

"Take five." Cooper stopped to check his map.

"I think I have diarrhea again. I'm going to find a spot," Masao told Garcia. Fifteen yards away from the squad, Masao found a spot by a swampland that had formed from all the rainfall. While looking for a hidden place, out of the corner of his eye, he saw a bush move. He stopped in his tracks and squatted, his body frozen with fear and adrenaline. His heart was pounding so loud and so fast he was sure he would be detected.

Then he saw it: an Imperial soldier with tree branches on his helmet. The soldier rose up from the brush at fifteen yards, scanning the dense foliage for his enemy target. Masao's breathing deepened. Sweat trickled from his forehead and mixed in with the raindrops hitting his face. *Is he alone?* He slowly pulled his sidearm out and cocked it, the sound absorbed by the rain. The Imperial soldier looked young. Masao aimed his weapon right at the soldier's chest. *Shoot!* He screamed to himself.

Suddenly, the enemy saw him and jerked. He didn't have a chance to draw his weapon. Masao had his sidearm pointed directly at him, ready to fire.

"You move, you're dead," Masao said calmly.

"I'd rather be dead than betray my country," the soldier spat back.

"If that's the way you want it." Masao took better aim. *Do it*, he tried to convince himself.

"You don't *belong* on their side." The soldier's desperation to get out of this standoff alive came through in the high pitch of his voice.

"I don't belong anywhere." Masao's own words surprised him. Maybe in the heat of the moment, the truth had finally come out. The Imperial soldier lurched to shoot his weapon. Without flinching, Masao fired twice.

At the sound of the gunfire, Dalton and Garcia took off in the direction of the shots.

Masao watched as the Imperial soldier fell back into the shallow pool of rainwater. *Is he dead? Dear God, what did I just do?* He stayed in a squatted position until Garcia and Dalton rushed in, assuming defensive positions. They looked around for other enemy faces.

"I still need to take care of business," Masao informed his bodyguards as he slowly rose up.

"We've got you covered," Dalton assured him. Masao lit up a cigarette and went into the brush. When he came out, he glanced at his bodyguards. The rain stopped, and the quiet became loud with the unthinkable. He went to the body and picked up the soldier's rifle.

Blood was now coloring the water around the dead soldier, his body slowly settling into the swamp, his face breaking the surface.

Garcia and Dalton looked at each other. They could see that Masao needed time. There were levels to this that they would never understand.

Masao thought about checking the soldier's pack for food or cigarettes, then stopped himself.

He flicked his cigarette butt into his own reflection in the swampy water. "Son of a bitch," he said under his breath.

"Abe. You okay?" Garcia asked.

"No." He handed the soldier's rifle to Dalton. "Let's go."

★ ★ ★

"I didn't like that. Nobody wants to take a life, a-no? Gee, that was a hard thing to get through." Masao looked off in the distance, deep in thought. "That soldier, he was just a kid. . . . I wouldn't have done it, but I wanted to live."

We sat there, on the curb, in our own silent world while celebrations continued all around us at the Bon Odori festival.

"You know, the Japanese military . . . they didn't retrieve the bodies. Not a one. Our military, we buried our fallen guys, a-no? But not theirs. They just let their guys *rot.*"

I looked up at him. His gentle face was stressed at the thought of soldiers being left on the battlefield. "That first one was *really* hard, boy," he said. "But after that, it got easier." He paused and seemed to digest the audacity of that statement. "That sounds funny."

"Well, isn't it that way in war? You either kill or you are killed. Right?"

"That's right," he nodded, content that I was not going to judge him. "You know, that guy, I think he was recon for the Japanese military. He must have been; he was all alone out there. Either that, or he got separated from his unit. It wasn't long after that, our unit, we encountered heavy fire. And, ah, we lost a lot of guys. But we got a lot of theirs too."

OCTOBER 1944—PELELIU, PALAU

Cooper, on the radio, glanced at the three as they rejoined the unit. He nodded at Masao, which was his way of saying "I'm glad you're okay." Every man on the squad was soaked through with the return of the heavy rain. They all crouched low to the ground, waiting for orders, scanning the dense brush for any movement, scouring the hillside for any hint of life. His bodyguards enveloped Masao between them.

"It feels like we're being watched," Masao whispered to Garcia.

"Don't say that. You're giving me the heebie-jeebies." Garcia sank lower in the brush.

Cooper hung up the radio and motioned that they were going forward. "There's a pocket ahead. We're going to circle them," Cooper ordered his men, even though his instincts were telling him to retreat. The platoon fanned out in different directions, crouching in the tall, thick grass. It poured on them, sheets of rain coming down. Masao and his bodyguards kept moving out, keeping an eye on their comrades, feeling more and more insecure as the distance between them and the rest of the squad grew. They had advanced forty yards when machine-gun fire erupted. They immediately squatted, their backs to each other.

"*Damn.* Did they get anyone?" Garcia blurted, his eyes wildly searching for the enemy.

"*Hey,*" Masao pointed to an Imperial soldier who had popped up from the grass a mere twenty yards away and was now aiming his automatic rifle directly at them. Without thinking, they fired off shots simultaneously. The soldier went down, riddled with bullets.

More machine-gun fire came at them from the other side in a shower of violent rounds. They all fired back. Masao was sure this was the end. Then the firing stopped as abruptly as it started.

"Hold your fire." This voice was one they recognized—Cooper. Masao strained to see where Cooper was and spotted him. He was waving his hand, calling his squad back together. Masao and his bodyguards stayed low to the ground and made their way to him. They scanned the area around them with each step.

"Recon was right on the money that time. A goddamn miracle in itself." Cooper grabbed the radio. "Let's see what else they know." Masao strained to scan in all directions.

"Sounds like we're about to link up with the marines. They're moving along this line approaching Hill B." Cooper pointed to his rain-soaked map. "They're getting help from *our* guys. Three or four companies are up there already. We're ordered to move along this way—to take care of any enemy that might flee out the back side here." He looked at his men. All eyes were on him; he wanted to be smart about how they proceeded. He didn't want to lose any guys. "Let's go. Stay low to the ground. They're coming out of nowhere and armed to the hilt."

Cooper's platoon stalked in the brush. They advanced into a shallow valley through severe terrain, hills flanking the sides of the small basin. The rain stopped. Mist rose from the depths of the earth, the result of the moist ground heating up from the sun that was now breaking through the clouds. It was quiet, eerie.

"We're sitting ducks out here," Dalton whispered.

The unit was isolated. In the distance from behind one of the hills, they heard the sound of relentless battle, spurts of machine-gun fire, grenades exploding, and mortar fire being launched with even louder blasts upon impact. In the small world of their hundred-yard vicinity, though, everything was quiet. Without the rain, their footsteps were no longer muffled. Every step they took seemed to echo throughout the valley.

"They're watching us," Masao breathed out. In a low position he ran to Cooper's side.

"Coop."

"I know. I feel it too," Cooper whispered back before Masao had a chance to elaborate. Cooper motioned for the unit to fall back.

"Screw orders. We're going to fall back and sit it out for a while. Over there," he pointed to an area that would take them out of ambush range.

Suddenly, machine-gun fire came directly at them from the front as six enemy soldiers sprouted up from the dense brush. The three soldiers at the front of the unit were sprayed down in a split second.

"*Take cover!*" Cooper shouted.

Soldiers dropped to the ground and fired off shots in all directions. More incoming fire sprayed the area with rapid machine-gun fire as they scattered. The Japanese soldiers yelled out instructions to each other, wanting to eliminate this Yankee squad.

"*They're everywhere, goddammit,*" Cooper shouted. The now separated and vulnerable unit was surrounded on two sides. The enemy was closing in.

Masao, understanding the instructions being shouted in Japanese, looked up and spotted the cave on a ridge where they were setting up bigger fire power. "*They've got a grenade launcher. Up on the hill. Move!*" Masao yelled as loud as he could. He glanced at his bodyguards who were twenty-five yards away and camouflaged in thick brush.

"*Abe!*" Dalton motioned for Masao to make a run in their direction. Dalton fired off his Browning toward the men closing in on the unit from the front. He hit three of their soldiers. The other three Imperial soldiers dove to the ground in opposite directions.

"*Goddammit.*" Dalton ducked and squinted to see where the enemy was. Masao scurried to their position, diving in between them. He looked back to see a grenade hit the spot he had just left. Grass and rocks sprayed their faces.

Terrified, Masao wiped his face and assessed the damage. He saw no soldiers from his unit standing. They were all either on the ground or, God forbid, dead.

"There!" Garcia pointed up to the ridge. An enemy soldier was loading the grenade launcher again. His target: them.

"The trees. Hurry." Masao pointed to the nearby tree line. They made a dash for it and jumped into a clump of trees. Masao tucked himself behind a trunk and took inventory of his bodyguards, who were all there. The grenade launcher operator gave up on them and, instead, looked for another target.

"We don't stand a chance without mortar," Escola surmised, scanning the brush for the rest of their outfit.

"The bazooka —" Dalton looked at Masao. "Stevens."

"He's out there," Garcia pointed, "He's down."

"Cover me." Dalton set his rifle down.

"Jack. Don't. You'll never make it," Garcia said.

"*We don't have a chance without it,*" Dalton barked.

Dalton readied a grenade. On the ridge Masao noticed that, in addition to the grenade-launching soldier, other soldiers had emerged from other caves and were scanning the area and pointing, making all sorts of hand gestures and yelling out instructions.

Dalton sprinted out to the retrieve the bazooka, throwing a grenade toward the hill. The grenade hit the ridge and rattled it. The Imperial soldiers stumbled to regain their footing. Garcia and Masao covered Dalton at the front, scanning for the enemy to emerge from the brush. Dalton returned with the bazooka, and Masao hoisted up Dalton's Browning to use instead of his pistol.

"Let's see how brave they are now," Dalton hissed as he set up the apparatus to launch a shell.

Garcia continued to scan the area for the rest of the unit. He spotted them. Cooper and two soldiers were pinned under the ridge. Three more soldiers were twenty yards down the ridge, hovering behind some boulders.

"There they are." Garcia pointed.

"Where's the rest of the outfit?" Masao feared the worst. Garcia and Masao frantically scanned for other soldiers while Escola and Dalton finished setting up the bazooka. Neither had done it before.

"There." They spotted the lone radioman out in the middle of the action, scared to death and trying to hide behind a shrub. Masao looked up. The enemy had spotted the radioman too and took aim with the grenade launcher. Masao couldn't stand the thought of the radioman's horrid demise.

"*Run!*" Both Masao and Garcia yelled to the radioman, who heard them but didn't know what was about to happen. His body was frozen with fear. *Fffffftttt.* The sound of a grenade being launched was unmistakable. The radioman looked up just as the grenade hit. Masao had never seen such a horrible sight. The radioman was alive one second, his body shredded into a thousand pieces the next. Blood, flesh, bone, fingers, hair, and bits of uniform ripped apart and cast in every direction, showering the area. Every soldier in Cooper's squad was a helpless witness to the horror.

"*Jack!*" Masao was angry at the sight.

"Almost there . . ." Dalton looked around. "Get those assholes on the ground." He pointed to the movement in front of them. Imperial soldiers were closing in on Cooper and the other guys along the underside of the ridge. Masao spotted it and adjusted the automatic weapon.

"Eddie." He motioned for help. Garcia helped steady the bulky rifle. Masao sprayed the area where he had spotted the Imperial soldiers, his body barely able to absorb the reverberation from the weapon.

"Did I get 'em?" Masao's breathing was heavy. He hadn't realized how hard a Browning was to maneuver. Before Garcia could answer, Masao fired again.

Garcia looked up on the ridge. The enemy soldier looked for his next target. "*Jack—it's now or never.*"

"I've got to move out some. Cover me." Dalton had to clear the trees to get off a good shot. Masao and Garcia stood in full view of the enemy—shooting unflinchingly. It kept the enemy soldiers from gaining ground. Dalton had the bazooka set up and aimed it at the ridge. He launched the first shell then quickly ducked. "I don't know how to use this thing." The bad shot bought some time. The enemy up on the ridge stumbled and scurried to arm themselves, realizing they had a fight on their hands. Garcia and Masao ducked for cover behind the trees.

Machine-gun fire was coming at them from the ridge. Bullets hit the trees all around them. They all dove to the ground. Masao looked up at the ridge, where the soldier with the grenade launcher had recovered; he was wobbly, but he loaded the weapon again.

"Again, Jack." The soldiers, pinned against the ridge, saw the plan. They waited for the right time to make a run for it. Dalton was almost ready. He and Escola quickly positioned the weapon.

"*GO,*" Dalton shouted.

Masao and Garcia again stood and aimed at the ridge. Dalton fired off another shell. The blast knocked the enemy down. Garcia shot at the ridge. Masao aimed below so the isolated American soldiers could make a run for it.

"*RUN, DAMMIT, RUN,*" Dalton bellowed as he grabbed the Browning from Masao's shoulder.

"I got this," he handled the weapon as if it was a toy and fired relentlessly toward the front and the ridge, hitting two guys, who yelped as they went down. Garcia, Escola, and Masao took whatever weapon they could and fired it at the ridge. It was hard to tell where the incoming fire was coming from or where it was aimed, but Masao didn't care. He just kept firing. The US soldiers who were pinned against the ridge were half way to cover and running for their lives. Cooper was in the rear.

Enemy fire changed its target when they saw the soldiers who were running for cover. First came machine-gun fire. The American soldiers dove for safety. Another Japanese soldier appeared on the ridge from a different cave opening. He was setting up another grenade launcher. Dalton saw it first.

"*Son of a bitch.*" He threw down his gun and loaded the bazooka again. Escola assisted, cringing from the incoming fire that was hitting all around. Masao and Garcia ducked for cover as machine-gun fire turned on them again, this time with a vengeance. Dalton got off the shell just as fire sprayed his area, miraculously missing him and Escola as they ducked. He loaded again and fired without any assistance. It was a direct hit on the ridge, taking out one of their grenade launchers.

"You got him," Escola shouted as he positioned himself behind a tree with his rifle. The pinned American soldiers made another run for it while Masao and the bodyguards shot with punishing accuracy toward the ridge. But with every soldier they took out, two more would come out from the depths of the volcanic hill. Incoming fire hit all around, shattering trees and the brush around them. Masao looked for Cooper, still in the rear. The men crawled along the ground, trying to get to the safest place. Twenty-five yards away now, the soldier right in front of Cooper got hit in the back.

"Dickerson!" Cooper shouted.

Cooper caught up with him just in time to see Dickerson breathe his last breath, his body quivering, his head jerking back and forth until he went limp and lifeless.

"Goddammit," Cooper muttered. He looked up to see that his other soldiers had made it to cover.

Masao frantically motioned for Cooper to make a run for it. "*Come on, Coop. Come on!*" Without flinching, Cooper tore through the brush in an all-out run to get to safety. In a moment that stood still for Masao, Cooper and he made eye contact. Cooper was now a mere twenty yards away. Their eyes locked just as Cooper was hit from behind multiple times. His eyes told Masao he knew he'd been sprayed with bullets. He knew this was the end. His body fell forward in a slump and hit the ground hard. More incoming fire tore into his body. Masao looked up at the ridge where the Imperial soldiers were wildly shooting.

"*NO!*" Masao couldn't believe his eyes. The remaining four soldiers dove for cover behind trees. Masao still stood, staring at Cooper, incoming fire hitting all around him. Dalton reached up and pulled him down. The two hugged the ground, their faces covered in mud, blood, and flesh. Masao was in anguish, shaking his head and in shock.

"Let it go," Dalton's voice was low but empathetic. "But those assholes are going to pay for that." He shimmied over to the bazooka. Like a mad man, he reloaded and looked over at Masao and Garcia to give them the signal.

"Now," he hollered. Masao and Garcia stood and shot at the ridge. Dalton stood and fired off a shell. They all ducked and looked up at the ridge. A direct hit. Imperial soldiers dropped and fell off the ridge.

"Again," Masao heard himself shout. Dalton loaded another shell. "*Now.*"

Masao and Garcia stood and aimed high and low. Other soldiers joined in, seeing that the plan had worked. Another direct hit. The incoming fire slowed.

"I've got one more," Dalton shouted.

"Use it," Masao shouted back.

What was left of the unit stood and shot at the remaining enemy. Dalton fired off the shell. The remaining men in the unit hit the ground and waited for sounds, any sound that indicated the enemy was approaching.

Masao looked out in the valley. He spotted Cooper's body. He hated what he was about to do. He nudged Garcia, who was on the ground next to him, and pointed to Cooper.

"We need his map . . . and binoculars."

Garcia spotted the binoculars hanging off of Cooper's body. He knew Masao was right. Masao looked up at the ridge—it was secure for the moment.

"I'm going out." Masao started to move, but Garcia stopped him.

"Not you. I'll go." Masao thought about this and knew Garcia was right. Their orders were to protect Masao. If he'd been killed carrying out this task, Garcia, Dalton, and Escola would pay for it. Garcia bellied out the twenty yards into the wide open to retrieve Cooper's binoculars. Masao and the others waited, aiming at the enemy front, ready to shoot. Masao spotted movement and braced himself. He looked at Garcia, who had reached the body. He scanned the ridge—there was no sign of life. His eyes went back down the terrain on the valley floor. *They could be anywhere.* He thought he saw something move in the brush at seventy-five yards. Without hesitation, he shot at the spot. He looked at Garcia, who was still at the body.

"What's he doing out there anyway?" he asked no one in particular. "*Hey! Hurry up!*" he called to Garcia. Garcia bellied back with the binoculars and map in hand.

"What the hell took you so long?"

Garcia showed him Coop's last letter, addressed to Serena Cooper. Masao thought about the conversation he had with him about Serena and wondered if this woman was even worthy of Coop's last words. "I want to be sure this gets delivered."

Masao nodded.

"Guys. *Guys.* There's still more." Dalton's voice was shaky. Masao nodded and squinted through the binoculars. He motioned for the men to circle close.

"Keep your eye on that area, about the one o'clock position from here. I thought I saw movement. Let's keep pushing forward to the position on the far side. If we encounter live ones, we have a reason to go back." He motioned the unit forward. The scant platoon, half its original size, fanned out and advanced cautiously. They started coming across enemy bodies.

"Make sure they're dead," Garcia said as he picked up an enemy rifle equipped with a bayonet. Another soldier did the same, and they used the bayonet to stab the dead Japanese soldiers, more out of revenge than to ensure death. They made it to the end of the valley without incident.

"What do you think?" Dalton looked around.

"Let's keep looking."

Sniper fire abruptly came at them from the ridge. A bullet hit the ground next to Masao's feet.

"*Shit!*" Masao jumped. The soldiers ducked and scanned the ridge. Dalton hurled his rifle up and sprayed the ridge. There was an anguished cry then an enemy body dropped. The soldiers slowly rose up from the brush. Masao jerked his head when he spotted something ahead. He motioned to be quiet and then signaled forward, pointing to the area. Masao led as they approached a clump of torched trees that would have made a perfect hiding place. He raised his pistol and held it out in front of him. He could barely detect movement, but it was there.

Masao's heart pounded. He glanced around and motioned for others to cover the area. Dalton intuitively made his way around the other side of the charred tree trunk. Garcia stood to Masao's left, his gun ready. The other soldiers were nearby, standing guard, scanning the ridge. Masao looked at Dalton, who nodded. An enemy soldier was hiding inside, tucked away.

"You are surrounded. Come out and surrender," Masao shouted in Japanese.

"Go to hell," the Imperial soldier snapped back.

"Shut up and come out with your hands up."

"I'd rather die than surrender to you *Joes*."

"What's going on, Sarge? You two catching up on old times or what?" Dalton shouted.

"He's a stubborn son of a bitch. Can you see him, Jack?"

"I'll move in closer." Dalton edged in closer.

"Be careful, Jack." Masao didn't want to lose anyone else, especially not one of his bodyguards. Dalton moved in behind the Japanese soldier. He was armed, wedged in between tree stumps. When he saw Dalton, he panicked, trying to aim his gun at the US soldier.

"Abe! Say 'Don't move.' Never mind. Don't move!" Dalton rushed toward the soldier and knocked his rifle away. Masao came close.

"Check him for grenades," Masao ordered. Dalton patted him down.

"Nothing," Dalton assured Masao. Masao was eye to eye with this Imperial enemy, like before at the pond with the recon soldier. Only this time he had no empathy. This time he had only hatred in his heart. The heavy rain started again.

"You're going with us," Masao instructed the soldier, who had just become a prisoner.

"Just kill me here. On the battlefield. I don't deserve to live. I'm a disappointment to Japan."

Dalton tossed down the enemy's rifle. "He was out of ammo."

Masao looked at the rifle on the ground, then back at the enemy prisoner. "You don't deserve to live after what you did to my guys back there."

The Japanese soldier stood defiant, staring directly into Masao's eyes, daring him to act on his primal instincts. Masao stared back at him. He held onto his pistol, aiming it at the enemy soldier, wanting nothing more than to end this guy's life yet aware that there was a frail line between a battle kill and murder. And Masao was no murderer.

Garcia gently helped Masao bring his pistol down to his side, taking the aim off the enemy. Masao looked at Garcia, then noticed that all the soldiers had their eyes on him. He was the highest-ranking soldier left. He was in charge. The most protected among the platoon, now the protector.

"Sir," Dalton spoke up, "we have our orders."

Masao nodded. He regarded the young faces around him. They were tired, worn, and dirty. All he wanted to do now was preserve the remaining lives of the unit. "Let's get him back to camp. We'll go along the south." He nodded in the direction that would give them the most protection.

On the way back, Masao recognized the area they were passing through. It was the site of the cave that Cooper had left as a tomb just days before. Masao was content knowing that he had served under a sergeant like Cooper, brave and humane. As they neared the cave that they had carefully secured with boulders, he realized something was different. Debris was scattered everywhere. There were pieces of shredded uniform, bits of paper, fragments of flesh and hair strewn about. Masao feared the worst. They came closer and saw it: another unit had come along and decided the cave was better off obliterated than left alone. What was left of Cooper's platoon stood at a distance from the destroyed cave. There were no words, only a few glances.

"Look what barbarians you are," the prisoner snorted.

"Shut. Up." He looked at his soldiers. "Let's go."

The prisoner had been uncooperative all the way back to the line camp, trying to give signals to hidden comrades by talking loudly. Masao kept note of where he would erupt, sure signs that there were enemy foxholes nearby. The prisoner refused to give up any information about their command post or anything else. Masao thought about the radical Kunio. *This is what Kunio would be.*

Back at line camp, Masao looked around for the highest-ranking soldier and found a tech sergeant by the name of Thompson.

"Sir," Masao said. Thompson looked up from his map.

"We lost Cooper?"

Masao nodded.

"Damn." Thompson rubbed his chin. Masao couldn't help but feel responsible, even though he wasn't.

"The prisoner," Masao nodded toward the uncooperative Japanese soldier, "he was signaling on the way back. Here," Masao motioned toward the map. "It was right along here, this point, here, and down here." He pointed to different areas. "They might be hot spots, sir."

Thompson nodded. "Good job, sergeant." They both looked at the prisoner, who then went into another tirade.

"Just give me a grenade so I can end my life. I will not dishonor the emperor or bring shame to Japan," he shrieked in Masao's direction.

"Shut up, asshole," Masao called back in Japanese. "He wants a grenade to kill himself. I say we give it to him. Stuff it right in his mouth and let him have it. He's on my last nerve."

"Get the MPs. Let's get him back to headquarters ASAP," Thompson ordered. Masao nodded and started to leave. "Hey, soldier." Thompson stopped him. Masao turned. "Let's have you and your boys tag on to my unit from now on." This was a compliment and Masao knew it. He wasn't asking Masao to join his unit as an interpreter, he was asking Masao to join his unit as a soldier.

"Thank you, sir."

Masao spotted the MP by the ammo hut. As he passed by McCoy he signaled with a wave of his hand. It was understood—no food for this prisoner.

"Please take him quickly. He's making me crazy." He handed the prisoner off and then noticed that the camp felt empty. "Where's Galligan?" Masao asked. The MP shrugged.

On the perimeter of camp, waiting for their final ride off the battlefield, were the bodies of dead soldiers, lined up and covered. Masao hesitated, but knew he had to check. He stood looking down at the tattered canvas tarps covering the bodies, thinking about Cooper, who was still out in the middle of the valley. He pulled the tarp back from the first body. Not Galligan. He pulled the tarp off the second corpse. Not Galligan. Then, under the third tarp, he found him: Galligan. His body was lifeless; his canteen still hung from his neck. The tin cup he used to offer Masao coffee was attached to his ammo belt.

"Christ." Masao squatted, overwhelmed by death. Before this day, death had been something that happened to other men, not his own.

McCoy had silently joined him. He laid his hand on Masao's shoulder. "Sorry about Coop." His voice had a calming effect on Masao. It was as if they were at a funeral on the mainland. Masao could barely hear the constant blasts coming from a distance.

Masao nodded toward Galligan, "How did this happen?"

"He went out after one of ours—some idiot who went out to find souvenirs. Then a sniper got him. We had to go get him and lost two more in the process."

"You've gotta be kidding me."

McCoy shook his head. The heaviness hit Masao as he sank into the ground next to Galligan's body.

"Who do we have to retrieve *our* guys?" he asked in a desperate tone, referring to Cooper and the others. "They're still out there with those sons of bitches." Masao pointed frantically to the direction of the valley.

"We'll bring them back," McCoy patted Masao's shoulder. "Don't you worry, Abe."

★ ★ ★

Masao, the best narrator on earth, made great sound effects for various weapons and explosives. It was both riveting and heart-wrenching listening to his account of the battle that had taken the lives of so many of his buddies. We were still sitting on the curb, and the *taiko* drummers played in the distance. Masao wasn't even aware of his surroundings; all he could see was the part of the war that claimed his comrades.

"When I was kneeling over his body, I wanted to take his cup," Masao looked at me.

"The tin cup he always brought to you so you could make hot coffee?"

"That's right. I wanted to have it. To remember the guy. He was *really* nice, boy."

I nodded.

"But, it would have looked kind of funny. You know, a soldier taking something from a dead guy's body. A Japanese guy—digging around. It wouldn't look right."

I nodded that I understood. As the festival wound down and we walked back to the car, I couldn't help but feel what a magnificent warrior Masao was. A magnificent warrior with the kindest of hearts.

The Seattle Chapter of the Nisei Veteran's Committee, or NVC, is housed in a beautiful facility located in the heart of central Seattle, adjacent to Little Vietnam. The organization was established to support Japanese American veterans of war who were excluded from other agencies that served veterans. The well-run NVC offers various events and exhibits to celebrate the legacy of Japanese Americans. Alan and I were especially excited to take Masao to the 2012 Veteran's Day occasion there because we had a special birthday gift waiting for him.

Months earlier, we had learned of the Japanese American Memorial Wall located on the premises. At the far end of the parking lot, space had been allocated and designed to house hundreds of black granite tiles enshrining the names of Japanese Americans who were either interned during World War II or served in World War II or other wars, from the Spanish American War to the war in Afghanistan. All branches of the military were recognized.

The wall is approximately twelve feet tall and ninety feet long, extending the entire width of the parking lot. The overhead concrete beam was designed to accentuate the wall and meant to resemble traditional Japanese *tori* gates, structures that are spiritual in nature. The black granite tiles, similar to the tiles used in other memorial walls, provide a naturally reflective surface, creating an aura of tranquility. In keeping with the culture of Japan, it is sturdy and polished, but not pretentious or grandiose.

The wall is visually separated from the parking lot by five Japanese maple trees, interspersed with bamboo shooting up a good ten feet. There is a wide path lined with pea gravel before the wall, and benches to sit and reflect are nestled near the trees. The NVC Memorial Wall is peaceful, beautiful, and spiritual.

About one-third of the wall holds tiles of war veterans, the other two-thirds, tiles of Japanese Americans who were interned at any one of the ten internment camps or eight Department of Justice prisons. Alan and I had purchased a tile, and we were excited to show Masao that his legacy would live on for decades, if not centuries. We were limited, though, on what we could have engraved. We couldn't reference the battles that he had fought in—Angaur,

Peleliu, or Leyte. All we could include was his name, World War II, and MIS. But even so, we thought it was a spectacular gift.

We were an hour early and assumed there would be plenty of parking. As it turned out, we took the very last spot. Alan got Masao's walker, and I prepared an umbrella because it was a typical rainy November day.

"Let's go look over there," Alan suggested, pointing to the memorial wall. It looked stunning and attracted attention, even if you didn't know what it was, and Masao did not, yet it piqued his interest.

"What is that?" He started to roll his walker in the direction of the wall. The excitement built for me, and I think for Alan too. We knew exactly where his tile was, so we steered him to that particular column. What emotional response might we get from Masao when he saw his own name etched in the black granite?

As he got closer, we had to help him navigate the gravel with his walker. He examined the structure. "Gee, this is nice," he remarked. "All Japanese people . . ."

The designers would have been pleased. This was exactly the response they wanted, admiration and reflection. Masao rolled along and then came to the part where soldiers were honored.

"They have soldiers, too, a-no?" He continued rolling along. "Guys from the 442nd." He pointed to a tile or two. "Ohhhh . . . MIS," he said.

"Dad, look up there." Alan stopped him and pointed up high where Mas's tile was positioned. It took him a few minutes to see what Alan was talking about.

"Gee, is that me?"

I almost started to cry, knowing that at any second, Masao's gratitude would be overwhelming.

"What's it say, anyway?"

"It says: Masao Abe . . . US Army . . . MIS . . . World War II." Alan read it for him.

Masao looked at Alan. "Nothing about the battles? I—I fought in battles." He looked a little panicked.

"Mas, I asked if we could put those on there and they said no. Only the war and branch could go on there." My plan was quickly going awry. Where was the love? Where was the emotional burst of gratefulness that I was expecting?

"I was in battles. *Three* of them: Angaur, Peleliu, and Leyte." He counted them off with his fingers to prove his point. "It should be on there."

Alan looked at me as if this whole fiasco was my fault. And it *was*. This idea was my brainchild. I had coordinated with the NVC. I filled out the paperwork.

"But none of the tiles have battles. Don't you see?" I sounded like a little girl. But Masao had moved on. He had waved us off and was maneuvering the walker back to the pavement.

Back in the parking lot, more veterans were rolling themselves toward the entrance of the NVC hall, wearing their dress caps decorated with various war ribbons.

"Ohhhhh," Masao uttered in a startled tone. "My cap. I left it in the car."

"I'll get it," Alan assured him. And then I, the screw-up, continued to escort Masao into the building, with Alan catching up at the last minute to hand him the dress cap that he immediately put on.

The garrison dress cap he'd chosen to wear that day was dark blue with gold piping. Disabled American Veterans, or DAV, appeared on one side. The DAV patch was placed just above and off to the side of the embroidered words "Seattle Chap. 2." Above the stitching, Masao had placed various pins he had collected: a DAV pin with an eagle, a big V for veteran with an American flag, a World War II fiftieth anniversary pin that he had picked up in 1995, a Nisei Veterans Reunion pin from Reno in 1988, his precious Eighty-First Infantry

Division pin that had the wildcat in the middle, an MIS pin, and a Japanese American Veterans Association pin.

On the other side of the cap's fold were all of his well-earned and well-deserved military decorations. Above the embroidered "Life Member" stitched into the lower part of the cap and beneath the gold piping were all of his medals in cloth ribbon form, the kind you see soldiers wearing on the front of their formal uniforms.

The only metal pin on that side of Masao's dress cap was the army's Combat Infantryman Badge, or CIB. Many soldiers felt that this pin carried the most respect and was considered the most important decoration a soldier could wear, indicating that the individual had been in combat, had been an infantryman, and had seen battle. Rectangular, measuring one inch by three inches, it had a light blue background. In the center was a silver musket surrounded by an elliptical oak wreath. Masao's CIB was empty at the top center of the oak wreath, indicating that it was a first award. Had he been awarded more of these badges, stars would have been placed inside the wreath.

Below the CIB pin were three rows of ribbons, neatly arranged by order of their importance and merit. In the first row, his Bronze Star Medal, his Army Commendation Medal, and his Purple Heart. In the second row, his Army Good Conduct Medal, the American Defense Service Medal, and the American Campaign Medal. In the third row, his Asiatic-Pacific Campaign Medal flanked with two Bronze Campaign Stars and Bronze Arrowhead Device, his World War II Victory Medal, and his Philippine Liberation Medal that contained one Bronze Campaign Star. He wore his service proudly.

I later learned the difference between all the bronze stars. His Bronze Star Medal, taking the first and most important place, was awarded for a heroic act and/or meritorious achievement in connection with operations against an armed enemy or while engaged in some sort of military operation involving conflict with opposing armed forces. The Bronze Star Medal was specifically awarded to soldiers not involved in aerial warfare, but who were involved in ground combat. Bronze battle stars, on the other hand, indicate that a soldier had participated in a specific battle and is worn on the campaign ribbon that the soldier also earned. In the case of Masao's Asiatic-Pacific Campaign Medal, he earned two Bronze Campaign Stars

Masao on Veteran's Day

for the conflicts on Angaur and Peleliu. Also attached to his Asiatic-Pacific ribbon is a Bronze Arrowhead Device, indicating his involvement in the amphibious assault on Angaur. He earned a third Bronze Campaign Star for the battle on Leyte in the Philippines.

Inside the NVC hall, people gathered on the converted basketball court. I had never seen so many rolling walkers, canes, and wheelchairs, barring, of course, our trips to the casino. There were display tables lining the walls, vendors with various items to sell, and cookies to eat. The middle of the basketball court was filled with chairs, and a projector was being set up to show a film that was narrated by none other than George Takei. I immediately noticed that Masao's dress cap was the only dark blue one in the room. The majority of other veterans in the room were wearing maroon caps with gold piping. I didn't think much of it. Masao's cap looked far more striking and military, it seemed to me.

I anticipated that he would be a complete and utter chatterbox, mingling with war buddies and catching up on old times. But nothing was further from the truth. He stayed to himself, near to Alan and me. I wondered if he was still disappointed about the tile, but he wasn't one to carry a grudge. He took a couple of cookies, and I was quick to get a napkin to hold them for him, still attempting to redeem myself from the tile catastrophe.

Other soldiers, with the maroon caps, gathered in groups and chatted. Masao would glance up at them every so often, but then would continue on his voyage around the room.

"Do you know any of these guys?" I finally asked.

He glanced around, careful to give me the right answer, looking for any familiar face in the crowd. "Gee, I don't think so. I used to know a couple of guys," he said as he looked harder, "but I don't see them."

"Are there any MIS guys here?"

"Gee, I don't know, you know? All I see are the 442nd guys."

"Are those the guys in the maroon caps?"

"Yeah, I think so." He was still looking. At least I felt like I was off the hook with the tile issue. He had moved on, long before I had, not giving it a second thought.

There were some announcements and some acknowledgments before the short film began. We found cushy seats. I, like a proud daughter, took pictures of Masao looking dapper in his dress cap. But before the film began I became aware of a subtle nonverbal communication in the room—glances of the other veterans toward Masao. My emotions seemed to fine-tune the atmosphere. The 442nd veterans appeared to have a mistaken idea about the Military Intelligence Service, and Masao seemed to be the only MIS soldier in the room. Their faces indicated their thoughts: the MIS men weren't *real* soldiers. Everyone knew about the all-Nisei 442nd and the Hundredth Infantry Battalion, their valor in Europe, their courageous military efforts, and the hundreds of Purple Hearts they had collectively earned through their bloodshed. But very few people, even in this circle of war heroes, understood that MIS deployed soldiers to the southern and central Pacific. Even fewer were aware that these men were attached to regimental combat teams in battle zones on various islands.

With every glance of one of the 442nd in Masao's direction, I could feel it. Evidently, and wrongly, they must have thought that Masao was one of the many MIS soldiers who had been stationed at one of the huge communications centers far behind enemy lines. Those MIS men had intercepted chatter about military strategies and positions and helped to shorten the war significantly. But Masao was on the enemy line and had the ribbons to prove it. Unfortunately, he had served in near isolation among white soldiers, while Nisei soldiers in the 442nd had each other. Not any of his ribbons, indicating his medals earned, deterred the detached way they looked at Masao. Confused by his CIB and his Bronze Star Medal, not to mention the unmistakable Purple Heart, not one of the 442nd veterans interacted with Masao. Instead, they mingled amongst themselves.

Then I looked at Masao. His gentle face absorbed all the ignorance. He was used to this, I could tell. Here he was, a warrior who had seen the horror of war close up, a soldier who had looked into the eyes of his commander as he died on Peleliu, a guy who felt the loss of good and worthy men, and here, his service was discounted. No wonder he wanted the battles of Angaur, Peleliu, and Leyte on his tile.

"They don't know you served on the line," I whispered so only Masao could hear. He shook his head no, indicating that I understood correctly. "They think you were a desk man." He nodded only one short but affirmative nod.

"Why don't they know about guys like you?"

Masao looked around before whispering back, as though guarding his response. "Well, we couldn't talk about it. For thirty years, a-no?"

"How come?"

"Heh! The military didn't want us to." He paused, reliving a single point in history. "It was a secret, I guess. Secret operation. And now, now it's just lost. Our part, it's just lost."

The US Army had officially embargoed their speaking of it for three decades after the end of the war. However, by 1975, America was more enthralled with the disaster that was the Vietnam War; nobody wanted to hear about a highly secret operation that took place during World War II.

I offered him a cookie, because I had taken a few more to get me through the seventeen-minute film. Masao accepted one and looked at me, noticing I was a bit emotional with this discovery. He knew. I didn't have to say a word and neither did he. He just took the cookie, patted my leg, nodded, and continued to watch the short film that was mostly about the 442nd. For Masao, it was enough that I got it, that I understood the situation. What had frustrated him was this: outside at the memorial wall, I didn't understand that his place during the war was specific and unusual, and now, in here, in this hall, I finally realized that his role in the war was, indeed, quite unique. His accomplishments were different from the soldiers of the 442nd, the Hundredth Battalion, and even other MIS soldiers.

OCTOBER 25, 1944—PELELIU, PALAU

The platoon returned to line camp by noon, empty-handed; soldiers cooled off in the shade, where they could find it. In the distance, Masao heard more orders by radio; another cave to be checked out. The other Nisei assigned to the 321st, Frank, happened to be nearby and Masao spotted him gearing up. Relieved that it was Frank's turn to go out, he sat down and lit up. Then he felt a tap on his shoulder.

"Hey, Abe," he turned to see Frank, who had a worried look on his face.

"Yeah?"

"I need you to go out on this one."

"I just got back in." Masao couldn't believe his ears—the nerve of this guy.

"Abe. I just have a bad feeling about this. I think—if I go out, I won't come back," Frank pleaded. Masao understood the power of gut feelings. He studied Frank's face. It seemed tender to Masao and filled with tension and fear.

He nodded. "All right, Frank. I'll go."

Masao alerted his bodyguards, and while he was gearing up, a bad feeling came over him. He wondered if his own intuition was trying to tell him something. He decided to visit the ammo hut and get extra weapons, including two hand grenades and a rifle.

The platoon arrived at the suspected cave and surrounded it. A makeshift white flag hung on a blown-apart tree near the opening.

"Go ahead, Abe," the tech sergeant ordered.

"Come out. You won't be harmed," Masao called out in Japanese. He scanned the terrain, noticing that they were easy targets.

It was quiet. Masao's intuitive radar was screaming at him. "Sir, this feels like a trap," he suggested as he looked around. The tech sergeant contemplated his next move, deciding to move in anyway. "You three—" he pointed to three of his soldiers, his words suddenly interrupted.

The blast of a sniper's gun alarmed the soldiers. Masao looked up just as the bullet hit him. It threw him off his feet and he landed with a thud. Soldiers scattered and took cover. Masao, in the wide open, dragged himself behind a tree trunk. Blood was everywhere.

"*ABE!*" Dalton shouted when he realized Masao had been hit.

Another shot was fired and a soldier went down. His body jerked and trembled.

Dalton got to Masao. "It's my leg." Masao was in excruciating pain.

Another shot. The unit rushed to rescue the other wounded soldier. Masao's bodyguards surrounded him, ducking and searching for the best place to find cover.

"Where's it coming from? Get him to cover, dammit," Garcia yelled in the midst of all the confusion. Another bullet hit close by. This time it shattered what was left of the tree covering Garcia. "*MOVE!*"

Dalton dragged Masao, leaving a swath of blood as he pulled him into some brush.

"Where's the medic? Get the medic. Someone get the goddamn medic!" Dalton frantically looked around.

"There—up on that ridge. Get him!" someone shouted when they spotted the assailant.

Dalton strained to stop the gushing from Masao's thigh, feeling his way to the hole where the blood was escaping. Soldiers started firing at the ridge.

Masao began to lose consciousness. "I think my number is up . . ." His voice was weak. *Dying out here in the Pacific, in between the two worlds that have divided my soul. . . .* Masao closed his eyes with this thought.

"Stay with me, Abe. *SARGE.*" Dalton shook Masao to keep him awake.

Masao opened his eyes wide. He was confused and getting colder by the minute, even though it was ninety degrees. The sniper fire continued. Garcia ran over and bellied down near Dalton and Masao.

"We're sitting ducks here."

"I realize that, Tony. We gotta stop the bleeding." Dalton took Masao's belt off his pants and used it as a tourniquet around the bleeding leg. Blood was spewing. Sniper bullets hit all around them. Dust and dirt flew up everywhere.

In a brave but stupid move, Dalton picked Masao up, threw him over his shoulder like a potato sack, and ran for his life. Garcia followed, running toward denser brush while trying to cover them from the continuing assault. Dalton made it fifteen yards and fell, struggling to hold on to Masao.

"Did you get hit?" Garcia shouted, jerking his head back and forth between Dalton ahead of him and the sniper behind.

"No, goddamit. I fell. My legs are shaking so bad." Dalton got up, blood covering his uniform. "At least I think I fell. There's blood everywhere—I don't know if it's mine or his."

"Keep going—go, go." They ran until they found cover. Dalton laid Masao down and tightened the belt to try to stop the bleeding, then applied pressure with his hand.

"Hang on, Abe. Hang on." Dalton used his entire hand to put pressure on the bullet hole. Garcia put his shirt under Masao's head.

"Hold on." Garcia took Masao's hand, soldier style. Masao opened his eyes, saw his guys, looked at each one, and nodded.

The jeep screeched up on Beach Orange, where medics were waiting. Masao's bodyguards pulled the stretcher off the jeep and took it to the medic station. For a brief moment, the four were alone amidst the busy goings on around them on the beach.

Dalton squeezed Masao's hand. "Sarge," he said, "stay with us."

Masao opened his eyes. He searched the faces of Dalton, Garcia, and Escola. "Did you get the bastard?"

"Hell yes, we got him," Escola assured Masao.

"You guys . . . you're good soldiers," Masao struggled to get out.

A medic came over and showed Dalton where to keep pressure. "Right here," the medic pressed Dalton's hand on Masao's leg.

"I got it," Dalton's voice quivered. He looked at the blood seeping through his fingers, the Japanese blood of Masao. He looked at Masao's face just as Masao opened his eyes and looked back. "Sarge.

You're a good soldier." Dalton fought his emotions. "I should have trusted you from the get-go." With that, Escola helped apply pressure on the wound, and Garcia took Masao's hand.

Masao nodded. "It's okay, Jack." He looked at the three bodyguards. "We're just regular guys doing our best."

Medics rushed in and took over. Dalton held Masao's hand until the last possible moment. The bodyguards watched as they loaded Masao onto the amphibian, and the gate closed.

★ ★ ★

It was a beautiful spring day outside. Inside Masao's apartment, I waited while Masao finished his fried egg sandwich and then fussed around to get ready. I meandered over to his wall of pictures and examined the one that appeared to have been taken on a battlefield. He was squatting, rifle in hand, in between two other soldiers, one Japanese American and one Caucasian. As Masao rolled through the living room, I pointed to the photo.

"Where was this taken, Mas? Peleliu?"

He looked up and saw the photo. "Uh, no. Let's see now. That guy to my right is Bob Sakai, a *really* smart guy, boy. And that Caucasian gentleman, I don't know who he is. Uh, let's see now. Not Peleliu, that was taken on Leyte. In the Philippines," he said as he pulled his shoes on.

"It's a really cool picture," I said.

"Heh! We look tough, don't we?"

"I think you were pretty tough." I helped him get his jacket on. "You're still pretty tough."

"Heh! I'm a sad case, no? Can't even remember what day it is."

He was referring to the fact that he hadn't known it was our day together until I walked through the door.

"Mas. You're ninety-six. You still cook, do laundry, and iron. Can you be just a tad easier on yourself?"

"Heh!" He waved me off.

As we waited for the glacially slow elevator, I thought more about Leyte.

"What happened on Leyte? You never told me about that."

The elevator door opened. "When are we going to Vegas?" he asked as he rolled onto the elevator.

"This Sunday."

"Sunday. Good." Las Vegas was far more important to him than Leyte. "You know, I don't remember much about Leyte, to tell you the truth," he began. "After I was shot, they sent me to, ah, what's the name now, ah, New Caledonia. I was there for a couple of months. Then they sent me to Leyte. In the Philippines. The local people, they hated the Japanese, boy, I'll tell you that much. Whenever they saw me, they would point and their faces, they would look—terrified."

The brutality the Japanese military had inflicted on Allied Forces and the Philippine people was well known.

"I've never seen anything like it." He was thinking out loud.

JUNE 1945—LEYTE, PHILIPPINES

Although he was still attached to the 321st, everything felt different to Masao. The locals feared him and looked at him with loathing in their eyes. His bodyguards on Angaur and Peleliu now had different assignments; he hadn't even seen them since he left Orange Beach on Peleliu. His new bodyguards were aloof and distant. His leg bothered him most of the time, and he was astounded that he had been ordered back on the line with such a serious injury that hadn't healed completely. But the commanders in charge were more determined than ever to drive the Japanese out of every stronghold, including the Philippines. They needed every available man.

He was attached to a platoon that had been ordered on mop up behind enemy lines. Reports indicated that there were still active pockets. The platoon crept along silently, listening for signs of life. Suddenly, the platoon sergeant halted and crouched low, signaling everyone else to do the same. He motioned for the unit to stay put while he and two soldiers moved closer toward the sound, disappearing into tall grass that closed up behind them. The rest of the outfit waited, ready to fire.

"I need that interpreter," the tech sergeant shouted from a short distance. Masao followed his voice, wondering why his bodyguards weren't coming with him. He came upon the group in a small clearing where there was a Japanese officer on the ground, slowly bleeding to death. It looked as if he had been bleeding out for hours.

"What's he saying?" the tech sergeant asked in his gruff voice.

Masao squatted down next to the officer. "He wants to know what you are saying," he asked, keenly aware of the man's agony.

"I was asking him to let me use his gun. I could end my life."

"He wants to use your gun, sir, to end his life."

The tech sergeant softened. "I wonder where his unit is."

"Where is the rest of your outfit?" Masao took charge and asked.

"They fell back, under my orders." He pointed to a direction. "That way."

"Is that the direction of your command post?" Masao proceeded with his usual questioning. Then he realized that this tech sergeant might not have worked with an interpreter, so he explained. "His unit headed that way. I'm asking if that's where the command post is."

"Our command post was there, yes." The Japanese officer was losing strength by the minute.

"Their CP was in the same area, sir," Masao interpreted.

"I'd like to get him some help, but it would take half my guys to do it." The tech sergeant's humanity appeared out of nowhere.

The Japanese officer looked back and forth wanting desperately to know what was being said. Masao noticed. "Sir? May I?"

The tech sergeant nodded.

Masao said, "My commander is thinking this through. He would like to get you some help."

The Japanese officer shook his head. "It's too late for help. Please. A gun with one bullet is all I need."

"Sir, he's pleading for us to let him end his life here."

The tech sergeant wrestled with his thoughts, and Masao saw it. "You guys, head back with the others." His soldiers were bewildered. "*Go on.*" He jerked his head, motioning for them to go. Masao looked at the Japanese officer, who looked back at him. Masao nodded slightly, then left.

They weren't yet back with the others when they heard a single shot ring out. They flinched and looked back. They knew what had just happened. The tech sergeant couldn't have given an enemy soldier a loaded gun. He had to do the unthinkable—the unthinkable and the most humane.

★ ★ ★

"I'll never forget that, boy. That guy was in bad shape, a-no? But the tech sergeant, he did what he had to do." He was lost in the past. "You know, ah, Japan. It's the only country in history, ever, to have an atomic bomb dropped on it. Two, in fact." He held up two fingers to drive his point in.

I slowly nodded.

"Thousands of innocent people died. They didn't have to, a-no?" His heart was torn, as it had been for most of his life. "Hiroshima, then Nagasaki," he reminisced, "August 6 and August 9. I don't know why those damn Japanese guys just didn't surrender after the first one, you know?"

"Why those two cities?"

"I don't know. Those bombs killed a *lot* of people, not just military. Tsk."

It was quiet for a few minutes while he was back in 1945. I waited, knowing that there was more wisdom coming my way.

"They had brought in a lot of young people, school-aged, a-no? To the city, to Hiroshima. From the country. Thousands of young kids, doing the work of men."

I thought about asking where all the men were but then realized— they had all been called to duty. Children were called to a different duty, to perform the jobs that would otherwise go to adult men and women.

"The girls, they had them working in a military factory, sewing military uniforms. Thousands of girls. The boys, they had them tearing down buildings to make, ah, breaks, what's it called now . . . firebreaks. Because Hiroshima was one of the last major cities in Japan that hadn't been attacked by air raids. So they were expecting it. And they had these boys tearing down buildings so that when the air raids started, fires wouldn't spread." His emotions were evident. "And, ah, when that bomb dropped, those kids . . . they were all *vaporized* in a second." He stopped to collect his thoughts.

"Thousands died that day, or within a few days after, a-no? Half the population of that city. Civilians." He looked over at me and saw that I was feeling it, the horror of the moment on August 6, 1945, at 8:15 a.m. I wanted to get my head around the destruction. It was hard to imagine what an atomic bomb did to the earth that it struck.

"Did it leave a huge crater? Is there a crater there now?"

"No, no. It exploded above the city. I don't know, maybe five hundred meters above it, I can't remember. And it just flattened everything for a mile or so. And caused damage all over." He paused, and then another memory surfaced. "One gentleman, he was waiting on the steps of a bank near the exact place of the bomb. And, ah, when the bomb struck, he was just instantly burned up. But, ah, what was left on the concrete steps was his shadow. That was all that was left of him. A shadow."

I heard myself gasp. He looked at me and nodded. "Just a shadow. You can see those steps if you go to the museum there. You and Alan should go someday."

I nodded, but I wanted to get back to 1945. "You were still in Leyte? When the bomb dropped?"

"Yep, that's right, Leyte."

"Did you know at the time? That the bombs had been dropped?"

He nodded and looked away. I could see the emotion swelling inside him and felt horrible for bringing up such a painful memory.

"All I could think about was my mom."

AUGUST 10, 1945–LEYTE, PHILIPPINES

Soldiers were exhausted by seeing death play out in front of them day in and day out, and longing for home. Nobody cared that Masao was the lone Asian in the unit. Everybody had the same goal in mind—to get back to family and to where things made sense.

They were squatted down while the tech sergeant looked at his map. Suddenly a shout came from the hills.

"The war is over! The war is over!" an American voice yelled out to the world.

Within moments it was confirmed. Once back at the military base, Masao was eager to pack up and get back to San Bernardino to figure out his uncle's situation. After weeks, he was finally summoned to the captain's office on base.

"Sergeant Abe, you're now considered what the military calls an essential. And it's my duty to tell you what your next orders are," the Captain said. "You ship out for Tokyo on eighteen September. You'll be on the first transport ship to arrive for occupation efforts."

"Japan. Sir. With all due respect, I have enough points to be honorably discharged just like the other guys," Masao pleaded. He was right. The point system for an honorable discharge was a calculation based on factors including the number of battles in which a soldier had fought. The cut off score was seventy-five points. Masao had eighty-two.

"I understand." The captain felt for Masao, knowing he would still be the target of hate, only now it would be directed at him as an American in Japan, a different kind of traitor.

Masao learned that three of his Nisei interpreter buddies had been given the same news. On September 18, Masao boarded the military transport vessel for the seven-day voyage to Japan. He would be in the first wave of American soldiers to dock.

Masao (center) with Robert Sakai (right) and an unidentified soldier (left) on Leyte

Masao (third from right) stands for inspection

PART III

CHAPTER NINE

BEGINNING OF THE END

"Hellloooo?" Masao answered the phone. *He must have been sleeping,* I thought. He sounded groggy.

"Mas? This is Sandie."

"I—hellooo-wann—nooo—fllll—" He was completely incoherent.

I became alarmed. "Are you okay?" I pulled out of my parking spot in a hurry.

"Wannn—fllll—ahhh—slllll—" I couldn't make out a word. My heart started pounding.

"Masao. I'm going to call you back. Okay?"

"Ooookkk."

I hung up and dialed Alan's sister-in-law, Stephanie, while trying to drive at the same time. Thank God she answered.

"Steph? It's Sandie. Something's wrong with Masao. I'm on my way over there but can you please go check on him right now?" She could hear the panic in my voice.

"Sure thing. I'll head over there right now." She lived close to the retirement home and would be there within minutes. My heart raced as I merged onto the freeway. I dialed Alan.

"Something's wrong with your dad. I'm going over there, but I called Steph. She's on her way there too."

"Okay, well, call me when you get there. He's probably just tired."

Alan didn't seem too concerned, but something in my gut indicated urgency.

For the next week, Masao's not feeling well persisted and worsened. As it turned out, he had come down with pneumonia. He was admitted to the hospital, where he stayed for days. Instead of the casino, I would visit him in the hospital, often with food from his favorite restaurants. Sometimes he would have an appetite for it, and sometimes he wouldn't. Sometimes, he was strong enough to eat on his own, and other times, we would help him eat.

One day when I arrived, there were already visitors in the room, and Masao was awake. Alan, Mike, and Stephanie were all trying to get him to eat something, suggesting different things off the hospital menu or from local restaurants. He just kept shaking his head— he wasn't interested. *At least he has the strength to refuse*, I thought. Then I had an idea.

"What about a fried egg sandwich?" I asked him. He looked at me like I was on to something.

He nodded. "That sounds good." Everyone else in the room looked at me like I had some sort of extrasensory perception. I did not. I had just seen him eat a lot of fried egg sandwiches. Since I was last to arrive that day, I was the last to leave. I stayed with Mas while he ate part of the fried egg sandwich and watched him doze off and on. Just as I was about to leave, he woke up and looked alert.

"Where's Alan?"

"He went home." I patted his knee. "How are you feeling?"

"Oh, so-so." I nodded and waited to see if he was going to nod off again. "When are we going to Vegas?"

Alan had cancelled our trip the day before. It was evident that Masao was not strong enough to walk on a plane.

"Well, uh, when you're strong enough." I didn't have the heart to tell him the trip had been cancelled.

"Oh, this month, a-no?"

"Uh—I hope so. We need you to get better so we can go."

"Oh." He sounded dejected. I had to think fast. I didn't want him to get depressed.

"Hey, Mas, where did you meet Doris? Was that in Hawai'i, after the war?"

"No," he quickly corrected me, "I met my wife in *Japan*." He looked at me knowing I would be confused.

"I didn't know she was in Japan."

"Heh! Gee, that was a long time ago, now. Seventy years . . . I arrived in a place called Aomori, in the north."

SEPTEMBER 25, 1945–JAPAN

The transport ship maneuvered through the Tsugaru Strait. Its destination was Aomori, a port tucked inside Mutsu Bay in the very northern part of Japan. Masao and Naki stood at the rail, watching the shore approach.

"You're going to have to show me around, old boy. Introduce me to your family and friends." Naki nudged Masao with his elbow.

Masao smiled and lit up a cigarette. "My friends. I wonder what happened to them. They all went into the war. I doubt any of them made it," Masao concluded. He watched Japanese locals scurry from the dock area and close themselves up inside their homes, afraid for their lives. "I never thought I'd be coming back here as an American soldier."

Naki looked at his friend. He couldn't begin to understand what Masao was feeling. What kind of fate had been dealt to Masao, bounced back and forth between two countries that would end up as enemies? Forever feeling like a foreigner, never feeling as if he had a home.

"Does your mom know you're here?"

Masao shook his head. "No." His feelings swirled, not knowing which end was up, not knowing how he should feel being reunited with his family. By now, he'd been apart from them more than he had been with them.

Soldiers took the train from Aomori to Tokyo, which the military would soon occupy in great numbers. Masao was assigned to the US Army censor operation and worked at the post office, following certain dignitaries' mail. He and Naki would take a jeep to drive around town when they had free time—the military gave them free reign.

Seeing Japan and all the destruction wasn't easy. Witnessing the situation of Japan's people was heart-wrenching. But the hardest thing for Masao to contemplate was a visit with his family. The last time he'd seen his parents had been in 1936, almost a decade earlier.

For Masao, reuniting with his parents felt complicated.

It was a crisp October morning, and Tomie was helping Yasoshichi in the orchard. They had received periodic letters from Tatsuo, who was still in a Department of Justice facility in America. He had kept them loosely informed as to Masao's whereabouts in the world. Tomie had fretted when she heard Masao had been shot, praying, hoping her oldest child would somehow survive. She had spent many sleepless nights fearing for his safety and worried that he would fall into the hands of the Japanese military.

She kept herself sane by focusing on her remaining children. Her oldest daughter was grown and had married, and her youngest child, Yoichi, was still a teenager. While she was devastated that Japan had endured the atomic bomb attacks, she was more than relieved that Japan had finally surrendered. At least her youngest son wouldn't have to face conscription.

The air was refreshing on this particular morning, and it was quiet in the village as she took apples from Yasoshichi, who handed them down from the top of his ladder. Then she heard something. It was a vehicle of some sort, but the engine sounded unlike anything she had ever heard before. It stopped near their home. She shielded her eyes from the morning sun and strained to see.

For some unknown reason, Tomie's heart started pounding. She instinctively dropped the apples and walked toward the vehicle, hoping that her senses were accurate. Her heart seemed to pull her toward the car.

Then she saw him. Her Masao. Her body went limp with emotion when she saw her oldest son step out of the

Yasoshichi on a ladder with Tomie below at Abe orchard in Fukushima-ken, Japan

strange-looking car. He didn't notice that she had already extended her arms out. He didn't notice that her maternal energies had already wrapped him inside her heart and held him tight. Tears welled in her eyes as each step brought her closer to him, to the little boy she had abandoned when he was nine, to the young adult they forced to leave Japan when he was nineteen, to the man that he had now become.

She stepped on a twig and it cracked. Masao heard it and looked over to see his mother, her arms stretched out in front of her, her gait short but swift.

The soldier, the warrior, the survivor of bloody battles, now felt as if he were nine all over again. As they embraced, Tomie held onto her son tightly, sobbing tears of joy and love, sorrow and regret, and relief.

"My Masao . . . oh, Masao . . ." she sobbed as she held him even tighter. They didn't want to let go of each other for several moments.

Yasoshichi looked on. His reunion with his son would be different. He knew Masao harbored deep resentment toward him for the decisions he had made as a father. Yasoshichi had regrets—many of them. But he did not regret for one moment sending Masao back to the States before the Japanese military could grab a hold of him. The only chance Masao had for surviving the war was to be away from Japan, far from the Imperial military. Masao's presence there now had proven that.

After several minutes of embracing his mother and reconnecting with her love he so missed, he turned to his father and extended his hand to shake. His father held out his hand in return.

"Hello, father." Masao's Japanese was as perfect as ever.

"Son. I'm very glad to see you." Yasoshichi greeted Masao with a smile.

MARCH 1946—HONOLULU

With the war over, things in Honolulu slowly returned to normal. Doris still worked as a civil servant. She and Stanley were still dating, and Doris hoped he would commit to her soon. When Stanley announced that he was applying to go to Japan to work as a civil servant, she, at first, had been beyond disappointed. But then he suggested that she apply as well. She thought this was a magnificent idea. Maybe in Japan their relationship would solidify at last.

It took some badgering of her parents to let her go, but she eventually got her way. She found a group that was heading for Japan, one that had solid supervision and guidance and that eased her parents' concerns. Stanley had left two months before her, but she would be on her way soon. She was more than excited the day she left Honolulu. She desperately wanted to join Stanley to start their adventurous life together in Japan.

APRIL 1946–TOKYO

The Japanese government had instilled fear into the hearts of the citizens regarding Allied Forces. They warned that the occupying American troops would be brazen and would take the Japanese girls away; they would be savage on all accounts. But when American troops arrived with medicine, food, and clothing, Japanese locals started to emerge from out of nowhere.

Masao and Naki were acutely aware of the locals and lack of supplies. Every time their plentiful rations of cigarettes and alcohol were distributed they would take a jeep, drive to the shipyards, and share with the workers who were getting off their shifts. Most of the time, Japanese locals were happy to see the US uniform. Still, some people spat at them, wondering how Japanese men could possibly wear the uniform of the enemy.

The Imperial Japanese soldiers who survived the war had returned to Japan in shame. None of Masao's childhood friends made it back alive. Miyoko had long since married, Masao heard. On the brighter side, Cooper's outfit, or what was left of it, made it out of the war alive. His bodyguards were all awarded with Bronze Stars, two of them with Silver Stars. Masao thought it well deserved. He missed his guys from Angaur and Peleliu and thought of them often.

Back at the post office, Masao continued to censor mail. Naki had met a Japanese girl and was spending a lot of time with her at the expense of his buddy-time with Masao. While his feelings of loneliness had subsided since he had reconnected with his family, Masao still felt something was missing in his life. He envied Naki for finding a girl with whom he wanted to start a life.

"I've met a girl," Stanley said with little empathy over dinner on Doris's first night in Japan.

Doris thought she was hearing things. "What do you mean you 'met a girl'? *I'm* your girl."

"I found a Japanese girl. And . . ." He looked at Doris to gauge her reaction. "I think she's the one for me."

"You found a Japanese girl? I'm a Japanese girl. I'm the Japanese girl who *followed* you here from Honolulu." Her voice reflected her disbelief, her shock.

"Doris, please calm yourself. She's . . ." He smiled as he thought about how to describe his new girl. "She's a *real* Japanese girl."

Doris was angered by that insult. "A *real* Japanese girl, huh? You know what you are? You're a *damn bastard*, that's what you are." Her voice was loud.

"This is exactly what I'm talking about. Shizuko would never behave in this manner. Using profanity and yelling."

"Yelling? YELLING?" Doris shrieked, drawing attention in the restaurant. "What's going on with you, pal? Why are you talking that way?" Her eyes teared up, her voice turned soft, "This isn't the Stanley I know. And love."

"I'm a changed man." He looked at Doris with uncaring eyes, daring her to challenge his statement. "Shizuko. She made me see the real me."

A mixture of seething and heartache filled her beautiful face. "You don't know *who* you are." She got up, collected her belongings, resisted the urge to throw water in his face, and walked out.

Back in the hotel room, Doris was surrounded by a group of girls who consoled her. She sobbed helplessly for days until the group leader, Mrs. Okasako, found her a nice civil servant job that would help to get her mind off Stanley. Within her first week in Japan, Doris was longing for home.

"A new group is coming through," Naki nodded in the direction of the ladies walking toward them. Masao looked at him, uninterested in the husband-seeking girls coming from America.

Masao brushed off the notion that he would find anyone of interest. Many groups of newly arriving civil servants had come through the post office and he'd never noticed any girl that captured his interest. But he casually glanced at this new group.

He spotted Doris right away. She was different, not giggly like the other girls were. She seemed—*angry*. While the other girls darted their heads around in search of officers to glom on to, Doris looked off in a daze, eager to get down to business so she could get her mind off of whatever was ailing her. Masao studied her while she was introduced to the clerk who would give them their assignments and show them how to perform the tasks. She went right to work, kept to herself, and concentrated on the mail she was sorting.

"That one looks interesting," Masao said in a low voice. Naki looked up as Masao made a slight nod in the direction of Doris. Naki watched Doris for two seconds before he made his assessment.

"Are you crazy? She looks like she's the type who would bite your head off."

Masao just smiled, "That's okay."

He waited for a while before he moseyed over to her desk. She didn't see him approach. He lit up a cigarette and then offered one to her. That was when she noticed him for the first time. She accepted the cigarette and the light.

"I'm Masao," he said.

She looked at him as though she was going to burn him with the cigarette. "Hi, Masao." Her voice had anything but enthusiasm in it.

"You know, you don't look like the typical girl who comes here."

She set her mail down. She was annoyed to be taken off her task and was not interested in this soldier's opinion of her. She sighed and sat back. *Go ahead, I'll listen to your babble*, she thought.

"Well, the typical girl who comes here is like a pan-pan girl. You know, a working girl." He thought he was being funny and smiled, anticipating a connection.

But instead of smiling back, she pursed her lips together and put out her cigarette, extinguishing the gift, the offer, Masao's gesture to be friendly. "Listen here, Masa, or whatever your name is. You just mind your own *goddamn* business and *leave me alone.*"

This was not the response he anticipated.

He slowly backed away and returned to his desk. Naki had been a witness to the epic failure, but he had to ask anyway, smiling at his buddy's attempt. "How'd it go?"

Masao looked at Doris over his glasses and studied her. "I have a good feeling about her."

★ ★ ★

"That's what she said to me, 'You mind your own *goddamn* business,' heh!" Masao chuckled as he remembered their first encounter. "I liked her right away."

I reveled in Masao's wonderful and vivid memory. This was not the Doris I had known. This young Doris was someone I would have wanted to hang out with. I would have wanted to watch her put people in their place and would have admired her for saying things to others that I never could.

"Doris was sassy."

"Heh! She was," he chuckled. His recollection of their first meeting had warmed his heart. "I knew she was the one. After a while, I thought I should ask her to marry me. So, I sent a letter to my uncle in San Bernardino and asked him to send a ring."

Masao looked at me and I nodded.

"Where were you when you asked her? In a Japanese garden somewhere?"

"Heh! No. It was on a bus."

SUMMER 1946—TOKYO

Doris had thawed toward Masao, and they began to see each other. She wanted to tour Japan and Masao had access to a jeep, so they were a good combination. They traveled all over the country together, meeting Masao's family and visiting the Japanese relatives Doris had never met. The more time they spent together, the stronger their connection grew.

One evening they had gone to a show in town. They took the bus and were on their way back to Doris's place. They sat together, holding hands. Masao reached into his pocket and pulled out a ring.

"Doris," he said sincerely, "would you consider marrying a soldier like me?" Doris looked at Masao, surprised and delighted by the ring he was holding.

"I would love to marry you, Masao."

★ ★ ★

Doris surrounded by children in Japan who had never before seen a Japanese American woman

"Heh! I almost fell off the bus chair. I was so surprised that she would marry a bum like me." His love for Doris was so deep, you could feel it.

"What are you talking about? You were a catch, just like she was."

"Nah. She was pretty. So pretty. Too pretty for a guy like me. Until the day she died, a-no?"

I nodded in agreement. "She was pretty."

I stayed until he was almost asleep. "Mas," I tapped him and whispered, "I'll see you tomorrow."

"Okay, thank you," he said as he dozed off.

"No, Mas," I squeezed his hand, "Thank *you*."

"Ohhhh, boy, that looks good." His eyes devoured the food I brought from Ginza, Masao's favorite Japanese restaurant. It made me happy that he was hungry and that I brought food he would eat. And to have a coherent Masao to converse with—that was a gift.

"You want tea?"

"No, water is fine." He was dribbling food down his chest, so I helped him with his napkin.

"I'm a sad case, a-no?"

"You're just trying to get better, that's all." I sat down and watched him enjoy the fish head, something he ordered many times at Ginza, a dish I did not understand and never wanted to try. In his better days, Masao would tease me about eating the fish eyeballs, knowing I would be completely grossed out by the notion.

"Hey, Mas? Can you tell me about your Uncle Tatsuo? What happened to him after the war?"

"My uncle, he was a *really* good guy. Everyone loved him. He ended up living in, ah, the barrio. Heh! He saved every penny and sent it back to Japan. Then the war happened and all his money—gone. Just like that."

"Did he still have the little store?"

"Nope. Let's see now. What happened to that store . . ."

1946—SAN BERNARDINO

The internment camps and Department of Justice prisons were closing one by one, sending their incarcerated back out into society. Tatsuo had been moved from the Santa Fe facility, where Masao had visited him before shipping out, to yet another detention center in Crystal City, Texas. Tatsuo and Yukie had been separated for years when the War Relocation Authority finally approved Yukie and her two young daughters to join Tatsuo at Crystal City.

Upon their arrival, Tatsuo's daughters looked at their father as though he were a complete stranger. He was a stranger to them. He had never met his youngest daughter and hadn't seen his oldest daughter since she was an infant. They welcomed a third child, a son, while incarcerated at the Crystal City facility.

Now that they had been given clearance to leave the prison, they would return to San Bernardino to start all over again. They were thankful they had a home to return to, grateful to Masao for putting the house in his name. At least they had a place to land; the overwhelming majority of Issei and Nisei did not.

San Bernardino had changed dramatically. There was not even a hint of the Japanese legacy that had long-occupied Third Street. Every last shop that had been owned and operated by Tatsuo's friends was gone. Many of the previous Japanese residents refused to come back at all.

His little grocery store, still under the ownership of his former manager, was run down and losing money. The manager had refused to turn the ownership back over to Tatsuo. So, Tatsuo found a job as a custodian, worked hard and saved his money, and eventually found a site for a new grocery store in the barrio, where he felt welcomed by the warmth of the Latinx and African American communities.

A year after his release from prison, Tatsuo had established the new Star Cash Grocery deep in the barrio in San Bernardino. Since the old Star Cash Grocery had been run into the ground and no longer existed, Tatsuo took the name back. He was open for business, and his old customers had found him. He felt right at home in the barrio, filled with people of various ethnicities. Working away, he hardly noticed as Ben Miller entered through the front.

"Ben—my old friend. Good to see you. Come in, come in," Tatsuo welcomed Ben.

"It's good to see you back here." Ben's voice was shaky. He had aged since Tatsuo had last seen him. "We were all worried about you and your family."

Tatsuo nodded. He appreciated Ben's concern. "Here, have a seat. It's good to be home. I missed all of my customers." Tatsuo had to help a slightly unstable Ben sit on a stool. "And I missed seeing you, dear friend, from time to time. Uh, I don't have the back set up for you just yet. Although we don't have to be so secretive in this neighborhood, do we?" He chuckled at the newfound freedom. But Ben was shaking his head. It wasn't whiskey he was seeking. It wasn't food. He didn't want anything from Tatsuo.

"I'm not here for that." Ben looked at Tatsuo. "I just . . . I just wanted to welcome you home. Nothing else, my friend. Just to welcome you home."

Ben's thoughtfulness and concern washed over Tatsuo in a heartfelt wave, warming his entire body with gratitude. It was clear that Tatsuo's presence in this new community was greatly valued.

"That's . . . thank you, Ben."

And Tatsuo was home, at last.

★ ★ ★

Masao dozed off to the good memories of his Uncle Tatsuo. I stayed with him until Alan showed up after work. I reported that Masao had eaten a little bit, and that made Alan happy.

"Hey, Alan? Did he ever talk about the war with you guys?"

Masao was most likely tight-lipped about the war, even with his own family. Like all the other MIS soldiers, he kept the details to himself.

"Sometimes, sure," Alan thought about this. "I remember him talking about how after the war it was hard for him to eat. He didn't have an appetite. I guess the sick smell of all the dead bodies, you know—the stink had infiltrated his nostrils and just stuck with him. He couldn't shake it for years. Sometimes, the smell would come back for no reason at all. He would just have to get up from the dinner table and leave."

I looked at the sleeping Masao. "What else?"

"I don't know. He just seems to really like to talk about the war with you more than anyone." I sat back with that thought. I knew I had a special connection with Masao, I knew he had been a gift to me, and I couldn't stand the thought of losing him. My face contorted as I tried to hold in the emotion that leaked out. I felt the sudden urge to leave the room before my emotions erupted. I didn't want to cry around Masao—whether or not he was awake.

Alan found me outside on an isolated bench where I had collected myself. He rubbed my back to comfort me. "He's lucky he has you around. You know? You listened to him and took notes on everything, recorded his thoughts. You listened, and he loves that. He loves you."

"Just—*shut up*," I said. I started to sob again. Alan was completely confused. Here he thought he was comforting me, but it had the opposite effect.

"What's wrong? What'd I say?"

"It's not him who's lucky," I choked out. "It's me." I looked at him. He was clueless. "Don't you see? *I'm* the lucky one."

I was glad to be done with the morning CrossFit class and eager to check my phone for messages. There were two messages, and I had to look at them twice, blinking my eyes as I read.

"Dad's not doing well. I'm on my way up there now," the first text read. That was at 9:20. I quickly scrolled to get to the next message; it had come at 9:35.

"Dad just died."

I felt like the air was suddenly sucked out of my lungs. At the same time my legs felt as though they had been cut off at the knees. I just wanted to get to Masao. All I wanted to do was get to Masao.

I called Alan simply because I didn't know what else to do. "Where are you?" My voice was frantic.

"I'm at the bottom of the hill," Alan's voice sounded equally as distressed. The bottom of the hill meant that he would be with his dad within minutes. Meanwhile, I was a good forty-five minutes away. It somehow felt reassuring knowing that Alan would be there, would be with the lingering spirit of Masao.

At the entrance of the facility, family members gathered. Everyone had arrived before me, and there I was in my sweaty workout gear. I saw Alan and he walked me into Masao's room, where more family was gathered. I sat down in the chair next to his bed, and it was there that I broke down. I looked at his still body. No sound would come out of my mouth. I could only inhale in gulps. I rested my hand on his arm and continued to suck air in while tears dropped out, one after another.

My sobbing was deep. Someone handed me tissue, someone else was rubbing my back. I noticed that I was far more visibly upset than anyone else in the room and felt foolish for a fleeting second.

Alan was crying, but he wouldn't allow himself to sob. I noticed Katharine, Masao's granddaughter, across the bed.

"Was anyone with him?" I tried to get out. Nobody understood me.

"What?" Katharine asked compassionately, straining to make out my words. She was crying too. *Thank God I'm not the only one,* I thought.

"Was he alone, or was someone with him?" I managed to get out.

Stephanie stepped in to assure me. "I think one of the nurses was with him." She didn't sound too convincing.

"Are you sure? Someone was with him?" I couldn't bear the thought of him dying alone. This warrior, this wonderful man who had served his country heroically—he deserved to die surrounded by love.

Stephanie nodded. "He wasn't alone."

"Okay," I blurted out in between bursts of sobs. At the time I couldn't think of anything but the incredible loss I felt, the void that would now fill my life in the absence of my good friend Masao.

August 6. I didn't connect the date until later. Masao left us on August 6, 2013, sixty-eight years to the day after the bomb was dropped on Hiroshima. If it's true that we decide when to leave, then this made sense. Masao's heart had forever been shared between two countries that he loved. It was not a coincidence that he died on a day so historically fraught for Japan and the United States.

CHAPTER TEN

FINAL JOURNEY

NOVEMBER 6, 2013

It was the first time I noticed that all three sons were emotional. The playing of taps. The urn sitting in front of them. The finality of it all. It must have been heartbreaking for them. Life just wouldn't be the same without Masao, without his stories, without his wit, without his sass.

As the bugle player sounded the last note of taps, many tears were shed. Everyone remained standing while the two soldiers who held the flag now folded it with great precision and care, placing three bullet casings, symbolic of three volleys and representing duty, honor, and country, inside the folded flag. Once it was folded back into the triangle with the stars on the outside, the soldier kneeled down and the flag was presented to Alan's brother Michael.

We all gathered around as the grounds worker respectfully unscrewed the face of the niche, placed Masao's urn inside next to Doris's, and closed it back up. Leis were laid in front, along with flowers. The only comfort my aching heart had was that Masao was with Doris at last.

I stood off at the side and watched Masao's family and friends as they comforted each another and fussed over the flowers. *There must be some reason that I intersected Masao's life when I did.* It was

Masao's funeral service

Doris and Masao in Japan, circa 1946

the perfect meeting of souls; he had a fascinating story to tell, and for whatever reason, I was fortunate enough to be a listener. Why he chose me to tell it to, I'll never know. Maybe it was because I had joined the family late in his life, so I didn't have any preconceived notion of Masao, and he didn't have any of me. We had several precious years of true friendship.

I watched the cemetery worker screw in the last bolt, sealing up Masao and Doris's niche forever. I thought of them together in the mid-1940s when they blissfully traversed Japan as a pair, providing Masao with a sense of belonging that he so longed for and giving Doris the sense of adventure she craved.

In that moment at the Punchbowl, watching the niche close up, I knew that Masao's legacy was one that must not be forgotten.

EPILOGUE

In October 2010, President Barack Obama signed an order to honor World War II Japanese American soldiers with the coveted Congressional Gold Medal. Masao proudly accepted this great honor at a ceremony in Seattle, where he and other soldiers from World War II were recognized. As wonderful as that medal is, what might be more important to Masao's generation is social recognition. Receiving an award from the highest office in the land is one thing, but having acknowledgment, or even better, appreciation from your own generation and your children's generation and their children's generation is quite another. It's the collective awareness of those quiet heroics that make this country great.

The generation of Nisei that lived through the World War II era was among the greatest. They gave up everything, quite literally, to prove their loyalty. All the suspicion about Japanese Americans was for naught. After all the investigations, all the evacuations, all the injustice levied against an entire ethnic group, only ten people living on American soil were found guilty of espionage or fifth element activity. All of them were white.

When Nisei and Sansei soldiers were finally discharged from the military, they weren't allowed to join veterans' associations. Masao wasn't even issued a lapel button, a standard issue for soldiers. Yet, this group of citizens was the first to provide a strong voice on behalf of Muslim Americans after 9/11, and to this day, they strive to prevent any hysteria that would lead to the same injustice they had once endured. This is the importance of history—to learn from our shortsightedness, to grow as a people, and to become stronger by listening to those who have gained wisdom through endurance.

No generation understands this more than our Nisei.

Masao with his Congressional Gold Medal

BIBLIOGRAPHY

Adler, David Gray. "Minidoka and Flagrant Violations." *The Blue Review*, 2013. Accessed March 2014. www.thebluereview .org/wwii-japanese-incarceration.

Aimone, William F. *A Personal Reflection on the Author's Life Before, During, and After World War II.* Written postwar, no date indicated.

Aimone, William F. "The Nisei and the CIC." *Japanese American Veterans Association (JAVA) Newsletter*, March /April 2003.

Ano, Masaharu. "Loyal Linguists: Nisei of World War II Learned Japanese in Minnesota." *Minnesota History 45, no. 7* (1977): 273–287.

Antill, Peter. "Peleliu, Battle for (Operation Stalemate II): The Pacific War's Forgotten Battle, September–November 1944." *History of War Military History Encyclopedia on the Web.* Accessed May 2014. www.historyofwar.org/articles /battles_peleliu.

Army Pictorial Service Signal Corps. *Action at Angaur.* 1945. Accessed April 2014. www.archive.org/details /22014ActionAtAngaurVwr

Asia-Pacific Digital Library, Kalamaku Press. "Traditions of Oʻahu: Stories of an Ancient Island. Kaʻahupahau." Last modified September 11, 2010. apdl.kcc.hawaii.edu/oahu /stories/ewa/kaahupahau.htm.

Bailey, Ronald H. "The Incredible Jeep." *World War II,* September 2009. Accessed May 2014. www.historynet.com /the-incredible-jeep.htm.

Blair, Bobby C., and John Peter DeCioccio. *Victory at Peleliu: The 81st Infantry Division's Pacific Campaign.* Norman: University of Oklahoma Press, 2011.

Brown, DeSoto. *Hawaii Goes to War: Life in Hawaii from Pearl Harbor to Peace.* Honolulu: Editions Limited, 1989.

California Japantowns. "Terminal Island." Accessed April 2014. www.californiajapantowns.org/terminalisland.html.

Chicora Foundation, Inc. "Lessons from the Past: Japanese-Americans." Accessed May 2014. www.chicora.org/Japanese -Americans.html.

Conn, Stetson, Rose C. Engelman, and Byron Fairchild. *Guarding the United States and Its Outposts.* Washington, D.C.: Center of Military History, United States Army, 2000. Accessed April 2014. www.history.army.mil/books/wwii /Guard-US/index.htm#contents.

Cook, Haruko Taya, and Theodore F. Cook. *Japan at War: An Oral History.* New York: New Press, 1992.

Custermen. "The Points System or Advanced Service Rating Score." Last modified October 25, 2008. http://custermen .com/AtTheFront/Points.htm.

Densho Encyclopedia. "Santa Fe (detention facility)." Accessed April 2014. encyclopedia.densho.org/Santa_Fe_(detention _facility).

Densho Encyclopedia. "Timeline." Accessed April 2014. encyclopedia.densho.org/timeline.

Dower, John W. *Embracing Defeat: Japan in the Wake of World War II.* New York: W. W. Norton & Company, 1999.

Dower, John W. *War Without Mercy: Race & Power in the Pacific War.* New York: Pantheon Books, 1986.

The 81st Wildcat Division Historical Committee. *The 81st Infantry Wildcat Division in World War II.* Washington: Infantry Journal Press, 1948.

The 442nd Regimental Combat Team Historical Society
Digital Archives. "What was the 442nd Regimental Combat
Team?" Accessed April 2014. www.the442.org/442ndfacts
.html.

Franklin D. Roosevelt Presidential Library and Museum. "FDR
and Japanese American Internment." Accessed April 2014.
www.fdrlibrary.marist.edu/archives/pdfs/internment.pdf.

Gayle, Gordon D. "Bloody Beaches: The Marines at
Peleliu." *Official US Marine Corps Marines in World War II
Commemorative Series.* Accessed May 2014.
www.marines.mil/News/Publications/MCPEL/Electronic
-Library-Display/Article/898180/Bloody-Beaches-the
-Marines-at-Peleliu-pt-1.

Go For Broke National Education Center. "Military
Intelligence Service (MIS)." Accessed February 1, 2010. www
.goforbroke.org/learn/history/military_units/misls.php.

Go For Broke National Education Center. "Timeline." Accessed
February 1, 2010. www.goforbroke.org/learn/history
/timeline/1943.php.

Hirohata, Joyce, and Paul T. Hirohata. *Nisei Voices: Japanese
American Students of the 1930s—Then & Now.* Oakland,
California: Hirohata Design, 2004.

Historical Museum at Fort Missoula. "Fort Missoula
Alien Detention Center." Accessed April 2014.
FortMissoulaMuseum.org/exhibit/fort-missoula-alien
-detention-center.

History Matters "Executive Order 9066: The President
Authorizes Japanese Relocation." Accessed March 2014.
www.historymatters.gmu.edu/d/5154.

Ichihashi, Yamato. *Japanese Immigration: Its Status in
California.* San Francisco: The Marshall Press, 1915.

Institute of Heraldry, Department of the Army. "Military

Awards." Accessed June 2018. https://history.army.mil
/html/forcestruc/docs/r600_8_22.pdf.

Ishimaru, Stone S. *Military Intelligence Service Language School:
Camp Savage, Minnesota 1942–44.* Southern California:
Military Intelligence Service Club, 1992.

Johnson, Robert Flynn. "Manzanar: The Wartime Photographs
of Ansel Adams." Los Angeles, California: Photographic
Traveling Exhibitions. Presented at the Jundt Art Museum
at Gonzaga University, Spokane, Washington, January 2014.
Accessed March 2014. www.p-t-e.org/manzanar/text.pdf.

McNaughton, James C. *Nisei Linguists: Japanese Americans
in the Military Intelligence Service during World War II.*
Washington, D.C.: Department of the Army, 2007.

Military Intelligence Service—Northwest Association. *Unsung
Heroes: Military Intelligence Service, Past, Present, Future.*
Seattle: MIS—Northwest Association, 1996.

Minnesota History Center, Gale Family Library. "Military
Intelligence Service Language School at Fort Snelling:
Overview." Last modified July 14, 2016. www.mnhs.org
/library/tips/history_topics/120language
_school.html.

National Graduate Institute for Policy Studies. "The 1930s and
War Economy." Accessed May 8, 2010. www.grips.ac.jp
/teacher/oono/hp/lecture_J/lec09.htm.

Odo, Franklin. "100th Infantry Battalion." *Densho Encyclopedia.*
Accessed March 2014. encyclopedia.densho.org/100th
_Infantry_Battalion.

Public Broadcasting Service. "The War, At Home, Civil Rights:
Japanese Americans." Published September 2007. Accessed
April 2014. www.pbs.org/thewar/at_home_civil_rights
_japanese_american.htm.

San Pedro Peninsula Chamber of Commerce. "Japanese

Memorial Terminal Island." Accessed April 2014. SanPedro
.com/san-pedro-area-points-interest/japanese-memorial
-terminal-island.

Sledge, E. B. *With the Old Breed*. New York: Ballantine Books,
2007.

Smith, Robert Ross. "The 321st Infantry Moves North." In *U.S.
Army in World War II: The War in the Pacific. The Approaches
to the Philippines*. Washington, D.C.: Center of Military
History, United States Army, 1996. Accessed May 2014.
www.ibiblio.org/hyperwar/USA/USA-P-Approach/USA-P
-Approach-23.html.

Smithsonian Institute, National Museum of American
History, Behring Center. "A More Perfect Union: Japanese
Americans and the US Constitution." Accessed May 2014.
AmHistory.si.edu/perfectunion/non-flash/index.html.

Terminal Island—Our Stories. "The Lost Village of Terminal
Island." Accessed April 2014. www.terminalisland.org.

United States Department of the Interior, National Park
Service. "A History of Japanese Americans in California:
Terminal Island." Last modified November 17, 2004. www
.nps.gov/parkhistory/online_books/5views/5views4h87.htm.

United States Department of the Interior, National Park
Service. "Patriotism and Prejudice: Japanese Americans and
World War II." Accessed April 2014. www.nps.gov/goga
/planyourvisit/upload/MIS-bulletin_5-13.pdf.

United States Department of the Interior, National Park
Service. "World War II Harbor Defenses." Accessed April
2014. www.nps.gov/goga/learn/historyculture/world-war-ii
-harbor-defenses.htm.

United States Department of the Interior, National Park
Service. "World War II in the San Francisco Bay Area."
Accessed April 2014. www.nps.gov/nr/travel

/wwIIbayarea/pre.htm.

United States Department of Veterans Affairs. "National Memorial Cemetery of the Pacific." Last modified February 9, 2016. www.cem.va.gov/cems/nchp/nmcp.asp.

United States Office of War Information. *Japanese Relocation* (film). 1943. archive.org/details/Japanese1943.

University of California, as part of the Japanese American Relocation Digital Archive (JARDA) project, California Digital Library. "Essay: Relocation and Incarceration of Japanese-Americans During World War II." Accessed April 2014. calisphere.org/exhibitions/essay/8/relocation.

University of Denver Museum (DUMA) Online Exhibit. "Behind Barbed Wire at Amache." Accessed April, 2014. www.du.edu/behindbarbedwire/history.html.

Weber, Mark. "The Japanese Camps in California: World War II West Coast Camps for Japanese-Americans." *The Journal of Historical Review* 2 (1981): 45–58. Accessed March 2014. www.ihr.org/jhr/vo2/vo2p-45_Weber.html.

Wong, Morrison G. *"The Japanese in Riverside, 1890 to 1945: A Special Case in Race Relations."* PhD dissertation, University of California, Riverside, 1977.